THE ES

MANAGEMENT AND FINANCE

SOURCEBOOK

LEO GOUGH

Series Editor: Ros Jay

London · Hong Kong · Johannesburg · Melbourne
Singapore · Washington DC

PITMAN PUBLISHING
128 Long Acre, London WC2E 9AN
Tel: +44 (0)171 447 2000
Fax: +44 (0)171 240 5771

A Division of Longman Group Limited

First Published in Great Britain 1996

British Library Cataloguing in Publication Data
A CIP catalogue record for this book can be obtained from the British Library.

ISBN 0 273 61935 7

10 9 8 7 6 5 4 3 2 1

Typeset by Pantek Arts, Maidstone, Kent
Printed and bound in Great Britain by Bell and Bain Ltd, Glasgow

The Publishers' policy is to use paper manufactured from sustainable forests.

SURVEYS AND REPORTS, 1996-1997

The following surveys, reports and publications are produced by the organisations which have contributed to this book. You will find listed many of the full reports from which we have reproduced extracts in this book, along with other relevant publications. If you would like to order any of the surveys, reports or other publications listed here, the full contact details of the organisations are in Appendix II on page 287. Prices may not include extras such as VAT, postage and packing.

Start-ups, small business and expansion

Title: **Annual Review**
Published by: Association of British Factors and Discounters
Publication date: Annual   Price: Free

Title: **Starting up in business**
Published by: Barclays Bank plc.
Publication date: 1995   Price: Free

Title: **Bridging the Skills Gap**
Published by: Barclays Bank plc
Publication date: 1995   Price: Free

Title: **A Guide to Venture Capital**
Published by: British Venture Capital Association
Publication date: September 1995   Price: Free

Title: **Directory of Members**
Published by: British Venture Capital Association
Publication date: Annually in September   Price: Free

Title: **Sources of Business Angel Capital**
Published by: British Venture Capital Association
Publication date: Annually in November   Price: Free

Title: **Report on Investment Activity**
Published by: British Venture Capital Association
Publication date: Annually in April   Price: £30.00

Title: **Performance Measurement Survey**
Published by: British Venture Capital Association
Publication date: Annually   Price: £50.00

Title: **Report on Business Angel Investment**
Published by: British Venture Capital Association
Publication date: Annually in November   Price: Free

Title: **Report on Venture Backed Flotation**
Published by: British Venture Capital Association
Publication date: December 1995   Price: Free

Title: **Quarterly Survey of Small Firms**
Published by: The Forum of Private Business
Publication date: Quarterly

Title: **Office World Quarterly Small Business Survey**
Published by: Globus Office World
Publication date: Quarterly   Price: £100.00

Title: **Face to Face**
Published by: Kidsons Impey
Publication date: 1995   Price: Free

Title: **Business Brief**
Published by: Kidsons Impey
Publication date: 1995   Price: Free

Title: **The Budget Booklet**
Published by: Kidsons Impey
Publication date: Annual 1995   Price: Free

Title: **Directors' Responsibilities**
Published by: Kidsons Impey
Publication date: 1995   Price: Free

Title: **Starting a Business**
Published by: Kidsons Impey
Publication date: 1995   Price: Free

Title: **Ten Ways to Leave Your Company**
Published by: Kidsons Impey
Publication date: 1995 Price: Free

Title: **Kidsons Impey Small Business Tracking Survey XIV**
Published by: Kidsons Impey
Publication date: January 1995 Price: Free

Title: **Quarterly Small Business Management Report**
Published by: Lloyds Bank/ Small Business Research Trust
Publication date: Quarterly

Title: **Small Firms in Services – The 1994 Survey**
Published by: Small Business Research Centre, Kingston University
Publication date: May 1994 Price: £40.00

Title: **Small Firms in Services – The 1995 Survey**
Published by: Small Business Research Centre, Kingston University
Publication date: November 1995 Price: £40.00

Title: **Small Firms and Local Economic Networks: The Death of the Local Economy**
Published by: Paul Chapman, London
Publication date: 1994 Price: £29.95

Title: **Soft Loan Schemes and the Finance Gap – An Evaluation Study**
Published by: Small Business Research Centre
Publication date: August 1994

Managing resources

Title: **Company Relocation – Policy and Practice**
Published by: Ernst & Young/CBI
Publication date: June 1994

Title: **International Mobility – 1994 Survey Overview**
Published by: Ernst & Young
Publication date: 1994 Price: Free

Title: **International Mobility – Localisation Policy and Practice (Survey Overview)**
Published by: Ernst & Young
Publication date: April 1996 Price: Free

Title: **European Logistics Comparative Costs and Practice 1995**
Published by: Deloitte Touche Management Consulting Group
Publication date: 1995

Title: **Theft Prevention Guide**
Published by: Free Freight Transport Association
Publication date: October 1994

Title: **Finding the Time. A Survey of Managers' Attitudes to Using and Managing Time**
Published by: The Institute of Management Foundation
Publication date: March 1995   Price: £25.00 to members; £50.00 to
non-members

Title: **Are Managers Getting the Message?**
Published by: The Institute of Management
Publication date: 1993   Price: £15.00 to members; £30.00 to
non-members

Title: **Going Green, the Logistics Dilemma**
Published by: P-E International plc
Publication date: 1993   Price: Free

Title: **Supply Chain Partnerships – Who Wins?**
Published by: P-E International Logistics Consulting Services
Publication date: 1994   Price: Free

Title: **Contracting Out or Selling Out?**
P-E International plc
Publication date: 1993   Price: Free

Title: **Quarterly Small Business Management Report**
Published by: Small Business Research Trust/Lloyds Bank
Publication date: Quarterly

Executive management

Title: **The Changing Role of the Finance Director**
Published by: The Institute of Chartered Accountants in England and Wales
Publication date: November 1993   Price: Free

Title: **Non-Executive Directorship – A Guide for Chartered Accountants**
Published by: The Institute of Chartered Accountants in England and Wales
Publication date: December 1995   Price: Free

Title: **Chairmen & Non-executive directors: Fees, Facts and Attitudes**
Published by: PRO NED Ltd
Publication date: 1994

Title: **Coming on Board, The Non-executive Director's Role in Strengthening Boardroom Leadership**
Published by: The Institute of Management
Publication date: 1995   Price: £25.00 to members;
                                                     £50.00 to non-members

Title: **Survey of Non-executive Directors**
Published by: KPMG Peat Marwick
Publication date: 1994

Title: **Executive Share Options and Performance Targets**
Published by: KPMG Tax Advisers
Publication date: 1994

Title: **Corporate Governance: Remuneration Disclosures. A Survey of Directors' Pay Disclosures Within 100 Top Companies**
Published by: Ernst & Young
Publication date: 1995

Title: **Restructuring and Failure in Buy-out and Buy-ins,** *Business Strategy Review*
Published by: London Business School
Publication date: Summer 1994

Export management

Title: **Internationalisation for World Class Business Strategies**
Published by: Association of British Chambers of Commerce
Publication date: 1995

Title: **Winning the Export Race**
Published by: CBI
Publication date: February 1995   Price: £20.00

Title: **Investing in Emerging Markets**
Published by: Ernst & Young
Publication date: Price: Free

Title: **European Logistics; Comparative Costs and Practice**
Published by: Deloitte & Touche Consulting Group
Publication date: June 1995   Price: £100.00

Title: **The Third Survey of International Services Provided to Exporters**
Published by: Institute of Export
Publication date: July 1995   Price: £45.00

Title: **The Fourth Survey of International Services Provided to Exporters**
Published by: Institute of Export
Publication date: July 1996   Price: £45.00

Title: **The Royal Bank of Scotland Quarterly Survey of Exporters**
Published by: Royal Bank of Scotland
Publication date: Quarterly

Title: **VAT & the Single Market 1995 Report**
Published by: KPMG Tax Advisers
Publication date: 1995

Title: **A Profile of UK Exporting Companies – An Empirical Study,**
Journal of Marketing Management
Published by: The Dryden Press
Publication date: 8 times per year   Price: Annually, £175.00

Current management issues

Title: **Fraud – The Unmanaged Risk**
Published by: Ernst & Young
Publication date: 1995

Title: **European Cities Monitor**
Published by: Healey and Baker
Publication date: Annually   Price: £20.00

Title: **The Good Office – Management & Staff Requirements**
Published by: Healey and Baker
Publication date: 1995   Price: £20.00

Title: **European Property Transactions**
Published by: Ernst & Young
Publication date: Price: Free

Title: **Detectives' Tips for Business and Industry**
Published by: Hoffman Investigations Ltd
Publication date: Monthly   Price: Free

Title: **Tales of Hoffman: the Experiences of an International Business Investigator**
Published by: Hoffman Investigations Ltd
Publication date: 1989   Price: Free

Title: **Walking the Tightrope. A Survey of Ethics in Management**
Published by: The Institute of Management
Publication date: October 1994   Price: £25.00 to members;
                                         £50.00 to non-members

Title: **Management Development to the Millennium**
Published by: The Institute of Management
Publication date: July 1995   Price: £25.00 to members;
                                         £50.00 to non-members

Title: **Managing IT at Board Level, 2nd Edition**
Published by: Pitman Publishing
Publication date: 1995   Price: £25.00

Title: **Information Technology Review**
Published by: Price Waterhouse
Publication date: Annual   Price: Free

Title: **The Ernst & Young/Business & Technology International Information Security Survey**
Published by: Ernst & Young
Publication date: April 1996   Price: Not yet known

Title: **Managing Acquisitions – Key Success Factors in Managing Acquisitions**
Published by: Ernst & Young   Price: Free

Current financial and accounting issues

Title: **Annual Review**
Published by: Association of British Factors and Discounters
Publication date: 1995   Price: Free

Title: **Bank Relationship Survey**
Published by: The Bank Consultancy Group
Publication date: 1995   Price: £550.00

Title: **Bank Report**
Published by: The Bank Consultancy Group
Publication date: 1993   Price: £250.00

Title: **Late Payment of Commercial Debt**
Published by: The Creditors Group Ltd
Publication date: March 1994   Price: Free

Title: **Payment Procedures and Late Payments in Italy and Europe**
Published by: Dun & Bradstreet Kosmos
Publication date: 1995   Price: Free

Title: **The Dun and Bradstreet Country Risk User Guide**
Published by: Dun & Bradstreet
Publication date: Monthly   Price: £595.00

Title: **Transfer Pricing: Risk Reductions and Advance Pricing Agreements**
Published by: Ernst & Young
Publication date: 1995   Price: Free

Title: **Is Your Organisation in a Position to Monitor Internal Control?**
Published by: Ernst & Young
Publication date: 1995   Price: Free

Title: **Hunter Clark Associates' Bank Report**
Published by: Hunter Clark Associates
Publication date: 1993

ACKNOWLEDGEMENTS

We would like to thank the following people and organisations for their help and contributions in putting together this book:

Aspen Business Communications
Association of British Chambers of Commerce
Association of British Factors and Discounters
The Bank Consultancy Group
Barclays Bank plc
David Bellamy Associates
Board for Chartered Accountants in Business
British Venture Capital Association
Business Strategy Review
CBI National Manufacturing Council
Centre for Management Buy-out Research, University of Nottingham
Iayn G. Clark, The Bank Consultancy Group
Karen Cole, the Institute of Management
Consensus Research Ltd and Critical Research Ltd
The Creditors Group Ltd
Professor James Curran
Deloitte & Touche Consulting Group
Dun & Bradstreet
Ernst & Young
European Logistics Association
The Forum of Private Business
Freight Transport Association

Globus Office World plc
Professor Kit Grindley
Healey and Baker
Hoffman Investigations Ltd
Hunter Clark Associates
The Institute of Chartered Accountants in England and Wales
The Institute of Export
The Institute of Logistics
Institute of Management
Journal of Marketing Management
Kidsons Impey
Jeremy Kourdi, The Institute of Management
KPMG Peat Marwick, Tax Advisers
Lloyds Bank plc
London Business School
Manchester Business School
NCM Credit Insurance Ltd
Office World Quarterly Small Business Survey
Paul Chapman
P-E International plc
Pitman Publishing
Price Waterhouse
PRO NED Ltd
Royal Bank of Scotland
Small Business Research Trust
Small Business Research Centre, Kingston University
Nigel Smith, Ernst & Young
University of Bath

We would also like to thank Alison Alsbury for her work in editing this book.

CONTENTS

Surveys and listings   v

Acknowledgements   xiii

Introduction   xxx

START-UPS, SMALL BUSINESSES AND EXPANSION

FINANCING START-UPS   2

Choices of debt/equity   2

Which of the following types of debt are small businesses most
likely to consider? ■ Which of the following types of equity
scheme are small businesses most likely to consider?

Venture capital   4

What is venture capital? ■ What are the advantages of venture
capital ? ■ What do you need in order to raise venture capital?
■ How much can you raise from venture capitalists? ■ At what
stage of the business can you raise venture capital? ■ What can
put off venture capitalists from investing? x

The Alternative Investment Market (AIM)   9

What are the benefits of AIM? ■ What kind of companies are
likely to be interested in AIM? ■ Are small businesses aware of
the Alternative Investment Market, the replacement for the
Unlisted Securities Market (USM)? ■ How attractive would
small businesses find the AIM as a means of raising finance, if
they wished to raise extra finance for their business?

Factoring and discounting   14

What are factoring and invoice discounting? ■ What are the
benefits of factoring and discounting? ■ Does factoring offer a
relatively low cost option for raising finance? ■ Does invoice
discounting offer a relatively low cost option for raising finance?

Soft loans for small businesses

13

Is there a 'finance gap' for small businesses? ■ Are there many soft loans available? ■ How do soft loan schemes operate? ■ What was the average loan given? ■ Were there write-offs? ■ What factors make your business more likely to receive a soft loan? ■ Do businesses which start with finance from soft loan schemes have any other sources of finance? ■ What is the main source of finance used by start-up businesses in soft loan schemes? ■ Is a business plan helpful in the running of your business? ■ What quality is the help you get in preparing the application for a loan? ■ What sort of amounts do companies apply for? And what sort of amounts do they receive? ■ What do companies use the loans for (%)? ■ How long do you have to wait for approval of the application?

SMALL BUSINESSES

20

Reasons for starting businesses

20

Why do people start businesses? ■ Do these motives vary with the size of the enterprise? ■ Do the motives for starting a business vary between sectors? ■ Do the motives for starting a business vary between regions?

Small firms in services

23

Do small firms in services use computers? ■ How are computers used in small businesses?

Advice for small businesses

24

Where do you go for advice? ■ How do you view your bank? ■ What type of businesses use Training and Enterprise Councils (TECs)? ■ Do small firms in services use consultants? ■ What do those who use consultants think of them?

BUSINESS STARTERS

27

Survival

27

What are your chances of survival? ■ Do small businesses grow? ■ How does recession affect small businesses? ■ What type of small businesses in services are most likely to survive a recession? ■ What strategies do small firms in services use to cope with a recession?

CONTENTS

Characteristics   30

What was the employment situation of business starters at the time of starting up? ■ How old are business starters when they first start their own business? ■ Which characteristics will your business need to survive? ■ What are the main strengths that help small business starters run their business? ■ How hard do the self-employed work? ■ Do starters have no time for a personal life? Do they find running a business sufficiently fulfilling that the sacrifices are worth it? ■ Do starters expect an increased demand for better value and service? ■ Do starters think competition is increasing?

Public opinion   35

Are people who start their own businesses different from the rest of the population? ■ What do the general public think make MEN better business starters? ■ What do the general public think make WOMEN better business starters?

Women and small businesses   36

How many start-ups are by women? ■ Do women face more problems than men when starting-up? ■ What business characteristics do women need for survival? ■ What problems do female business starters experience? ■ What kinds of businesses do women start? ■ What legal form of business do women choose? ■ What business premises do women use?

Concerns   40

What were the most important concerns affecting small businesses in mid 1995? ■ What issues are significant to small businesses? ■ Are other small businesses appealing against UBR revaluations? ■ Which sectors are appealing against UBR revaluations the most? ■ What are the problems of expanding small businesses? ■ What problems do female business owners have? ■ Are small businesses expanding? ■ Are small businesses with a high turnover expanding faster?

MANAGING PEOPLE   46
Decision-making   46

What's the most important attribute for a manager of a small firm? ■ What are managers' views on motivating others? ■ What are managers' decision-making styles? ■ Are managers born or made?

Delegation 49

What tasks are not delegated? ■ What tasks are delegated?
■ So are managers satisfied with the extent to which tasks can
be delegated?

MANAGING RESOURCES

TRANSPORT 52

Theft from commercial vehicles 52

Do you experience a problem with theft from commercial
vehicles? ■ Are your vehicles being fitted with anti-theft
devices? ■ Are some devices more effective than others?
■ Why are some fleets crime-free? ■ Where and when are
your vehicles most at risk? ■ Are supervised lorry parks
safe? ■ Are motorway service areas safe? ■ What about
roadside thefts? ■ Are there regional differences in thefts?
■ Proportionately, where are the most thefts occurring?
■ Why are there regional differences? ■ What makes your
vehicles vulnerable? ■

Company vehicles and smaller firms 58

■ How many vehicles does your company have? ■ How
much do you spend on company vehicles? ■ Does your
company buy cars for business use, or as a personal benefit
for staff? ■ How does your company finance its vehicle
purchases? ■ How often does your company replace its
vehicles? ■ What makes of car does your company choose?

RELOCATION 62

Domestic relocation 62

How many companies relocate their employees within the UK,
how many staff do they move, and how often? ■ Does your
company pay for employees' expenses when they are buying and
selling their properties in the UK? ■ Does your company pay for
removals in the UK? ■ Does your company pay expenses for travel
and subsistence in the UK during relocation? ■ Does your
company pay for 'duplicate' expenses? ■ Does your company
pay for expenses such as bridging loans? ■ Does your
company provide expenses for additional housing costs in
the UK? ■ What other provisions does your company make for
temporary movers in the UK?

CONTENTS

International relocation   66

Does your company provide housing expenses for international moves? ■ Does your company provide expenses for education and settling in during international moves? ■ Does your company provide expenses for removals during international moves? ■ Does your company provide expenses for travel and leave? ■ Does your company provide expenses for tax and other payments during international moves?

TIME MANAGEMENT   69

Restructuring   69

How much restructuring has occured recently? ■ How is restructuring affecting managers? ■ What has been the impact of restructuring on the number of managers? ■ What is the impact of restructuring on the number of management levels? ■ How do the achieved results of restructuring compare with those that were planned?

Workload   72

How have organisational changes affected your workload? ■ What is your official working week? ■ How many hours a week do you work in excess of your official working week?

The future   73

Do you anticipate further restructuring in your organisation in the next few years? ■ Do managers welcome such restructuring?

Practicalities   74

What type of working environment do you have? ■ Do you have or need help with routine tasks? ■ Do you file more paperwork than necessary?

Priorities   75

What is the one aspect on which you would like to spend more time? ■ Do you feel that time management principles and techniques apply to you? If so, how? ■ Do you find business services and equipment help save time? ■ Do you find mobile phones very helpful? ■ How helpful is Electronic Mail (E-mail)?

COMMUNICATIONS   79

Flatter organisations   79

How has the culture for effective communications changed within organisations since restructuring? ■ How has restructuring affected managers' behaviour? ■ Are senior managers communicating more effectively? ■ Have communications improved? ■ Which means of communications are most effective? ■ Is there still too much paper? ■ Has information technology (IT) improved internal communications?

LOGISTICS   83

Purchasing   83

How does your company learn about new suppliers? ■ Does your company check the financial status of its new suppliers? ■ How many suppliers does your firm have? ■ How many years do firms stick with the same suppliers? ■ What are relationships like with suppliers? ■ Do suppliers give good value? ■ If suppliers give 'average' or worse value for money, why do companies stay with them?

Supply chain partnerships   87

What do supply chain relationships require? ■ Who drives outbound supply chains? ■ Who drives inbound supply chains? ■ Do companies think that ideas about integrating supply chains will become more important? ■ What are the triggers for information exchange?

Environmental considerations   90

Are companies really under increasing environmental pressures? ■ What are the major logistics environmental issues? ■ What are the sources of environmental pressure? ■ Will environmental policies increase operating costs? ■ Does your company have a specific environmental policy? ■ Does your company have a specific transport policy? ■ What policy does your company have for its road vehicles? ■ Does your company have a specific fuel efficiency related policy? ■ Does your company have specific emission reduction policies? ■ Does your company have specific policies in the office? ■ Does your company have specific packaging policies?

Costs   98

How willing are companies to discuss logistics costs openly with their partners? ■ What are the cost benefits of closer co-operation? ■ Does your company expect a reduction in the number of suppliers over the next few years? ■ What will be the effect on physical distribution? ■ What are the expectations of third party distribution companies?

Outsourcing distribution   104

Why do companies outsource? ■ Why do companies decide not to outsource? ■ How many contractors does your company use? ■ How long are contracts with the third-party service providers? ■ How are charges structured? ■ Are you satisfied with your contractors? ■ What are the main problem areas? ■ What are the causes of these problems? ■ Has the number of contractors used by your company decreased?

Logistics across Europe   109

What changes are taking place in the European logistics market? ■ What changes are predicted? ■ What are logistics costs in Europe? Which country is the most expensive? ■ How do logistics costs break down overall? ■ How much does storage cost across Europe? ■ How much does inventory cost across Europe? ■ How much does transport cost across Europe? ■ How much does administration cost across Europe? ■ How much does packaging cost across Europe? ■ How much do computers cost across Europe?

EXECUTIVE MANAGEMENT

NON-EXECUTIVE DIRECTORS (NEDS)   118

Becoming a NED   118

Are there any guidelines for NEDs? ■ Do you hold too many NED appointments? ■ How are NEDs approached and appointed? ■ What makes life difficult for NEDs? ■ Do NEDs' interventions affect the speed and quality of decisions? ■ What formal induction did you experience when becoming a NED?

The role of the NED   121

What do NEDs regard as their key roles? ■ What are the principal concerns of NEDs? ■ What information do NEDs need? ■ Is there an 'information gap'? ■ Does your company have a formal written strategic plan?

Chairs and NEDs   126

Is the proportion of NEDs increasing or decreasing? ■ What is the average size of a board of directors? ■ How are NEDs involved in companies? ■ How involved are Chairs in their companies?

Terms of office 127

How long is a NED's term of office? ■ What are NEDs' fees?

EXECUTIVE REMUNERATION 129

Performance targets 129

How many companies have performance target schemes? Is
there a difference between large and small companies? ■ What
is the difference between performance target and share option
schemes? Are there various different types of schemes? ■ What
sorts of performance targets do companies use? ■ Are larger
companies more likely to use different performance targets?
■ What do you measure performance targets against? ■ If
you use share price as a measure of performance, what do you
use as a benchmark? ■ If you use total shareholder return as
a measure of performance, what do you use as a benchmark?
■ Over what period do you measure performance targets?
■ Who sets performance targets? ■ Why did your company
choose the performance target it currently uses in its scheme?
■ What should performance targets achieve?

Share schemes 136

Are share schemes popular? ■ Who participates in executive
schemes? ■ What other schemes does your company operate?

MANAGEMENT BUY-OUTS AND BUY-INS 138

Success and failure 139

How many buy-outs and buy-ins fail? ■ Why are buy-ins more
susceptible to problems than buy-outs? ■ How does recession
affect buy-outs and buy-ins? ■ What are the advantages of
buy-outs?

EXPORT MANAGEMENT

WHY EXPORT? 144

What are the most common reasons for starting to export?
■ How do you find out about overseas business opportunities?
■ Which regulatory factors influence your decision on which
countries to do business with? ■ Which other factors influence
your decision? ■ If you don't export, why not?

CONTENTS

MARKETS 148

What export markets worth less than £1 billion have significant potential? ■ Where does the UK export to? ■ Which export markets are growing fastest?

STRATEGY 150

Recommendations 150

What are the core competencies? ■ How do you ensure 'state of the art' competitiveness in process, technology and people? ■ How do you apply a rigorous, professional, international approach to customer interfaces? ■ Where does a partnership with government help? ■ Who do you rely on for expertise in conducting your overseas business? ■ What are the greatest barriers to overseas business? ■ How do you go about choosing an overseas agent or distributor?

CREDIT, CURRENCIES AND PAYMENT METHODS 155

Credit control 155

How do you assess the creditworthiness of new overseas customers? ■ How do you ensure payments from your overseas buyers? ■ How serious is the problem of late payment by export customers?

Exporting to the EU 157

How many exporters trade within the EU? ■ Which currency is most often used? ■ What credit period is standard? ■ What payment methods are used?

Exporting to the rest of Europe 160

Is trade in this region falling? ■ Which currency is most often used? ■ What credit period is standard? ■ What payment methods are used?

Exporting to North America 163

Which currency is most often used? ■ What credit period is standard? ■ What payment methods are used?

Exporting to Asia 165

What currency, credit terms and payment methods are most often used?

Credit and country risk 166

What credit protection measures do you use? ■ How many exporters use letters of credit? ■ Which are the slow paying markets in the EU? ■ Which are the slow payers in other regions? ■ Who are the best payers?

FINANCING EXPORTS   169

What methods of financing do you use for exports? ■ What is your foreign exchange strategy? ■ Do you use credit insurance?

EXPORTING AND THE SMALL BUSINESS   171

Did your sales rise or fall in the 12 months to January 1995?
■ If you face competition in your export markets from any other exporters, which ONE country provides the most competition?

THE SINGLE MARKET   173

...and cross-border trading   173

How much trade is there between member states? ■ From which country do exporters most regularly acquire goods? ■ To which country do exporters most regularly dispatch goods?

...and VAT   175

Do the Single Market Rules put a strain on your company?
■ Which of the following activities are UK exporters involved in?
■ Do exporters register for VAT in other countries? ■ Why do exporters register? ■ Have you experienced problems with VAT in the EU?

Reporting   179

Do you find VAT reporting manageable? ■ Do you find EU sales lists easy to complete? ■ What is the average reporting commitment? ■ Do you find reporting requirements a burden or a benefit?

SALES CHAINS   181

What are sales chains? ■ How much trade is in this form?
■ Have the triangulation simplification measures made trade easier for you? ■ Have you been able to reduce your VAT compliance burden on sales chains? ■ Have Customs and Excise reviewed exporters' single market trade, ESL and intrastate returns?
■ How do you feel about the review by Customs and Excise?

CURRENT MANAGEMENT ISSUES

ETHICS IN MANAGEMENT   186

Ethical standards   186

Do you adopt an ethical approach to management? ■ Do your views on ethical issues differ from your organisation's? ■ Which ethical issues concern most organisation's? ■ How ethically responsible is your organisation?

Management and ethics   188

How do you regard various different ethical issues? ■ Do managers in financial services speak out against unethical practices? ■ Do you feel that, as a manager, your ethical responsibilities increase towards your immediate social and business circles? ■ Do you consider withholding information from shareholders unethical? ■ What are your organisational ground rules for ethics? ■ Does the need for efficiency override ethical issues?

Ethical codes   192

Do both organisations and managers favour the introduction of ethical codes? ■ How common are ethical codes? ■ How well do you know your organisation's code of ethics? ■ Are written ethical codes effective?

MANAGERS AND THE MILLENNIUM   194

Main challenges   194

What are the main challenges facing management in the next few years? ■ How are jobs changing? ■ How do changing work patterns affect managers? ■ Are managers getting the training they need? ■ What skills will managers need in the next millennium?

OFFICES AND LOCATIONS   197

Offices   197

How do businesses choose offices to rent? ■ What are the most important factors when choosing offices? ■ ...and the least important? ■ How satisfied are managers with their office environments? ■ What do office workers feel are essential features in their office environments?

Relocation within the UK   201

How far do most companies move? ■ Are some relocations more popular than others? ■ Why do companies move to new locations? ■ How do office workers rate locations? ■ So what factors influence employees' views about locations?

International business locations   205

Do some European cities dominate British choices of European location? ■ Are some European cities "on the up"? ■ Which cities do European companies favour? ■ Which areas outside Europe are favoured by British companies? ■ Which are the favourite non-European cities? ■ What are the key factors in deciding where to locate?

MANAGING INFORMATION TECHNOLOGY (IT)   209

IT directors   209

Why do companies appoint IT directors to their boards? ■ How many companies have IT directors on the board? ■ What are the main roles of IT directors?

Development   211

What problems have you experienced with systems development? ■ How has the use of software contractors grown? ■ Is there an IT 'culture gap'? ■ How long will the culture gap be a significant problem? ■ Do business people trust IT staff? ■ What are the remedies for the culture gap? ■ What are the reasons for programme maintenance? ■ Will programme maintenance continue in the future?

Outsourcing IT   216

Why do companies outsource IT? ■ Why use outside contractors? ■ What are programmers' views on outsourcing? ■ Do more companies outsource IT now than previously? ■ What are IT directors' roles in outsourcing? ■ What are the weak points in managing outsourcing? ■ What are the risks of outsourcing? ■ How can you solve your outsourcing problems?

Budgets and costs   220

What has been the average IT spend by large organisations over the last few decades? ■ What does your company spend its IT budgets on? ■ What is the average expenditure on IT? ■ What are IT budgets by total number of employees?

Benefits and problems   223

What are the benefits of IT? ■ Does your company suffer from a 'legacy' of obsolescent systems? ■ What are the constraints on rewriting legacy programmes? ■ What are the preferred solutions to legacy problems?

Scope of IT   227

How many PCs and terminals are there in large organisations? ■ How effective are IT services?

Emerging technologies 227

Glossary of IT terms ■ Which emerging technologies are popular? ■ Which emerging technologies are less popular? ■ Which emerging technologies are being considered? ■ Many of these developments may be very exciting for the technically-minded, but are they really going to be useful?

FRAUD 232

Extent 232

Have companies taken action over the worst fraud they have suffered since January 1993?

Detection 233

What kinds of fraud are the most common? ■ How is fraud detected? ■ Do companies report frauds to the authorities? ■ So why do companies report frauds to the authorities? ■ Do companies have written fraud policies? ■ What are the most and least vulnerable sectors? ■ What types of fraud are the most common? ■ What proportion of frauds are committed by employees? ■ What do companies see as the worst feature of frauds? ■ What proportion of frauds receive media coverage?

Prevention and cure 237

Can fraud be anticipated? ■ Do companies take action to prevent similar frauds happening again? ■ What preventative measures can be taken? ■ Is fraud on the increase? ■ How many years of service have perpetrators of fraud given to their companies? ■ What is the average age of perpetrators? ■ Are the partners of people who commit fraud aware of their misconduct? ■ When are investigation firms called in?

CURRENT FINANCIAL AND ACCOUNTING ISSUES

BANKS 244

Relationships with banks 244

How many companies have a relationship with a bank, and with which banks? ■ Do companies stay loyal to one bank? ■ Have relationships with banks improved? ■ How much help do banks offer with currency risk and international trading? ■ How good are the banks' relationships with small companies? ■ How important are different sources of strains on bank relationships?

Quality of service 246

How do you rate your bank's quality of service? ■ How dependable are banks?

Credit 248

What are the most important factors when a bank assesses a company financially? ■ Are banks 'short termist'? ■ What are the major constraints on company growth? ■ What proportion of companies have changed their principal bank in the last 5 years? ■ Has the availability of credit changed over the last 3 years? ■ What causes most strains on companies' banking relationships? ■ Are banks refusing credit even for worthwhile projects? ■ Do banks pass on cuts in interest rates?

Bank charges 254

Who in your company is responsible for negotiating bank charges? ■ How do banks charge for facilities? ■ How do the types of charges vary? ■ Are bank charges sometimes reduced or waived? ■ What are typical bank charges? ■ What are typical charges on plastic cards? ■ What costs can be expected for cash transactions? ■ What are charges for cheques paid/deposited? ■ What were the cheapest and most expensive charges for manual credits? ■ ...and for automatic credits? ■ What charges can be expected for electronic transactions?

Banks and British business 261

How much European expertise do banks have? ■ What role do the 'big four' play in corporate banking?

DEBT AND COMPANY FAILURE 263

Debt 263

How big a problem is late payment of commercial debt (LPCD)? ■ What does LPCD cost companies in interest and loss of return? ■ What does LPCD cost to administrate? ■ What is the cost of financing the VAT element of unpaid debt?

Remedial action against debt 264

What are the remedies? ■ Have you ever invoked a remedial clause?

Factoring and invoice discounting 265

What are factoring and invoice discounting? ■ What are the advantages of factoring and discounting? ■ What could a factoring or discounting company offer you? ■ What is the cost of factoring? ■ What is the cost of invoice discounting?

Company failure   267

What are the causes of company failure?

EUROPEAN COUNTRY RISK   268

Country risk   268

How do you assess country risk? ■ How do risk indicators
work? ■ So how do you rate European countries for risk?

Delays in payment in Europe   270

How long does it take you to collect an invoice in Europe?
■ What proportion of payments do you receive at the due date
or with a maximum delay of 15 days? ■ What credit period
do you offer your customers? ■ What are the average delays in
payments in Europe? (1994) ■ How do you assess the
creditworthiness of new overseas customers? ■ How do you
ensure payments from your overseas buyers? ■ How serious is
the problem of late payment by export customers?

TAX ISSUES   275

Transfer pricing   275

What is transfer pricing? ■ Is transfer pricing a major tax issue?
■ Is transfer pricing an important issue to you? ■ How does the
threat of investigation affect your company's policy on transfer
pricing? ■ What form have transfer pricing enquiries taken?

International tax issues   277

■ What do you consider are the main international tax issues?
■ What are the most important international tax issues to
multinationals? ■ Which cross-border transactions do you find are
susceptible to disputes with revenue authorities?

INTERNAL FINANCIAL CONTROL   279

Internal audit   279

Does your organisation use internal financial controls? Does it work?
■ How many companies have internal audit departments?
How big are they? ■ What role do internal audit departments
play in your organisation? ■ How effective are internal audit
departments? ■ Does your internal audit department need
strengthening? ■ Do you rely on external auditing?
■ Are you envisaging introducing internal audit? If so, why?

Outsourcing of internal audit   282

If you have an internal department, do you outsource part of
your internal audit function? ■ Which areas of internal audit

do companies need most help with? ■ Why do companies
outsource their internal audit function and what are the major
objections to outsourcing? ■ How receptive are managers to
the idea of outsourcing?

Internal audit partnering   283

■ What is internal audit partnering? ■ Do companies prefer
partnering to outsourcing?

Appendix 1: How to read statistics   285

Appendix 2: Contact addresses of contributing organisations   301

INTRODUCTION

This is a business reference book with a difference. The information it contains is directly useful to you and your business. There's a lot of statistical material currently available, but it tends to be along the lines of industry-specific or whole industry figures. It's not terribly helpful to know what's going on in the baked bean industry if you run a chain of travel agencies. And knowing what the total UK transport spend is each year tells you precious little about your own transport budget.

This book will give you generic – not industry-specific – business data, so it will apply to you whatever business you're in. And the information in this book is all relevant to the UK. Businesses overseas do some things very differently, and building their research information into the results would dilute the accuracy of the figures. The book also gives you average data for the individual organisation, so you can see how it compares with yours.

You can use *The Essential Management and Finance Sourcebook* for four main purposes:

- Benchmarking: you'll find plenty of information about how other businesses conduct various management and finance activities, and you can measure your own performance against the average.

- Planning: before you launch into a new initiative, you can look through the relevant section to see what the key factors are to consider. For example, if you're thinking of using a factoring or discounting company, you'll find that the relevant section of this book will tell you what problems you might encounter, and what the main benefits are likely to be.

- Decision making: you'll find the answers to all sorts of questions here, to help you reach decisions. Suppose you need to find finance for expansion, or to start a new venture. The relevant section of this book will tell you which sources of finance are best suited to your needs.

- Supporting proposals and presentations: the information in this book comes from reliable and authoritative sources. Consequently you will find it invaluable for adding weight to your own arguments. Suppose you want to persuade the board of directors that they should insure the company against country risk because they are about to start trading with Turkey. After referring to this book, you will be able to inform them that the credit risk in Turkey is significantly higher than that in France or Italy - and pinpoint the reasons why.

The Essential Management and Finance Sourcebook pulls together information on finance and management topics from start ups and venture capital through to the need for external auditors, calling in on logistics, time management, restructuring, exporting, tax issues and many others along the way. It should quickly become one of the most well-thumbed books on your shelf.

The series

This book is one of *The Essential Business Sourcebooks*. The other books in the series are *The Essential Marketing Sourcebook* and *The Essential Personnel Sourcebook*. Between the three of them, these books cover just about every area of business.

You may find that certain topics you are interested in are included in one of the other books. For example maternity pay, which you might reasonably consider to be an aspect of finance, has been included in *The Essential Personnel Sourcebook* since most of the information available on the subject relates to employee benefits, or policies about career breaks.

However, where only one or two pieces of data overlap between the books, we have included them in both books to make it easier for you to find them. For instance, you will find that part of the section of this book on exporting also appears in *The Essential Marketing Sourcebook*.

The data

We have used only the most reliable data we could find in this series of books. Clearly the methodology varies widely between studies, but if we included the full details of it each time, there would be no room to include the findings. Each piece of data is clearly sourced where it appears in the text, and you will find a complete list of contact details at the back of the book (Appendix II) should you wish to find out more.

We have studied the data ourselves, of course, and we have not included any material that we consider to be unreliable. In a few cases, we felt that the information available needed to be treated with a measure of caution; in these instances we have made this view clear in the surrounding text. We took the view, however, that any information is more useful than no information, as long as you are aware of the possible risks in treating it as gospel. Where we felt that data was seriously flawed or biased, we excluded it.

The research findings included in the series are the most up-to-date we could find. In the vast majority of cases the research was published within the last two or three years. In a few cases the research is older than this, but often the reason no one has updated it is precisely because they do not expect it to have changed. We have not included any information that we considered to be unreliable because of its age.

The Essential Business Sourcebooks are a comprehensive guide to useful UK business data. But since the series is based on research data, we are obviously limited by the research that is available. We have found useful material on all the major areas of business, but it is possible that you may be interested in a particular aspect of one of these areas that you cannot find listed in the contents. If this happens, it will be because (after months of research, and contacts with hundreds of organisations) we have failed to track down any reliable data on the subject. If you know of any survey or other research data that is relevant to this series but which we have not included, we would be very pleased to hear from you so that we can include it in the next edition.

The contributors

The data in these books has been contributed by many of the most highly respected institutes and research organisations, by government departments, and by some of the top experts in various fields; we are very grateful to them for their co-operation.

Some of the reports that we have taken extracts from are publicly available from these organisations. In most cases, we have reproduced only a small part of the full research findings - the information we think will be of the widest interest. But if you have a special interest in any subject you may well want to see the full report. A listing of surveys and reports that are published by our contributing organisations appears at the front of this book. This listing not only includes the reports from which we have taken extracts, but also gives details of any other reports and surveys that you might find interesting.

How to use the book

The book is divided into broad management and finance categories (for example 'managing resources'), which are subdivided into more specific categories (such as 'logistics'). These are then divided further into areas within this (for example 'outsourcing distribution'). Finally, the data in these sections has been split into individual subject areas, each headed up with a question (e.g. 'Why do companies outsource?'). You will find a very comprehensive contents at the front of the book to help you find your way around this system, and menu headings indicating the current category across each double page.

We have presented each piece of data in the form which illustrates it most clearly. In many cases, this involves using charts, graphs, matrices and other things that make some people feel slightly unnerved and confused. If you're one of these people, you may find Appendix I helpful; it is a user-friendly guide to reading statistics which briefly explains each type of graph, chart and so on that you may come across while using the book. Let me reassure you, however, that we have not tried to be clever, but have used only those graphics which are in relatively common usage.

Although we have designed the books to be functional, we were surprised when we put them together to find just how fascinating much of the research material is, even when the subject matter is not immediately relevant to you. You should find it easy to track down the information you want; we hope however that you will find the book sufficiently interesting that you will not only use it for its primary purpose – as a reference book – but will also find it entertaining to browse through for general interest.

START-UPS, SMALL BUSINESSES AND EXPANSIONS

Financing start-ups 2

Choices of debt/equity ■ Venture capital ■ The Alternative Investment Market (AIM) ■ Factoring and discounting ■ Soft loans for small businesses

Small businesses 20

Reasons for starting businesses ■ Small firms in services ■ Advice for small businesses

Business starters 27

Survival ■ Characteristics ■ Public opinion ■ Women and small businesses ■ Concerns

Managing people 46

Decision-making ■ Delegation

FINANCING START-UPS

CHOICES OF DEBT/EQUITY

Just as the reason for starting a business varies, and the size varies, so does the need for finance, and the most appropriate route. Some businesses are low-capital – then financial needs can be met personally, with help from relatives and friends, or with a short-term loan. You may well not be in this fortunate position. So where can you turn for finance? Who takes which route? And when?

■ *Which of the following types of debt are small businesses most likely to consider?*

Small businesses may well have different needs for capital than do larger enterprises. If you are a small business, it will help you to know where others go for finance. In the *Kidsons Impey Small Business Tracking Survey* in January 1995, small businesses were asked about their debt and equity choices. When it came to debt, 72% said they would consider an overdraft (more than one response was allowed):

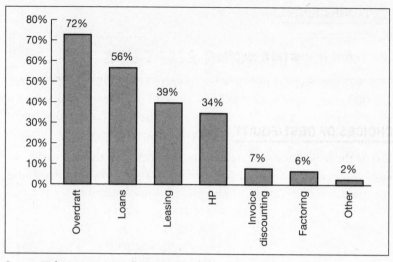

Source: Kidsons Impey Small Business Tracking Survey XIV, prepared by Consensus Research Ltd and Critical Research Ltd, January 1995

■ Which of the following types of equity scheme are small businesses most likely to consider?

The same survey asked which types of equity scheme the respondents would consider. Interestingly, 55% said they would consider venture/development capital:

Venture/development capital	55%
Personal equity purchase by existing shareholders	52%
Personal equity purchase by new shareholders	52%
Enterprise investment schemes	41%
Corporate venture schemes	41%
Venture trusts	24%
Debenture issues	24%
The Alternative Investment Market (AIM)	21%
Business Angels	14%

Source: Kidsons Impey Small Business Tracking Survey XIV, prepared by Consensus Research Ltd and Critical Research Ltd, January 1995

VENTURE CAPITAL

■ *What is venture capital?*

The venture capital industry has invested over £13 billion in over 13,000 companies since 1983. In 1994 £2.1 billion was invested in 1,208 companies and £2.6 billion was raised for future investment. This is not unimpressive considering the industry only formally emerged in the late 1970s.

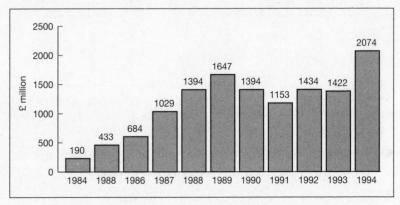

Source: BVCA. Note figures are not srictly comparable

Venture capital provides long-term, unsecured, commited, risk sharing capital, which helps unquoted companies grow and compete. The ability to provide capital *and* experience and contacts sets venture capital apart from other sources of business capital. Although venture capital requires the owner to sell some shares and sometimes to give the venture backer a non-executive board position, it seeks to *increase* value to the owner, *without* taking control. Unlike a conventional lender, an equity investor makes returns from the growth and profitability of the business. Lenders have a legal right to interest on a loan and its repayment, irrespective of the borrower's success or failure, a venture capital investor's returns are dependent on the company's performance.

Source: British Venture Capital Association

■ What are the advantages of venture capital?

Venture capital is a less familiar route than approaching the bank – so why use it? The real advantages of venture capital finance over other forms of finance are:

- It provides a solid capital base for the future – to meet your growth and development plans.

- There is no repayment during the term of investment and no interest costs – therefore no detrimental impact on cash flow (unless the equity risk includes preference shares which pay a fixed dividend and may also have redemption terms, or if debt is not included in the package).

- The venture capitalist is a true business partner, sharing in your risks and rewards, with practical advice and expertise (as required) to assist your business success.

- There will be no charges on your business assets and no personal guarantees.

- There is a wide range of sources, types and styles of venture capital organisations to meet many different needs.

Source: A Guide to Venture Capital, British Venture Capital Association, 1995

■ What do you need in order to raise venture capital?

If you want to raise venture capital, what will you need? The British Venture Capital Association stresses the importance of your track record, reporting that you will need:

1. A business with high growth potential.
2. An experienced and ambitious management team.
3. A business with a proven product or service.
4. A market where your company has, or can gain, a protected position.
5. A complete management team of proven marketing, production and finance specialists with an effective team leader – to make things happen as planned.
6. A business plan which covers all the above areas and demonstrates succinctly why your business should be given the finance and how you will deliver attractive returns for your investors.

Source: British Venture Capital Association.

5

■ *How much can you raise from venture capitalists?*

This varies with stage of investment, but few investments are made of less than £100,000. If you are looking for less that £100,000 there are various seed funds, both independent, government sponsored and part of larger venture capital organisations. Also, business angels (private investors and their syndicates) which are a useful source of smaller amounts of equity financing particularly for start-up and early stage businesses.

■ *At what stage of the business can you raise venture capital?*

While finance can be raised at any stage, most venture capital companies invest at the expansion stage. There is less investment in smaller earlier stage companies, mainly due to the additional risk associated with these investments. The British Venture Capital Association defines the various stages as follows:

Seed
Financing provided to allow a business concept to be developed, perhaps involving production of prototypes and additional research, prior to bringing a product to market.

Start-up
Financing provided to companies for use in product development and initial marketing. Companies may be in the process of being set up, or may have been in business for a short time, but have not sold their product commercially.

Other early stage
Financing provided to companies that have completed the product development stage and require further funds to initiate commercial manufacturing and sales. They may not yet be generating profit.

Expansion

Capital provided for the growth and expansion of an established company. Funds may be used to finance increased production capacity, market or product development and/or provide additional working capital. Capital provided for turnaround situations is also included in this category, as is the refinancing of bank debts.

Management buy-out

Funds provided to enable current operating management and investors to acquire an existing product line or business.

Management buy-in

Funds provided to enable a manager or group of managers from outside the company to buy in to a company.

Secondary purchase

Purchase of existing shares in a company from another venture capital firm, or from another shareholder or shareholders.

Source: Report on Investment Activity 1995, British Venture Capital Association

■ *What can put off venture capitalists from investing?*

The received wisdom is – avoid frivolity!

Signs of frivolity
1. Flashy, expensive motor cars
2. Company yacht/aeroplane
3. Personalised number plate
4. Carpets with the company logo
5. Company flagpole
6. Directors who use military titles
7. Fountain in the forecourt
8. Too many bankers involved
9. Fish tank in the board room
10. Too many auditors involved
11. Founder's statue in reception

Source: A Guide to Venture Capital, British Venture Capital Association, 1995

THE ALTERNATIVE INVESTMENT MARKET (AIM)

If companies are too small, unprofitable and/or young for flotation on the Official List of the London Stock Exchange, they have had no choice but to turn to banks or traditional venture capitalists. The Alternative Investment Market –AIM – was introduced to provide companies have another means of raising equity finance.

The Stock Exchange believes that private investors and institutions will be attracted to the AIM and will provide it with the liquidity lacking in the Unlimited Securities Market (USM). The AIM is intended to replace the USM; it should have a wider appeal than the latter because it is open to companies with a shorter track record, and regardless of where they are incorporated.

■ *What are the benefits of AIM?*

Perhaps your company is still in its early stages, and does not have the kind of track record that listing requires. If you are considering turning to the AIM, then the benefits include:

1. Access to public finance.
2. A reduction in the reliance on debt finance at a later date, and with greater ease.
3. Credibility and public profile for the company.
4. Scope for long term stability.
5. Potential for sustained growth.
6. Confidence in the company for bankers, suppliers and customers.
7. For tax purposes, AIM companies will be regarded as unquoted, which is an advantage.

Source: Kidsons Impey Small Business Tracking Survey XIV, prepared by Consensus Research Ltd and Critical Research Ltd, January 1995

■ *What kind of companies are likely to be interested in AIM?*

Put another way, this asks whether your company is the right type of company to be considering finance the AIM way. The types of companies fall broadly into the following categories:

- Regional firms needing to raise small amounts of capital with local investors.
- Companies already trading under the Stock Exchange's 4.2 Rule, a trading facility which is to end. These are likely to be private or family controlled companies looking for a quotation to raise their profile locally, or to provide more liquidity in the family shares, and who are not particularly looking to raise finance itself.
- Owners of private companies who do not want to sell as many shares as institutional venture capitalists would probably require, but who require small amounts of developmental capital.
- Management buy-outs.
- Growing companies with a short track record which are looking to expand, or increase product development, and which require a sizeable amount of capital.

■ *Are small businesses aware of the Alternative Investment Market, the replacement for the Unlisted Securities Market (USM)?*

The AIM is a recent development. Have you heard of it? If you haven't, you're not alone. Only 38% were aware of the AIM without prompting:

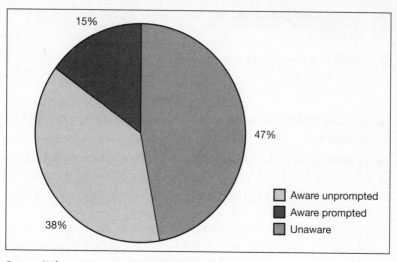

Source: *Kidsons Impey Small Business Tracking Survey XIV*, prepared by Consensus Research Ltd and Critical Research Ltd, January 1995

■ How attractive would small businesses find the AIM as a means of raising finance, if they wished to raise extra finance for their business?

So has the AIM lived up to the Stock Exchange's expectations in introducing it? If smaller businesses are not happy with it, then it is not helping the companies it was designed to help. If your company is considering using the AIM, it helps to know whether other companies find it an attractive source of finance. A sample of small businesses were asked for their reactions, and the percentage giving each assessment is listed below:

Very attractive	2%
Quite attractive	11%
Not very attractive	30%
Not at all attractive	40%
Do not know enough about it yet	11%

Source: *Kidsons Impey Small Business Tracking Survey XIV*, prepared by Consensus Research Ltd and Critical Research Ltd, January 1995

11

FACTORING AND DISCOUNTING

■ What are factoring and invoice discounting?

Factoring and invoice discounting are financial services designed to improve cash flow, primarily by providing finance secured against the outstanding invoices of a business. They offer companies a flexible means of growth by allowing them to make maximum use of their assets.

Source: Association of British Factors and Discounters Annual Review 1995.

■ What are the benefits of factoring and discounting?

This form of financing can enable companies to make better use of management time and the money tied up in trade credit to customers. So if you are considering using a factoring or discounting company, they will offer you the following services:

- Buying your unpaid invoices as they arise.
- Providing immediate finance of up to 80% of the value of your invoices, with the balance (less administration and finance charges) payable after a set period, or when the invoice is paid.
- Advising on credit risks.
- Protecting you against bad debts.

Companies which do not use factors or discounters wait on average for about 75 days before invoices are paid. At any one time, there are £57 billion of payments due to small businesses tied up in unpaid invoices. Businesses using factors and discounters get paid 80% of the value immediately, with the balance paid on average only 58 days later.

Source: Association of British Factors and Discounters Annual Review 1995.

■ Does factoring offers a relatively low cost option for raising finance?

Obviously, neither factoring nor invoice discounting come without cost – the credit company takes the risk, and expects to be paid for doing so – normally as a percentage of the bill you have sent out. If you are considering taking this path, it might help to know how others feel. So what do small businesses feel about factoring? Is it seen as a relatively low cost option? The following responses were obtained to "is this a relatively low cost option?"

Strongly agree	5%
Agree	24%
Neither agree nor disagree	14%
Disagree	31%
Strongly disagree	27%

Source: Kidsons Impey Small Business Tracking Survey XIV, prepared by Consensus Research Ltd and Critical Research Ltd, January 1995

■ Does invoice discounting offer a relatively low cost option for raising finance?

What about invoice discounting? If 58% of small businesses do not see factoring as a low cost option, maybe invoice discounting is a better solution? Possibly, as only 52% of respondents disagreed that this was relatively low cost:

Strongly agree	8%
Agree	26%
Neither agree nor disagree	14%
Disagree	41%
Strongly disagree	11%

Source: Kidsons Impey Small Business Tracking Survey XIV, prepared by Consensus Research Ltd and Critical Research Ltd, January 1995

SOFT LOANS FOR SMALL BUSINESSES

The availability of finance for small firms has led to considerable debate. Small enterprises, it has been argued, frequently find it difficult to obtain finance in amounts below £100,000, or even £50,000.

One little discussed option which can help small businesses, especially those having problems obtaining finance from conventional sources, is the 'soft loan'. This provides finance at below market rates, often combined with other support such as counselling.

■ Is there a 'finance gap' for small businesses?

If small businesses cannot find finance anywhere, then there is a finance gap. If you are looking for finance, then this gap would be worrying. Academics have tended to reject the idea of a 'finance gap', arguing that the finance market has changed to serve the needs of smaller businesses more effectively.

Yet even if the finance market is functioning effectively, there can still be unsatisfied demand. Unsatisfied demand can exist either if borrowers are unwilling to pay the price (interest rate) at which finance is offered, or if suppliers of finance reject a proposal where it is too risky. A study undertaken for the Small Business Research Centre found examples of both.

Source: Soft Loan Schemes and the Finance Gap – An Evaluation Study, by James Curran, Robert A Blackburn and Martina Klett-Davis, Small Business Research Centre, August 1994

■ Are there many soft loans available?

If you are unable to afford current interest rates, or are deemed by normal lenders as too risky, where can you turn to for loans? How many soft loan schemes are there? The same research found that there were some 82 schemes in the UK. Public bodies sponsoring soft loans included local authorities, enterprise agencies and British Coal, while private sector sponsors ranged from Sainsbury's to the merchant bank Kleinwort Benson, to major companies such as Shell UK. Others included the Mercers' Company, a City livery company, and the Royal British Legion.

Source: Soft Loan Schemes and the Finance Gap – An Evaluation Study, by James Curran, Robert A Blackburn and Martina Klett-Davis, Small Business Research Centre, August 1994

■ How do soft loan schemes operate?

Supposing that you are considering a soft loan. The crucial question is – how do they work? The easiest answer is to examine one or more schemes in detail. The high street banks are very commonly involved as sponsors of such schemes. The Small Business Research Centre examined 8 soft loan schemes operated by Midland Bank.

The study covered 63 applications, of which 47 applied successfully, 15 were refused and 1 declined the offer of a loan.

- The schemes themselves had highly individual characters. Each seemed to have come into existence in a fairly ad hoc fashion through the activities of particular individuals.
- The size of the schemes varied considerably. One had only £10,000 at its disposal, enough for only 3 or 4 loans at most, while the largest had just under £1 million.
- The emphasis of the schemes was on start-ups, although almost a third of the loans went to established businesses.

Source: Soft Loan Schemes and the Finance Gap – An Evaluation Study, by James Curran, Robert A Blackburn and Martina Klett-Davis, Small Business Research Centre, August 1994

■ What was the average loan given?

The average loan of the sample was £6,700. The largest was £25,000.

Source: Soft Loan Schemes and the Finance Gap – An Evaluation Study, by James Curran, Robert A Blackburn and Martina Klett-Davis, Small Business Research Centre, August 1994

■ Were there write-offs?

Overall, write-offs had affected 17.3% of the businesses who received loans from the schemes up to the time of the interviews. Of the businesses interviewed, the average amount written off was considerably less than £6,700, the average size of the loan, indicating either that these were smaller loans and/or that some businesses were able to repay part of the loan before defaulting.

Source: Soft Loan Schemes and the Finance Gap – An Evaluation Study, by James Curran, Robert A Blackburn and Martina Klett-Davis, Small Business Research Centre, August 1994

■ What factors make your business more likely to receive a soft loan?

The businesses, measured by turnover and employment levels, emerged as successful compared with conventional small businesses.

- Applications to the schemes, which tend to be poorly publicised, are likely to come from people who are adept at finding out about local opportunities and confident enough to approach bodies such as local enterprise agencies, TECs and banks to find out more about the schemes.

- Applicants were likely to be better educated than average, and to have the skills needed to take advantage of the opportunities offered. They also have the stamina and patience to fill in forms and write business plans with the help and advice on offer from those running the schemes.

Source: Soft Loan Schemes and the Finance Gap – An Evaluation Study, by James Curran, Robert A Blackburn and Martina Klett-Davis, Small Business Research Centre, August 1994

■ *Do businesses which start with finance from soft loan schemes have any other sources of finance?*

If you are considering taking out a soft loan, is it likely to be your only source of finance? Few borrowers relied exclusively on a soft loan – the majority used their own capital as well. The figures again relate to the 47 successful applicants for the Midland Bank schemes.

Own capital/savings	81%
Family and relatives	22%
Bank loan	34%
Friends	6%
Other soft loan help	16%
Outright grants	16%
Bank overdraft	9%
Enterprise allowance scheme or equivalent	37%
Other sources	6%

Source: Soft Loan Schemes and the Finance Gap – An Evaluation Study, by James Curran, Robert A Blackburn and Martina Klett-Davis, Small Business Research Centre, August 1994

■ *What is the main source of finance used by start-up businesses in soft loan schemes?*

So if other sources of finance were used, was the soft loan filling a gap, or just topping up funds? For about a third of start-ups, the soft loan was the main source of finance:

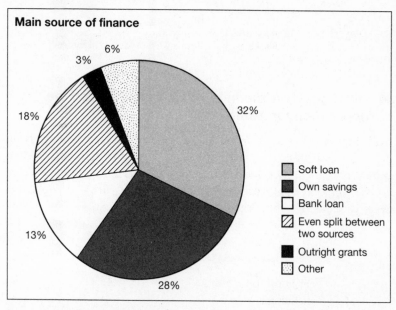

Main source of finance

- 6%
- 3%
- 18%
- 32%
- 13%
- 28%

Legend:
- ▨ Soft loan
- ■ Own savings
- □ Bank loan
- ▨ Even split between two sources
- ■ Outright grants
- ▨ Other

Source: *Soft Loan Schemes and the Finance Gap – An Evaluation Study*, by James Curran, Robert A Blackburn and Martina Klett-Davis, Small Business Research Centre, August 1994

■ *Is a business plan helpful in the running of your business?*

An integral part of any application for a soft loan – and, indeed, most other loans – is a business plan. Drawing one up takes considerable time and effort – from detailed market research to working out cash-flow forecasts. But is this effort worthwhile, even if the application for a loan is turned down? The Small Business Centre study asked soft loan applicants if their business plans had been helpful in the running of their businesses.

Over half thought that it had.

Yes	57%
No/only helpful in obtaining loan	25%
Helpful only at the beginning of the loan	11%
Other	7%

Source: Soft Loan Schemes and the Finance Gap – An Evaluation Study, by James Curran, Robert A Blackburn and Martina Klett-Davis, Small Business Research Centre, August 1994

■ What quality is the help you get in preparing the application for a loan?

Soft loan schemes are not unique in offering assistance in applying for a loan. If you have not applied for a major loan before, you would probably appreciate some guidance. This question was specific to the Midland Bank soft loan schemes. The majority of applicants were very positive about the help given:

Opinion	Percentage
Very good	45
Satisfactory	26
Mixed opinions	13
Unsatisfactory	4
Poor	6
Did not receive any assistance	6

Source: Soft Loan Schemes and the Finance Gap – An Evaluation Study, by James Curran, Robert A Blackburn and Martina Klett-Davis, Small Business Research Centre, August 1994

■ What sort of amounts do companies apply for? And what sort of amounts do they receive?

If you are looking at soft loans as a possible source of finance, it helps to know the size of sums which are normally provided this way. So each applicant was asked to give the two figures – amount applied for, and amount received.

	Applied for	Received
£1,000 – £2,500	26%	30%
£2,501 – £5,000	36%	34%
£5,001 – £10,000	13%	15%
£10,001 – £15,000	21%	19%
£15,001 – £25,000	4%	2%

Source: Soft Loan Schemes and the Finance Gap – An Evaluation Study, by James Curran, Robert A Blackburn and Martina Klett-Davis, Small Business Research Centre, August 1994

■ *What do companies use the loans for (%)?*

New finance is not just needed for new equipment, or more plant in order to expand. For many businesses, the greatest need at start-up is for working capital – to survive those first few months until the money comes in. So do the needs for finance change between established businesses and start-ups? The survey also analysed how the loans were used:

	All businesses	Start-ups only
Capital equipment and buildings	81%	87%
Working capital	38%	37%
Marketing & development	15%	12%
Other	8%	12%

Source: Soft Loan Schemes and the Finance Gap – An Evaluation Study, by James Curran, Robert A Blackburn and Martina Klett-Davis, Small Business Research Centre, August 1994

■ *How long do you have to wait for approval of the application?*

If you are planning to use a soft loan, then the time-lag between application and approval is a vital element of that planning. The Midland Bank applicants were asked this question. The majority received approval within 6 weeks:

Within 6 weeks	68%
7 – 12 weeks	20%
13 – 24 weeks	7%
Over 25 weeks	5%

Source: Soft Loan Schemes and the Finance Gap – An Evaluation Study, by
James Curran, Robert A Blackburn and Martina Klett-Davis, Small Business Research
Centre, August 1994

SMALL BUSINESSES

REASONS FOR STARTING BUSINESSES

■ *Why do people start businesses?*

Small business ownership is a high risk venture. A recent lifespan
analysis by the DTI found that almost 40% of new registrations for
VAT cease trading within 3 years. Small business owners work long
hours -often more than 50 hours a week. An estimate for the early
1990s suggested that almost 80% of all businesses in the UK had
turnovers of £100,000 or less; the majority of these had turnovers of
under £50,000. Once all the costs of running the business have been
deducted, these figures suggest that many small business owners will
earn quite modest returns for their investment and hours worked.

So, why do people go into business for themselves? Perhaps you
are thinking of starting a business, and wonder what motivates other
entrepreneurs. One survey asked people who had started new businesses what was the main reason that they had decided to branch
out. They were given six possible reasons: independence; unemploy-
ment/insecurity; to make money; saw a market opportunity; inherited
the business and other/don't know. They replied:

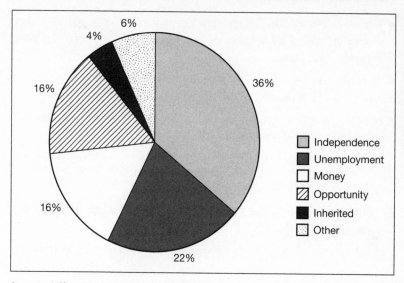

Source: *Office World Quarterly Small Business Survey*, Vol2, No1, Globus Office World plc in association with the Small Business Research Centre, September 1995

■ *Do these motives vary with the size of the enterprise?*

The bigger the enterprise, the greater the risk. Putting your own livelihood at risk is a different ball-game from risking other people's. So does the primary motive for starting the business relate to the size of the enterprise? Certainly, the picture varies when the data was broken down by the size of the firm:

	No. of employees					
	1-4	5-9	10-19	20-49	50-99	100-200
Independence	37%	37%	29%	26%	33%	31%
Unemployment/insecurity	27%	16%	10%	9%	–	6%
To make money	14%	15%	21%	31%	27%	44%
Saw a market opportunity	13%	21%	27%	17%	27%	19%
Inherited the business	2%	6%	9%	10%	10%	–
Other/don't know	7%	5%	5%	7%	–	–

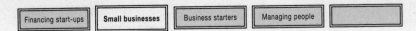
- Unemployment and economic insecurity was a much more common motive for owners of small businesses (1-9 people) than for owners of larger businesses.

- Making money was much less important for owners of smaller businesses (1-9 people) than for owners of larger businesses.

- Owners of larger businesses were much more likely to have inherited the business they run.

Source: Office World Quarterly Small Business Survey, Vol 2, No1, Globus Office World plc in association with the Small Business Research Centre, September 1995

■ *Do the motives for starting a business vary between sectors?*

The same survey found that there were some differences between owners of businesses in different sectors, for example:

- Owners in the agriculture, forestry and fishing sector were much more likely (19%) to have inherited their businesses than owners in other sectors (3%).

- Owners in this sector were the least likely (8%) to have started the business because of unemployment/economic insecurity, compared with 22% of other business owners.

- Independence was still the primary motivation in all sectors.

Source: Office World Quarterly Small Business Survey, Vol 2, No1, Globus Office World plc in association with the Small Business Research Centre, September 1995

■ *Do the motives for starting a business vary between regions?*

There were few regional differences, except that owners in Wales were the most motivated by independence (50% compared with 36% for others) and the least motivated by making money (10% compared with 16% among other owners). They were also somewhat less likely to have been motivated by seeing a market opportunity (11.5% compared with 16.4% among other business owners).

Source: Office World Quarterly Small Business Survey, Vol 2, No1, Globus Office World plc in association with the Small Business Research Centre, September 1995

■ Do small firms in services use computers?

Even the smallest business has some functions which can be computerised – like accounting. Perhaps you are computer-phobic, or feel that the expense will not be recouped by the time savings. If this is your attitude, are you the odd one out? Certainly not. Nearly 35% of those interviewed did not use a computer.

Source: Small Firms in Services – The 1994 Survey, by James Curran, Robert A Blackburn and Martina Klett, Small Business Research Centre, May 1994

■ How are computers used in small businesses?

Many companies have to have computers to produce their basic product – a secretarial agency wouldn't get very far without a word-processor, for example. So is this the principal reason for using computers, or are they used to make record-keeping more efficient? The same survey – of small firms in services – asked how companies used their computers. More than one answer was allowed. Predictably, word-processing and accounting topped the list:

Word processing	56%
Accounting/bookkeeping	52%
Invoicing/billings	47%
Sales/purchases	44%
Payroll administration	33%
Processing orders	31%
Stock control/inventory	25%
Other use	32%

Source: Small Firms in Services – The 1994 Survey, by James Curran, Robert A Blackburn and Martina Klett, Small Business Research Centre, May 1994

23

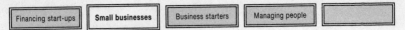
ADVICE FOR SMALL BUSINESSES

■ Where do you go for advice?

Are you thinking of starting a small business? For many, the whole process seems like trying to run through a minefield. And the only safe way through a minefield is to find someone who knows where the mines are. So who can you turn to? Barclays Bank asked a sample of starters who they turned to, and received the following answers:

Advisor	Percentage of starters seeking advice
Bank	30
Training and Enterprise Council	16
Friends/relatives	15
Enterprise agency	12
Accountant	11

- Women are also more inclined than men to seek advice and training before starting up, with one in three women undertaking training as compared with one in five men.

Source: Starting in business. Barclays Research on Small Business Characteristics, Barclays Bank plc, 1995.

■ How do you view your bank?

Businesses owners were asked about their banks' attitudes to charges and borrowing, and whether they had considered changing their banks. As well as a national average, the responses were split according to gender, with a category for mixed ownership.

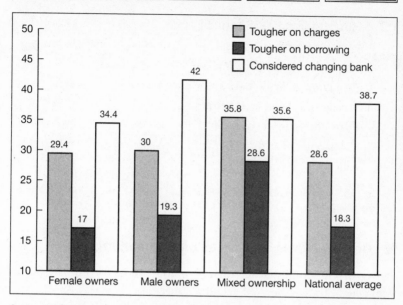

Source: *38th Quarterly Survey of Small Firms, Quarter 2, 1995*, The Forum of Private Business.[1]

■ *What type of businesses use Training and Enterprise Councils (TECs)?*

Training and Enterprise Councils provide a variety of services. Through Business Link, they operate the Government's Start-up scheme, giving grants and training to new businesses. They act as a training referral agency, putting the providers in touch with the users, and vice versa. And they provide on-going training and consultancy for small businesses – free in the first 18 months, and at reduced costs subsequently.

If you have recently set up a business, or know someone who has, then you will probably want to know whether the TECs can help. Knowing which sectors find the TECs helpful is one way of assessing their contribution. This survey covered small businesses in services only, and discovered that computer service firms were the most likely to use TECs:

---

[1] See also Current Financial and Accounting Issues – Banks – pp 246–250

Advertising, Marketing and Design	21%
Computer Services	36%
Employment, Training and Secretarial Agencies	33%
Free Houses, Wine Bars and Restaurants	5%
Garage and Vehicle Repairers	17%
Plant and Equipment Hire	15%
Video and Leisure	9%
All	19%

Source: Small Firms in Services – The 1994 Survey, by James Curran, Robert A Blackburn and Martina Klett, Small Business Research Centre, May 1994

■ *Do small firms in services use consultants?*

Perhaps you would rather turn to a consultant for advice. So do other small firms in services feel the same?

● Over the 12 months to March/April 1994, only 12.3% of respondents had used a consultant.

Source: Small Firms in Services – The 1994 Survey, by James Curran, Robert A Blackburn and Martina Klett, Small Business Research Centre, May 1994

■ *What do those who use consultants think of them?*

You may have used a consultant, and lived to regret it. If so, are you alone? No, you are not, although 60% of those who had used consultancy thought its quality was 'good':

Assessment of consultant	Percentage of respondents
'Good'	60
Mixed views	36
'Bad'	4

Source: Small Firms in Services – The 1994 Survey, by James Curran, Robert A Blackburn and Martina Klett, Small Business Research Centre, May 1994

BUSINESS STARTERS

SURVIVAL

■ What are your chances of survival?

Anyone who takes the enormous risks involved in starting up a business must ask themselves one basic question – will I survive? Obviously, your personality, your product, the nature of your finance and your market will all affect your chances of survival. However, it is interesting to know how many new businesses survive.

- Despite a recent improvement in the survival rate amongst UK start-ups, around 20% of all new businesses are failing to survive their first 18 months of trading.

- More than 50% close within 3 years.

Barclays Bank believes such high closure rates in the early stages of the business reflect, to a significant extent, inadequate planning and preparation by business owners before starting up.

Source: Starting up in business. Barclays Research on Small Business Characteristics, Barclays Bank Plc, 1995.

■ Do small businesses grow?

Perhaps you feel that small is beautiful, and have no desire to grow beyond a certain limit. Or perhaps you feel the sky's the limit. Either way, it helps to know how other small businesses fare.

- The majority of small businesses remain small; over two-thirds of small businesses record an annual turnover of less than £20,000.

Source: Starting up in business. Barclays Research on Small Business Characteristics, Barclays Bank Plc, 1995.

■ *How does recession affect small businesses?*

Supposing the going gets tough – as in the last few years, with the recession. Is your business more likely to go to the wall? Sadly, yes – during the recession, there was a dramatic rise in business closures, and the total number of businesses fell in 1993:

	Numbers of businesses (000s)	
Year	Opening	Closing
1990	520	454
1991	352	554
1992	372	443
1993	414	372
1994	446	386

Source: Starting up in business. Barclays Research on Small Business Characteristics, Barclays Bank Plc, 1995.

■ *What type of small businesses in services are most likely to survive a recession?*

One way of finding out what your chances of success are is to find out how other people have fared. The early 1990s saw many small service companies begin – and a fair number go to the wall. So what was the survival rate? The Small Business Research Centre monitored the success of a sample of small businesses in various sectors from 1990-1994. Overall, 60.1% of them survived the period. The failure rate was highest in employment, training and secretarial agencies; there only 40% of the original sample survived:

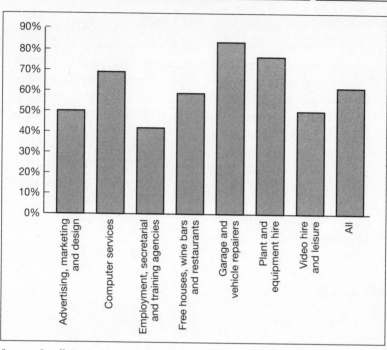

Source: Small Firms in Services – The 1994 Survey, by James Curran, Robert A Blackburn and Martina Klett, Small Business Research Centre, May 1994

■ What strategies do small firms in services use to cope with a recession?

The economic climate has been unpredictable in recent years – although some commentators think that the economy is on the upturn, others are still rather depressed about it. 1992-1994 were some of the toughest years for small firms in services. If you are thinking of setting up a service company, it might help to know how similar firms survived these years.

The same survey asked companies what strategies they had adopted between 1992 and 1994. More than one answer was allowed.

In 1992-1993, there was a clear emphasis on defensive strategies (cutting costs and pressuring debtors to pay more quickly, for example) and a lack of proactive strategies such as spending on marketing and advertising or investing in new equipment. In 1994, there was a shift to proactive strategies, without abandoning the defensive ones:

Strategy	1992	1993	1994
Cut fixed costs/overheads	75%	56%	83%
Cut labour costs	56%	34%	50%
Delayed payments to creditors	50%	39%	43%
Pressured debtors to pay more quickly	70%	66%	70%
Introduced new services/products	48%	52%	56%
Expanded into new markets	36%	37%	40%
Introduced new equipment	36%	40%	48%
Introduced new working methods	47%	36%	44%
Reduced marketing and/or advertising expenditures	46%	48%	36%
Increased marketing and/or advertising expenditures	18%	19%	34%
Reduced borrowing	48%	36%	42%
Increased borrowing	16%	12%	18%

Source: Small Firms in Services – The 1994 Survey, by James Curran, Robert A Blackburn and Martina Klett, Small Business Research Centre, May 1994

CHARACTERISTICS

For many, the desire to be their own boss and start up in business stems from a strong sense of independence and self-reliance. Some are also spurred on by the conviction that they can do better than the companies for which they work. This entrepreneurial spirit is reflected in the consistently high level of start-ups seen over the last decade; even during the recession, there was no dramatic fall in the level of start-ups.

■ What was the employment situation of business starters at the time of starting up?

Perhaps you have a secure job, but have simply caught the business bug. Or perhaps you cannot get a job, and have decided to branch out on your own. Is it unusual to give up job security for the increased challenge of being your own boss? The figures suggest otherwise; 68% of business starters surveyed were employed:

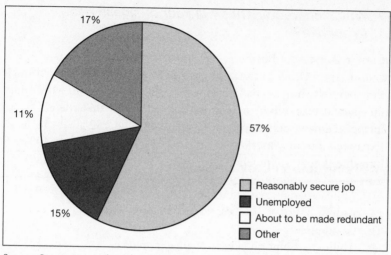

Source: *Starting up in business*. Barclays Research on Small Business Characteristics, Barclays Bank Plc, 1995.

■ *How old are business starters when they first start their own business?*

If you've lived half a life-span before you decide to do your own thing, are you a late starter? Is the desire to start a business a factor of youth? The picture has changed. Eight years ago, two-thirds of business starters were below the age of 35; now it's under half.

Age of business starter	1988	1995
16-24	22%	9%
25-34	41%	39%
35-44	24%	31%
45-54	11%	18%
55+	2%	3%

Source: *Starting up in business*. Barclays Research on Small Business Characteristics, Barclays Bank Plc, 1995.

■ Which characteristics will your business need to survive?

If you're starting a business, you must wonder whether you've got what it takes. Other business starters were asked to assess what qualities they felt they, or their business, needed to survive. More than one answer was allowed. The vast majority said that the ability to manage was important:

Key strengths for business survival	
1. Ability to manage the business	93%
2. Better quality products/services than competitors	90%
3. Good quality staff	86%
4. Ability to adapt quickly to change in market	85%
5. Well capitalised	68%
6. Lower costs than competitors	67%
7. High investment back into business	58%

Source: Starting up in business. Barclays Research on Small Business Characteristics, Barclays Bank Plc, 1995.

■ What are the main strengths that help small business starters run their business?

There is a difference between survival and security. So are the qualities needed to run a business successfully different from those required to ensure survival? Business starters seem to think so – interpersonal skills topped the list:

Being able to get on with customers and staff	90%
Motivation	88%
Sticking to the job (resilience)	84%
Being competitive	83%
Being decisive	81%
Thinking through decisions	78%
Sound business acumen	69%
Knowing when to seek advice/help	68%

Source: Starting up in business. Barclays Research on Small Business Characteristics, Barclays Bank Plc, 1995.

■ *How hard do the self-employed work?*

Do the benefits really out weigh the cost? Most self-employed people must think so – despite their increased freedom, they claim to work very long hours. But is this really the case?

- A self-employed business person works on average $9\frac{1}{2}$ hours a day, six days a week.

Source: Starting up in business. Barclays Research on Small Business Characteristics, Barclays Bank Plc, 1995.

Averages do not give the full picture. Another survey – this time for the Small Business Centre – asked owner-managers how many hours they worked per week. Some did work less than 40 hours:

Hours	Percentage
40 or less	17
41 – 50	17
51 – 70	47
Over 70	19

Source: Soft Loan Schemes and the Finance Gap – An Evaluation Study, by James Curran, Robert A Blackburn and Martina Klett-Davis, Small Business Research Centre, August 1994

■ *Do starters have no time for a personal life? Do they find running a business sufficiently fulfilling that the sacrifices are worth it?*

There must be a good reason for sacrificing a secure job, and a nine-to-five Monday to Friday routine. If you are worried about this aspect of your choice to start in business, what do other business starters feel? Do business starters record a detrimental affect on their personal lives? Or are they happy with their choices?

- Over 55% of starters found themselves with less time for family and friends.
- Yet only 10% have found it worse than expected.
- A reassuring 37% claim that starting up has been a lot more satisfying than anticipated.

Source: Starting up in business. Barclays Research on Small Business Characteristics, Barclays Bank Plc, 1995.

■ *Do starters expect an increased demand for better value and service?*

- 55% of small businesses expect the trend for consumers to seek better value and service to continue.

Source: Starting up in business. Barclays Research on Small Business Characteristics, Barclays Bank Plc, 1995.

■ *Do starters think competition is increasing?*

- 67% agree that competition will increase, as businesses become more aggressive in their attempts to gain market share.

Source: Starting up in business. Barclays Research on Small Business Characteristics, Barclays Bank Plc, 1995.

PUBLIC OPINION

■ Are people who start their own businesses different from the rest of the population?

16% of Britons in employment have seriously considered starting up in business – about 3.5 million of the working population. So the desire to start a business is not unusual. But perhaps the real entrepreneurs are different? Barclays asked the starters themselves, and the general public, whether they felt that people who start their own business are different from the rest of the population. It is interesting to see the differences in the answers:

	Percentage	
	General Public	Small Businesses
Yes	30	59
No	68	38
Don't know	2	3

Source: Starting up in business. Barclays Research on Small Business Characteristics, Barclays Bank Plc, 1995.

■ What do the general public think make MEN better business starters?

A cross-section of the population were asked which characteristics made men more suited to starting a business. 13% felt that there was still some discrimination in the business world:

Aggressive	22%
Determined	19%
General discrimination against women in business	13%
Fewer family commitments	11%
More business experience	8%

Source: Starting up in business. Barclays Research on Small Business Characteristics, Barclays Bank Plc, 1995.

■ *What do the general public think make WOMEN better business starters?*

The same sample were asked what characteristics gave women the edge as business starters. Women's determination and their innate ability to organise featured prominently:

Determined	47%
Natural organisers	26%
Work harder/more conscientious	9%
Better with people	7%
Shrewd	5%

Source: Starting up in business. Barclays Research on Small Business Characteristics, Barclays Bank Plc, 1995.

WOMEN AND SMALL BUSINESSES

Women play an important role in the small business sector, typically accounting for around a third of all start-ups. In addition, almost half (45%) provide the sole or main income for their household.

■ *How many start-ups are by women?*

If you are a women and want to start up in business, are you joining a growing trend, or setting the pace? The proportion of women starting businesses seems to have lessened since 1988:

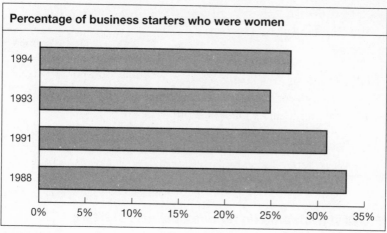

Percentage of business starters who were women

1994	~27%
1993	~25%
1991	~31%
1988	~33%

Source: Starting up in business. Barclays Research on Small Business Characteristics, Barclays Bank Plc, 1995.

■ *Do women face more problems than men when starting-up?*

The answer to this question may vary with gender – so Barclays split the findings accordingly. More women than men said they thought it was harder for women:

	Yes-more	About the same
Men	48%	30%
Women	63%	24%

Source: Starting up in business. Barclays Research on Small Business Characteristics, Barclays Bank Plc, 1995.

■ *What business characteristics do women need for survival?*

Do women feel that they need different characteristics when it comes to survival? They seem largely to recognise the same requirements for successful business management as their male counterparts:

	Percentage	
	Men	**Women**
Ability to manage the business	92	96
Better quality products/services than competitors	89	93
Well capitalised (cash to fall back on)	66	73
Lower costs than competitors	66	70

Source: Starting up in business. Barclays Research on Small Business Characteristics, Barclays Bank Plc, 1995.

■ What problems do female business starters experience?

If you are trying to balance a business and a family life, or coping with a reluctant partner's lack of support, are you alone? Or do a lot of women find the going difficult? The main source of worry was not domestic – a worrying 45% of women reported not being taken seriously by colleagues or business contacts:

Not being taken seriously by colleagues/business contacts	45%
The additional burden of family responsibilities	40%
Sex discrimination by suppliers/customers	26%
Pressure to stay at home and support partner	16%
Sex discrimination by institutions/government	14%
High cost of crèche/nannies/nursery facilities	9%

Source: Starting up in business. Barclays Research on Small Business Characteristics, Barclays Bank Plc, 1995.

■ What kinds of businesses do women start?

Are some sectors more 'female' than others? If you are a woman starting a garage, are you out on a limb? Certainly, more women start businesses in traditionally female-dominated sectors like retailing, as the following figures show:

	Percentage	
	Women	Men
Retailing	30	22
Catering/leisure	11	8
Property/finance	10	13
Production	9	18
Wholesale	5	5
Construction	5	6
Motor trade/transport	1	8

Source: Starting up in business. Barclays Research on Small Business Characteristics, Barclays Bank Plc, 1995.

■ *What legal form of business do women choose?*

Are women more likely to set up partnerships, and men more likely to go it alone?

There are some differences in the legal forms which women choose:

	Percentage	
	Women	Men
Self-employed	65	55
Partnership	25	20
Limited company	10	25

Source: Starting up in business. Barclays Research on Small Business Characteristics, Barclays Bank Plc, 1995.

■ *What business premises do women use?*

One obvious way for skilled women to re-enter the workforce after a break for child-rearing is for them to work from home – they might well be able to return sooner, and work more flexibly. So do more women then men decide to work from home? What about the other choices – are women less or more likely to set up a restaurant?

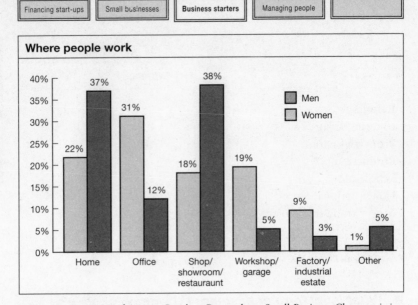

Where people work

Source: Starting up in business. Barclays Research on Small Business Characteristics, Barclays Bank Plc, 1995.

CONCERNS

Small businesses share many concerns with the business world at large. However, some of their main worries are a function of their size – inevitably, they are more vulnerable to late payment, or more likely to be crippled by a high business rate or tax demand.

■ *What were the most important concerns affecting small businesses in mid 1995?*

What problems do you have running your business? It may help you to know whether you are alone, or whether other small business owners find themselves in the same boat. Small business owners were asked what was their MOST important issue:

Late payment	16%
Uniform Business Rate	14%
Lack of sales	13%
Cost/availability of finance	11%
Red tape	8%
Tax burden	7%
Cost of tax admin.	6%
Unfair competition (from plcs)	4%
Bad debts	3%

- The black economy, lack of skilled employees, the cost or availability of insurance and crime were each cited by less than 3% of respondents.

- Court costs, unfair competition (from other small enterprises), supplies shortages and government procurement all registered less than 1%.

Source: *38th Quarterly Survey of Small Firms*, Quarter 2, 1995, The Forum of Private Business.

■ *What issues are significant to small businesses?*

Deciding what is your worst worry is one thing – identifying which of many issues are significant is another. The same survey allowed respondents to identify several areas of concern, so that it could discover which issues were significant to small businesses.

- 51% thought that the Uniform Business Rate (UBR) was a significant area of concern, in spite of Transitional Relief arrangements.

- 39.7% were concerned about red tape; the survey suggests that there is 'a considerable lack of understanding of the resources available to SMEs in attempting compliance' within government departments.

- Insurance difficulties continue to plague small businesses (38.8%); this is of course related to their worries about crime (25.8%). Most of the businesses recorded that the consequent increase in overhead costs has very serious implications.

Source: *38th Quarterly Survey of Small Firms*, Quarter 2, 1995, The Forum of Private Business.

■ *Are other small businesses appealing against UBR revaluations?*

Do you feel that the UBR is unfair to your business? If the Uniform Business Rate is such a source of concern, this must be reflected in the number of appeals. It is – 56.8% of small businesses said they were appealing or considering doing so. But the picture does vary by region, as the following graph shows:

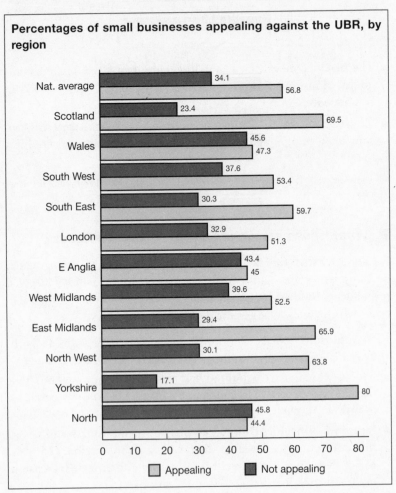

Percentages of small businesses appealing against the UBR, by region

Region	Not appealing	Appealing
Nat. average	34.1	56.8
Scotland	23.4	69.5
Wales	45.6	47.3
South West	37.6	53.4
South East	30.3	59.7
London	32.9	51.3
E Anglia	43.4	45
West Midlands	39.6	52.5
East Midlands	29.4	65.9
North West	30.1	63.8
Yorkshire	17.1	80
North	45.8	44.4

☐ Appealing   ■ Not appealing

Source: 38th Quarterly Survey of Small Firms, Quarter 2, 1995, The Forum of Private Business.

■ *Which sectors are appealing against UBR revaluations the most?*

If you are appealing against the UBR, it may help your case to know which sectors find it most unfair.

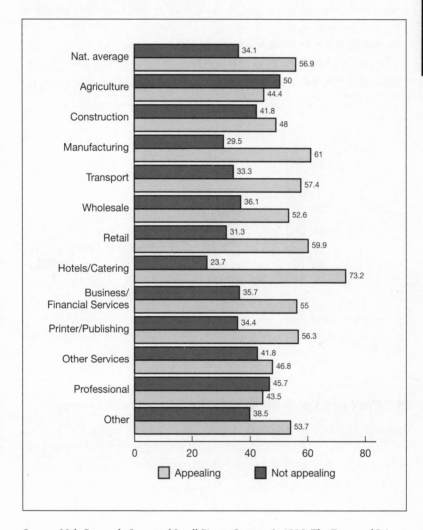

Source: 38th Quarterly Survey of Small Firms, Quarter 2, 1995, The Forum of Private Business.

43

■ What are the problems of expanding small businesses?

Perhaps you started a business a while ago, and are now looking to expand. Are the possible problems now old hat – ones that you came across at the beginning – or does expansion bring with it a new set of challenges?

Late payment and the shortage of skilled employees were significantly more important to expanding businesses than they were to the nation as a whole:

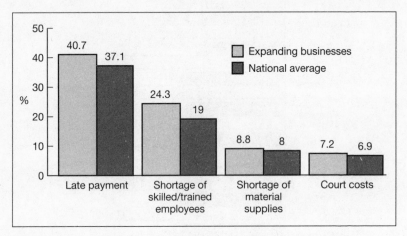

Source: *38th Quarterly Survey of Small Firms, Quarter 2, 1995*, The Forum of Private Business.

■ What problems do female business owners have?

Are any of these problems and concerns more pressing for women business owners? Do they experience more difficulty obtaining or financing insurance, for example? These three factors seemed to worry women particularly:

	Women	Men	Overall
UBR	56%	48%	55%
Lack of sales	47%	38%	40%
Cost/availability of insurance	42%	39%	38%

Source: 38th Quarterly Survey of Small Firms, Quarter 2, 1995, The Forum of Private Business.

■ *Are small businesses expanding?*

A major concern of all small business owners is growth. You can't stand still in the business world, so if you don't grow, you shrink. How healthy are your fellow small businesses? Are the majority expanding? The proportion of businesses that were expanding, categorised by number of employees, is:

No. of employees	Percentage
1 – 4	30
5 – 9	41
10 – 19	48
20 – 49	55
50 – 99	56
100+	43
National average	41

Source: 38th Quarterly Survey of Small Firms, Quarter 2, 1995, The Forum of Private Business.

■ *Are small businesses with a high turnover expanding faster?*

Expansion for small firms therefore seems more likely with more employees – does a larger turnover also make a difference?

Turnover size	Percentage of firms expanding
Less than £21,000	31
£21,000 – £44,000	29
£45,000 – £89,000	30
£90,000 – £149,000	31
£150,000 – £499,000	40
£500,000 – £999,000	47
£1 m – £ 4.9 m	56
5 m +	46
National average	41

Source: 38th Quarterly Survey of Small Firms, Quarter 2, 1995, The Forum of Private Business.

MANAGING PEOPLE

DECISION-MAKING

■ *What's the most important attribute for a manager of a small firm?*

How do you decide whether you are cut out for management? One way is to ask those who manage what qualities are needed. Small business managers were asked what they thought the most important attribute for managing a small firm was. Surprisingly, such qualities as delegation skills were thought to be less important:

Ability to determine priorities	22%
Perseverance	19%
Adaptability	19%
Ability to motivate others	12%
Communication skills	10%
High stress tolerance	7%
Ability to delegate	4%
Ability to learn from mistakes	3%
Creativity	1%
Emotional stability	1%
Self-analysis	1%
Negotiation skills	1%

Source: Quarterly Small Business Management Report No. 3, September 1993, Lloyds Bank/Small Business Research Trust.

■ *What are managers' views on the motivation of others?*

Do managers appreciate the staff that they work with? A lot can be discovered by examining managers' attitudes to employees in general. So are they valued? Respondents were asked to choose between two contrasting views of employees in general:

- 57% of those surveyed thought that:

  'The average person is not really a self-starter, has only a relatively modest level of ambition and does not usually go looking for responsibility.'

- 43% of those surveyed thought that:

  'The average person enjoys a challenge, is basically fairly ambitious and not only accepts but also seeks greater responsibility.'

The responses varied by sector and by region:

- More respondents (67%) in manufacturing tended to pick the first statement than those in other sectors, perhaps reflecting a 'traditional' view of employees in that sector.

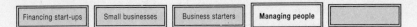

- More respondents (53%) in the South picked the second statement than those in other regions.

Source: Quarterly Small Business Management Report No. 3, September 1993, Lloyds Bank/Small Business Research Trust.

■ *What are managers' decision-making styles?*

Are these attitudes to employees reflected in managers' decision making styles? If the majority of managers think that their employees do not go looking for responsibility, then why give it to them? Despite the previous findings, most respondents (53%) said they had a consultative style:

Most problems placed with others	–
Obtain views – then decide	53%
Take decisions – then 'sell' them	20%
Take decisions – to get things done	26%

- Managers in the very smallest firms selected the authoritarian 'take decisions' more often than those in other firms.

Source: Quarterly Small Business Management Report No. 3, September 1993, Lloyds Bank/Small Business Research Trust.

■ *Are managers born or made?*

If managers are born, then there's little hope for those who are not natural leaders. So do managers feel that the relevant skills can be learnt, or are they innate? More than two thirds felt that management skills can be learned rather than being inborn:

Management skills can be learned	68%
Management skills are basically innate	32%

Source: Quarterly Small Business Management Report No. 3, September 1993, Lloyds Bank/Small Business Research Trust.

48

DELEGATION

■ *What tasks are not delegated?*

So if your style is naturally democratic, and you trust your employees to take responsibility, what are you most likely to delegate? Is it an issue of continuing doing what you are best at? Or is the decision to delegate made more on the basis of where the buck stops? The latter seems to be the guiding principle; 70% of managers keep responsibility for drafting proposals for finance, yet only 17% undertake stock checks:

Tasks least likely to be delegated

1. Personally draft proposals for raising finance
2. Handle important order enquiries
3. Undertake staff appraisals
4. Draft employment contracts/letters
5. Design company sales literature
6. Prepare regular sales figures
7. Personally evaluate potential major suppliers
8. Prepare regular management accounts
9. Open all company mail
10. Personally draft quality control procedures
11. Personally test prototypes
12. Prepare statutory returns
13. Formulate training programmes in detail
14. Man company's stands at exhibitions
15. Formulate equipment maintenance schedules
16. Undertake stock checks

Source: Quarterly Small Business Management Report No. 3, September 1993, Lloyds Bank/Small Business Research Trust.

■ *What tasks are delegated?*

Are all routine tasks delegated? If you no longer open company mail, or formulate equipment maintenance schedules, are you alone? Respondents were asked which tasks were delegated – multiple answers were allowed.

Prepare statutory returns	68%
Undertake stock checks	65%
Open all company mail	61%
Prepare regular management accounts	56%
Prepare regular sales figures	46%
Formulate equipment maintenance schedules	45%
Formulate training programmes in detail	43%
Personally draft quality control procedures	38%
Design company sales literature	35%
Personally evaluate potential major suppliers	35%
Draft employment contracts/letters	31%
Handle important order enquiries	26%
Personally test prototypes	25%
Man company's stands at exhibitions	21%
Undertake staff appraisals	21%
Personally draft proposals for raising finance	10%

Source: Quarterly Small Business Management Report No. 3, September 1993, Lloyds Bank/Small Business Research Trust.

■ *So are managers satisfied with the extent to which tasks can be delegated?*

Do you feel that your employees take enough of the strain? Given that managers make the decision about delegation, it might be reasonable to suppose that they were satisfied with the level of delegation. However, this is far from the case:

● Only 56% said they were satisfied.

Source: Quarterly Small Business Management Report No. 3, September 1993, Lloyds Bank/Small Business Research Trust.

MANAGING RESOURCES

Transport   52
Theft from commercial vehicles ■ Company vehicles
and smaller firms

Relocation   62
Domestic relocation ■ International relocation

Time management   69
Restructuring ■ Workload ■ The future
■ Practicalities ■ Priorities

Communications   79
Flatter organisations

Logistics   83
Purchasing ■ Supply chain partnerships
■ Environmental considerations ■ Costs
■ Outsourcing distribution ■ Logistics across Europe

TRANSPORT

THEFT FROM COMMERCIAL VEHICLES

■ *Do you experience a problem with theft from commercial vehicles?*

If you are running a haulage company, then theft can be a major concern. Yet theft of goods in transit affects most companies – and not just in terms of inconvenience. For many companies, there is a substantial element of consequential loss – if supplies are not received, then products cannot be manufactured, and will not be ready for sale. So how much of a problem is theft from commercial vehicles?

There are no national statistics on commercial vehicle theft. The only available figures group together the theft of motorbikes, caravans, diggers and cars as well as light vans and large goods vehicles. They were compiled by the Freight Transport Association (FTA), from a survey of its members:

- In 1992, 81% of all goods moved were transported by road.
- Approximately 4,000 FTA member companies suffered some form of vehicle or load theft in 1993.
- The estimated cost of criminal losses to FTA members is around £500 million.
- The total cost of thefts of, or from, the Freight Transport Association's members' vehicles in 1993, including estimates of consequential loss, is thought to be in excess of £1 billion:

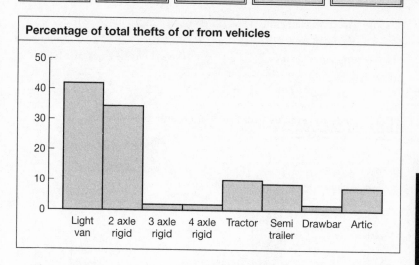

Percentage of total thefts of or from vehicles

- The popularity amongst thieves of light vans and two axle rigid vehicles reflects their proliferation – they are the most popular commercial vehicle types.

Source: Theft Prevention Guide, Freight Transport Association, 1994

■ *Are your vehicles being fitted with anti-theft devices?*

There are many anti-theft devices currently available. Surely it makes sense to fit one, given the size of the losses experienced?

- The same survey found that only 38% of respondents operating vehicle fleets had anti-theft equipment of any kind fitted to protect their vehicles.

- Even companies adding anti-theft equipment did not always do so across the whole fleet. If this trend is reflected nationally, only one in four vehicles is equipped with a security device.

Source: Theft Prevention Guide, Freight Transport Association, 1994

■ *Are some devices more effective than others?*

If you are considering fitting anti-theft devices, then which ones work best? One feature of crime-free fleets is that they have more immobilisers fitted. Yet alarms are the most popular retrofit device. These have an obvious drawback – many alarm systems are not self-arming and rely on drivers activating them.

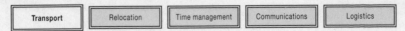

Companies making the decision to invest in security will undoubtedly equip those vehicles which are seen as most at risk. One way of discovering what works best is to analyse which devices are fitted in crime-free fleets:

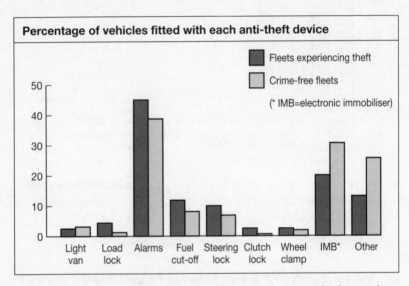

Percentage of vehicles fitted with each anti-theft device

■ Fleets experiencing theft

□ Crime-free fleets

(* IMB=electronic immobiliser)

The 'other' category included miscellaneous devices which members believed deterred thieves. Among these were the carriage of sticks, dogs, guns and raw sewage – these are clearly not means available to all vehicle operators!

Source: Theft Prevention Guide, Freight Transport Association, 1994

■ *Why are some fleets crime-free?*

Operators of fleets not suffering theft were asked why they thought that was. Many cited driver vigilance. Even more said they thought good luck was their only protection. Very few felt that the lack of theft arose from realistic measures to protect vehicles.

Source: Theft Prevention Guide, Freight Transport Association, 1994

■ *Where and when are your vehicles most at risk?*

If you are attempting to combat theft – or trying to decide which anti-theft devices to fit – it help helps to understand the nature and timing of the crime. Nearly half the thefts actually took place from the operators' home depot.

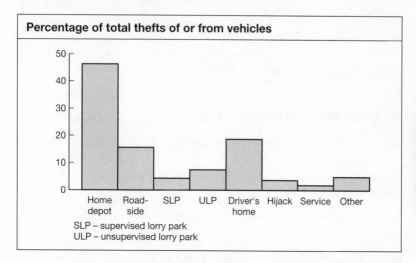

Percentage of total thefts of or from vehicles

SLP – supervised lorry park
ULP – unsupervised lorry park

- The home depot is a vulnerable location for two main reasons:

1. If a vehicle is parked in the same place on a regular basis it becomes easily known to thieves.
2. Once the perimeter of a site has been breached, the thief is left to work undisturbed.

- For similar reasons, nearly 20% of thefts took place outside drivers' homes.

Source: Theft Prevention Guide, Freight Transport Association, 1994

■ *Are supervised lorry parks safe?*

The next few questions relate to vehicles in transit. Is it possible to cut down on theft simply by giving your drivers guidelines as to where to park during rest periods?

Certainly, parking in a supervised lorry park will help – vehicles parked in these areas overnight suffered half the thefts of those kept at unsupervised parks. Although there are problems with the provision and availability of these parks, they were twice as popular with respondents.

Source: Theft Prevention Guide, Freight Transport Association, 1994

■ Are motorway service areas safe?

Motorway service areas are relatively crime free, principally because they are busy sites which vehicles generally only pass through. Typically, means of entry and exit to such sites are limited and easily blocked off, offering good security.

Source: Theft Prevention Guide, Freight Transport Association, 1994

■ What about roadside thefts?

Roadside thefts are frequently undertaken by opportunistic thieves. Only a small, but nevertheless significant, number of cases involved highly organised criminal gangs using prior knowledge of when and where a vehicle/trailer would be vulnerable.

Source: Theft Prevention Guide, Freight Transport Association, 1994

■ Are there regional differences in thefts?

The survey suggests that there are significant geographical differences in the occurrence of theft, allowing for the distances involved in members' work:

	Location of operating bases	Occurrence of thefts
London & SE	22%	20%
Scotland and NE	15%	3%
Midlands	22%	18%
Northern	23%	48%
Western	18%	11%

Source: Theft Prevention Guide, Freight Transport Association, 1994

■ Proportionately, where are the most thefts occurring?

The north of England appears to experience a disproportionate number of thefts even when compared with the south-east – generally considered to be a crime black spot. The rest of England and Wales suffers very few crimes by comparison, with significantly fewer thefts reported in Scotland and Northern Ireland.

Source: Theft Prevention Guide, Freight Transport Association, 1994

■ *Why are there regional differences?*

The most likely reason for these regional differences are underlying social and demographic trends. Recent police operations against organised lorry thieves have however, highlighted the following factors:

- The thief can operate most effectively where there is a good transport infrastructure which makes it easy to dispose of stolen goods quickly.
- The thief is at an advantage when operating in close proximity to the final market for stolen goods, for example businesses wanting to buy cheaper parts for their vehicles.

Source: Theft Prevention Guide, Freight Transport Association, 1994.

■ *What makes your vehicles vulnerable?*

Can the problem be addressed by being more careful? If some vehicles are more vulnerable than others to theft, does it help to understand why?

Vehicles and their loads may be vulnerable for a number of reasons:

1. They carry a high value of goods or the thieves have a good market for them.
2. Basic security measures are not taken and so they are fundamentally insecure.
3. Thieves are able to take advantage of the 'human factor', for example failure to activate an anti-theft device.
4. They are left in insecure locations, either because of the nature of the work they are involved in, or because the risks have not been anticipated.

Source: Theft Prevention Guide, Freight Transport Association, 1994

MANAGING
RESOURCES

COMPANY VEHICLES AND SMALLER FIRMS

Has the change in taxation policy over company vehicles affected you? If you are running a small business, and are reviewing your position on company vehicles, then a recent survey may well be of use. The Small Business Research Trust, in conjunction with Lloyds Bank, undertook a survey of small firms and company vehicles. It was fairly wide-ranging, covering issues as diverse as vehicle finance and which car to choose.

■ How many vehicles does your company have?

If you are wondering whether your company has rather too many vehicles, then you may be interested in how many vehicles other companies have. The vast majority (85%) of respondents' businesses have cars for every day use. The "no car" category includes non-respondents, and the survey suggests that this category may well run cars privately for tax reasons.

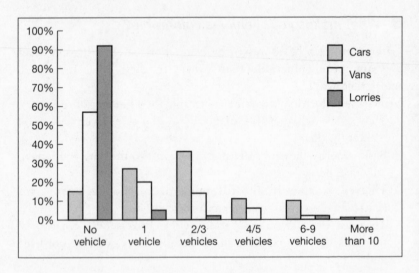

Fewer than half of respondents use vans; less than 10% use lorries.

Source: Quarterly Small Business Management Report, No.3, Vol. 3, 1995, Lloyds Bank/Small Business Research Trust.

■ How much do you spend on company vehicles?

If you find that company vehicles are a fairly major item on the balance sheet, then you are not alone. Expenditure on vehicles is a large item; even in the smallest firms (with 0 – 4 employees), 43% spend between £5,000 and £50,000 a year:

Expenditure on all vehicles (£'s)	Percentage
Under 5,000	38%
5,000 – 9,999	21%
10,000 – 49,999	32%
50,000 – 99,999	5%
100,000 – 249,999	1%

Source: Quarterly Small Business Management Report, No.3, Vol. 3, 1995, Lloyds Bank/Small Business Research Trust.

■ Does your company buy cars for business use, or as a personal benefit for staff?

Knowing how other businesses answer this question might help you shape your company vehicle policy – clarifying whether vehicles are normally bought as a perk, or only when necessary for business purposes. The majority of respondents stated that company cars are acquired primarily for business use:

Mainly for business	47%
Mainly as a perk/reward	10%
Both for business and as a personal benefit	32%

- Looking at the breakdown by number of employees, cars as rewards are more likely in the larger businesses.

Source: Quarterly Small Business Management Report, No.3, Vol. 3, 1995, Lloyds Bank/Small Business Research Trust.

■ *How does your company finance its vehicle purchases?*

Perhaps you are considering a leasing arrangement for your company vehicles. If so, would you be alone, or is this the most common solution? Of course, some companies use more than one method:

Hire/Purchase	36%
Purchase without borrowing	30%
Purchase with some borrowing	26%
Lease/Lease Purchase	23%
Purchase with 100% borrowed	4%

- The manufacturing sector particularly favours the hire/purchase method (41%).
- The smallest firms (0 – 4 employees) are the most likely to purchase vehicles with some external borrowing, and are less likely than other firms to use hire/purchase and leasing.

Source: Quarterly Small Business Management Report, No.3, Vol. 3, 1995, Lloyds Bank/Small Business Research Trust.

■ *How often does your company replace its vehicles?*

Cars in other companies tend to be replaced within 1 – 5 years, with more towards the end of that period than at the beginning. None are replaced within 12 months; only 9% are replaced after five years. Larger firms, and firms in the South, seem to replace cars at significantly longer intervals. Vans are replaced at longer intervals than cars. While relatively few respondents own lorries, in no case did they say they replaced them in less than 3 years.

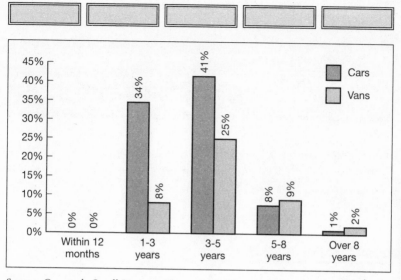

Source: *Quarterly Small Business Management Report, No.3, Vol. 3, 1995,* Lloyds Bank/Small Business Research Trust.

■ *What makes of car does your company choose?*

Your company may well have been loyal to one dealer until now, but is currently considering a change. Finding out which makes of car are popular with other companies will help you make a decision. Respondents stressed the economic advantages of higher-priced, lower depreciation cars, and favoured the following makes:

Ford	35%
Audi/BMW/Mercedes/Porsche	25%
Vauxhall/GM	21%
Rover/British Leyland	18%
Saab/Volvo	18%
Peugeot/Chrysler	16%
Toyota/Honda/Nissan	13%

Source: *Quarterly Small Business Management Report, No.3, Vol. 3, 1995,* Lloyds Bank/Small Business Research Trust.

RELOCATION

This section covers managing relocation in terms of provisions for employees. You'll find information on choosing where to locate under Current Management Issues on pages 203–210.

DOMESTIC RELOCATION

■ *How many companies relocate their employees within the UK, how many staff do they move, and how often?*

So often the answer to filling a management vacancy is to send someone from another branch or office whom you trust – rather than looking to recruit. If you require your employees to move to other UK locations, are you unusual? It seems not – in Ernst & Young's *Company Relocation & Practice*, nearly 2/3 of respondents had moved between 1 and 25 people in the last three years, and most expected a similar pattern of relocation over the next three years.

Source: Company Relocation & Practice, Ernst & Young/CBI, June 1994

■ *Does your company pay for employees' expenses when they are buying and selling their properties in the UK?*

If you are relocating employees within the UK, which expenses do you pay? Almost all companies pay for legal and estate agent fees:

Expenses	Percentage of companies who pay expenses	
	When selling	When buying
Legal fees	99%	100%
Estate agent fees	97%	-
Advertising charges	69%	-
Mortgage redemption fees	54%	-
Disconnection of utilities	46%	-
Survey fees	-	94%
Stamp duty	-	88%
Land registry fees	-	84%
Mortgage arrangement fees	-	46%

Source: Company Relocation & Practice, Ernst & Young/CBI, June 1994

■ *Does your company pay for removals in the UK?*

If you did not pay removal costs, you really would be out on a limb. Direct removal costs are always paid for, but for other costs the pattern varies:

Removal charges	100%
Insurance in transit	86%
Packing/unpacking charges	77%
Storage	75%
Attaching/adapting fittings	27%

Source: Company Relocation & Practice, Ernst & Young/CBI, June 1994

■ *Does your company pay expenses for travel and subsistence in the UK during relocation?*

Virtually all of the companies interviewed looked after their own employees well during relocation – but not all companies took such care of their employees' families:

Expenses	Proportion of companies meeting expense
Temporary accommodation for employees in new areas	95%
Accommodation while house hunting	88%
Travel & expenses on removal	77%
Weekend return	74%
Temporary accommodation for family in new area	64%

Source: Company Relocation & Practice, Ernst & Young/CBI, June 1994

■ *Does your company pay for 'duplicate' expenses?*

A strange term this; it refers to expenses you have to meet in both places for a while – like council tax – and to the things you have to change because you've moved, like the children's school uniforms, and curtains because the old ones don't fit. How generous are companies?

Replacement of domestic goods	79%
Council tax at old location	32%
School uniforms	27%
Loss on season ticket	14%
Unexpired subscriptions	13%

Source: Company Relocation & Practice, Ernst & Young/CBI, June 1994

■ *Does your company pay for expenses such as bridging loans?*

Most companies pay for bridging loans. Surprisingly, few reimburse employees for any loss on the purchase price of their old home:

Bridging loan	70%
Loss over guaranteed price	49%
Outright purchase by employer	36%
Return gain over guaranteed price	31%
Loss on purchase price	22%

Source: Company Relocation & Practice, Ernst & Young/CBI, June 1994

■ *Does your company provide expenses for additional housing costs in the UK?*

More than half of the companies interviewed give an additional housing cost allowance:

Additional housing cost allowance	68%
Subsidised mortgage	27%
Company loan for deposit/house purchase	25%

Source: Company Relocation & Practice, Ernst & Young/CBI, June 1994

■ *What other provisions does your company make for temporary movers in the UK?*

Supposing your employees decide to rent until they have sold their old houses – will your company pick up the tab? What about when they lodge with someone and travel back to the family at weekends? How do other companies tackle these situations?

● 86% of companies give a rental allowance and 70% provide assistance with travel.

● Company housing is provided by 19%.

Source: Company Relocation & Practice, Ernst & Young/CBI, June 1994

INTERNATIONAL RELOCATION

■ *Does your company provide housing expenses for international moves?*

The costs of relocation are different if you are moving your employees abroad. It is more likely that the first accommodation abroad will be rented; there may be increased living, taxation and insurance costs in a different environment.

The costs of relocation are also much higher, of course, if you are seeking to move your employees abroad. So does this affect the average company's generosity? Sadly, yes – the general picture is that fewer companies meet all the costs of relocation if employees are moving beyond the UK.

Housing allowance	79%
House hunting trips	64%
Utilities payment – host country	53%
Insurance maintenance – host country	40%
House sale – home country	39%

Source: Company Relocation & Practice, Ernst & Young/CBI, June 1994

■ *Does your company provide expenses for education and settling in during international moves?*

To achieve an acceptable education for employees' children abroad, fees may have to be paid for children who were previously state-educated. Or parents may well choose to let the children stay in the UK and board, in which case, there is the question of the children's travel costs in school holidays. What does your company do? Are other companies sensitive to such issues?

Although most companies provide settling in payments, the position over educational costs is mixed:

Settling in payments	83%
Education – host country fees	72%
Travel costs – children	64%
Education – home country fees	48%

Source: Company Relocation & Practice, Ernst & Young/CBI, June 1994

■ *Does your company provide expenses for removals during international moves?*

Removal expenses overseas do not come cheap – so how generous is your company? You may well want to match the going rate. So how generous are other companies? Insurance payments are more common than those for freight:

Insurance in transit	94%
Sea freight	83%
Storage	78%
Air freight	70%

Source: Company Relocation & Practice, Ernst & Young/CBI, June 1994

■ *Does your company provide expenses for travel and leave?*

If you decide not to pay your employees' and their families' travel expenses, you would be considered very mean, given the figures overleaf:

Expenses	Proportion of companies meeting expense
Employee air fare to and from host country	100%
Spouse – air fare to and from host country	99%
Employee – home leave fares	97%
Children – home leave fares	96%

Source: Company Relocation & Practice, Ernst & Young/CBI, June 1994

■ *Does your company provide expenses for tax and other payments during international moves?*

There will, inevitably, be other costs involved in an international move. The cost of living may well be higher in the host country – or taxation rates might be very different. How many other companies help their employees adjust to these costs?

Payment	Proportion of companies who provide payments
Medical insurance	90%
Cost of living	74%
Tax equalisation	59%
Tax protection	30%

Source: Company Relocation & Practice, Ernst & Young/CBI, June 1994

TIME MANAGEMENT

RESTRUCTURING

The classic rules of time management (distinguishing between the urgent and important, planning and prioritising, and delegation) are probably the best known, yet least applied, features of management. You will find them covered in this chapter, and also in **The Essential Personnel Sourcebook**. What is less well known is how UK managers are now using and managing their time in the flatter, leaner organisations of the 1990s. How much difference does restructuring make? If you are working in an organisation that has recently restructured, you may well be interested in some of the findings of the survey mentioned below.

■ *How much restructuring has occurred recently?*

The Institute of Management recently commissioned a study entitled *Finding the Time: A Survey of Managers' Attitudes to Using and Managing Time*. It asked managers about the level of restructuring.

- Nearly 70% reported that their organisation had restructured in the previous two years. This resulted in fewer management levels for 58% of organisations, and fewer managers for 70%.

Source: Finding the Time: A Survey of Managers' Attitudes to Using and Managing Time, by Karen Cole, the Institute of Management, March 1995.

■ *How is restructuring affecting managers?*

Are the changes worthwhile? Do they enable a better use of resources? If you are considering restructuring, then it is worth knowing how the managers interviewed felt about it.

- A reduction of fixed costs, as planned, has been achieved in almost two-thirds of restructured organisations.

- However, managers stated that improvements in efficiency, communication between departments and speed of decision making were less evident.

Source: Finding the Time: A Survey of Managers' Attitudes to Using and Managing Time, by Karen Cole, the Institute of Management, March 1995.

■ *What has been the impact of restructuring on the number of managers?*

Most respondents thought there were fewer managers:

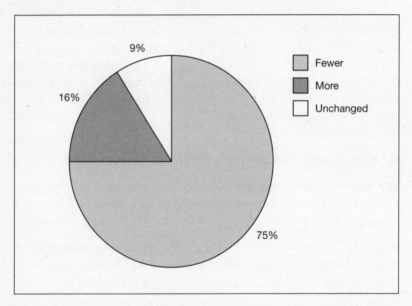

Source: Are Managers Getting the Message? An Institute of Management Report on Communications in the Flat Organisation by Aspen Business Communications, 1993

■ What is the impact of restructuring on the number of management levels?

Most respondents thought there were fewer levels:

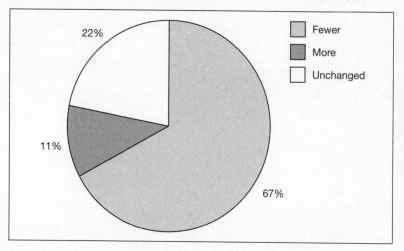

Source: Are Managers Getting the Message? An Institute of Management Report on Communications in the Flat Organisation by Aspen Business Communications, 1993

■ How do the achieved results of restructuring compare with those that were planned?

This is a particularly important question. It is one thing to plan – another to achieve expectations. Sadly, restructuring does not seem to have lived up to expectation on any level:

	Percentage	
	Planned	Achieved
Increased efficiency	74	41
Reduction in fixed costs	70	65
Improved communication between departments	62	37
Increased accountability	61	45
Increased responsibility	59	54
Faster decision-making	55	32

Source: Finding the Time: A Survey of Managers' Attitudes to Using and Managing Time, by Karen Cole, the Institute of Management, March 1995.

WORKLOAD

■ *How have organisational changes affected your workload?*

One of the comments the managers made in the survey was about fewer support staff. Many reported that they were now undertaking routine tasks themselves. One third were doing their own typing. So are managers having to work harder in restructured organisations? They were asked whether their workload had increased or decreased.

Decreased greatly	2%
Decreased slightly	5%
Unchanged	12%
Increased slightly	36%
Increased greatly	45%

Source: Finding the Time: A Survey of Managers' Attitudes to Using and Managing Time, by Karen Cole, the Institute of Management, March 1995.

■ *What is your official working week?*

Managers were asked to state what their official working week was. 78% of respondents officially work 35-40 hours a week.

No. of hours	Percentage
Under 35	4
35-40	78
41-50	11
51-60	4
61-70	1
Over 70	1

Source: Finding the Time: A Survey of Managers' Attitudes to Using and Managing Time, by Karen Cole, the Institute of Management, March 1995.

■ **How many hours a week do you work in excess of your official working week?**

The vast majority of managers put in extra time at work, though some were quite restrained :

No. of hours in excess	Percentage
None	5
1-5	16
6-10	38
11-15	21
Over 15	20

Source: Finding the Time: A Survey of Managers' Attitudes to Using and Managing Time, by Karen Cole, the Institute of Management, March 1995.

THE FUTURE

■ **Do you anticipate further restructuring in your organisation in the next few years?**

So if you are considering restructuring, are you the last organisation to do it, or is it an on-going trend? Most managers seem convinced that changes will continue:

	Next year (to Sept 95)	Next 3 years (to Sept 97)	Next 6 years (to Sept 2000)
Yes	70%	83%	71%
No	24%	6%	5%
Don't know	6%	11%	23%

Source: Finding the Time: A Survey of Managers' Attitudes to Using and Managing Time, by Karen Cole, the Institute of Management, March 1995.

■ *Do managers welcome such restructuring?*

Despite the extra workload and the long hours, 60% of managers said that they did. Perhaps the reason lies in the change of emphasis in their jobs. According to the survey, more managerial time is now being spent on new business development and planning and setting objectives than before – indicating a short-term emphasis on the 'harder' skills.

Source: Finding the Time: A Survey of Managers' Attitudes to Using and Managing Time, by Karen Cole, the Institute of Management, March 1995.

PRACTICALITIES

■ *What type of working environment do you have?*

If you are having to share an office, are you alone? No, but you are in a minority. And how many 'telecommuters' are there? Is it a growing trend? It seems not – only 15% of managers work from home. The vast majority of managers still have their own office – and work at work.

Have own office	65%
Work in open plan office	19%
Work on the move, e.g. on site, while travelling	17%
Work from home	15%
Share office with another person	12%
Share desk with another person	1%

Source: Finding the Time: A Survey of Managers' Attitudes to Using and Managing Time, by Karen Cole, the Institute of Management, March 1995.

■ *Do you have or need help with routine tasks?*

About three-quarters of managers are happy to do various routine tasks themselves, which could mean that they are making a virtue of a necessity. This was less likely at chief executive/managing director level:

Task	Percentage		
	Have help	Need help	Happy to do it myself
Basic typing	77	35	33
Opening/sorting post	74	23	43
Travel arrangements	70	25	43
Filtering phone calls	69	54	30
Photocopying	69	41	50
Filing	67	54	36
Sending faxes	67	28	51
Greeting visitors	65	23	54
Routine correspondence	57	41	55

Source: Finding the Time: A Survey of Managers' Attitudes to Using and Managing Time, by Karen Cole, the Institute of Management, March 1995.

■ *Do you file more paperwork than necessary?*

An estimated 85% of filed information is never looked at again.

Source: Finding the Time: A Survey of Managers' Attitudes to Using and Managing Time, by Karen Cole, the Institute of Management, March 1995.

PRIORITIES

■ *What is the one aspect on which you would like to spend more time?*

Perhaps you feel weighed down by pressures of work. You acknowledge that you need to take a break, and sort out your priorities. Do other managers feel the same? Yes – nearly 20% admitted that planning and setting of objectives is their main concern. One third of respondents wanted to concentrate more effort on new business development, because of its essential importance to organisations.

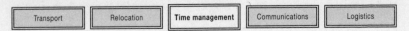
This was more of an issue in the construction industry, and in smaller organisations of up to 100 employees:

New business development	34%
Planning/setting objectives	19%
Personal training/development	14%
Representing organisation externally	7%
Staff training	5%

Source: Finding the Time: A Survey of Managers' Attitudes to Using and Managing Time, by Karen Cole, the Institute of Management, March 1995.

■ *Do you feel that time management principles and techniques apply to you? If so, how?*

You are probably familiar with time management principles. Do you find them a helpful concept? Do you feel that you prioritise well? Responding managers seemed fairly well organised and disciplined in terms of controlling their working day. They were asked whether they:

Discriminate between urgent and important tasks	91%
Find it easy to prioritise their daily tasks	84%
Run their meetings in a time-efficient manner	82%
Delegate tasks (upwards or downwards) in a time efficient manner	82%
Achieve their daily priorities	70%
Remember to review their long term work goals	55%

(Percentages indicate those who were confident of each skill).

Source: Finding the Time: A Survey of Managers' Attitudes to Using and Managing Time, by Karen Cole, the Institute of Management, March 1995.

■ *Do you find business services and equipment help save time?*

You probably have at least one piece of equipment that you swear by. When it comes to introducing new equipment, though, it is often difficult to choose. There is such a plethora of services – and equipment – at a manager's disposal. The choice is obviously personal – but what do other managers think? On-line databases, a desk fax machine and a portable laptop computer were regarded as key aids by those that had them, but video conferencing was definitely not liked:

Percentage who found them:	Very helpful	Fairly helpful	Not very helpful	Not helpful at all	Don't use/N.A.
On-line databases	28	30	7	2	33
Desk fax	23	21	7	4	44
Portable laptop computer	23	16	4	1	44
Mobile phone	22	18	4	2	54
E-mail	18	16	10	4	52
Car phone	18	11	3	2	66
Local/domestic Delivery services	12	33	11	4	40
International express Distribution	11	20	7	4	58
Electronic diary	11	13	13	8	55
Internal messengers	8	24	10	4	54
Pager	7	10	5	4	74
Voice mail	6	8	5	3	78
Video conferencing	4	8	5	3	78

● In organisations of over 5,000 employees, respondents felt that on-line databases were especially helpful.

Source: Finding the Time: A Survey of Managers' Attitudes to Using and Managing Time, by Karen Cole, the Institute of Management, March 1995.

■ *Do you find mobile phones very helpful?*

If you do, you are still in the minority. The survey broke down the above question by levels of management. So are mobile phones more useful to the higher levels of management, or the lower? They were found to be very helpful by 22% of respondents, in particular chief executives/managing directors (36%), 29% of directors, 29% of professional/consultants and 26% of those with over 50 direct reports.

Source: Finding the Time: A Survey of Managers' Attitudes to Using and Managing Time, by Karen Cole, the Institute of Management, March 1995.

■ *How helpful is Electronic Mail (E-mail)?*

If you are thinking of installing an E-mail system in your organisation, is it going to make things easier?

- 18% of respondents felt that it was very helpful.
- 27% of middle managers and of respondents from organisations with over 5,000 employees found this form of correspondence to be very helpful.
- Those in public administration found it to be very helpful (26% as against 18% overall).
- Almost 70% of those in organisations with under 100 employees do not use e-mail.

Source: Finding the Time: A Survey of Managers' Attitudes to Using and Managing Time, by Karen Cole, the Institute of Management, March 1995.

COMMUNICATIONS

FLATTER ORGANISATIONS

Since the mid-80s, almost every organisation has carried out a restructuring exercise, many of which have resulted in managerial job cuts. Most organisations have also implemented approaches like Total Quality and Just-in-Time, aimed at increasing the responsibility of 'front-line' employees and encouraging teamwork, but there has been little research on how internal communications have changed as a result of the flatter structures created by these initiatives.

The theory is that restructuring leads to easier and faster communications, with managers being given more authority and decision-making being pushed to its lowest level. The theory suggests that the use of traditional paper-based communication methods should decline, with more emphasis being placed on face-to-face communications and more advanced technological channels.

So does the practice match the theory? If you are dubious about the improvement in internal communications occasioned by restructuring, are you alone? The Institute of Management commissioned a survey *Are Managers Getting the Message?* to discover if, and how, internal communications had changed. This section assesses the nature and extent of those changes.

■ *How has the culture for effective communications changed within organisations since restructuring?*

• Managers felt that after restructuring their organisations had become slightly more open, honest, informal, consultative and progressive democracies but, at the same time, less caring:

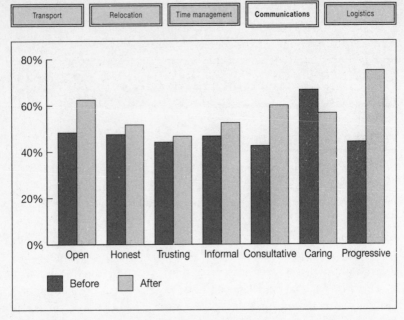

• Managers also felt that their organisations' cultures had become less ruled by a 'them and us' formal autocracy.

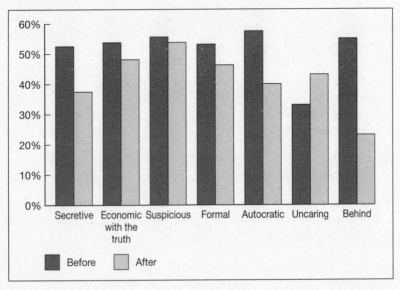

Source: Are Managers Getting the Message? An Institute of Management Report on Communications in the Flat Organisation by Aspen Business Communications, 1993

■ *How has restructuring affected managers' behaviour?*

Respondents were given three statements, with which they could agree or disagree – and the indecisive had a 'don't know' option. The percentages responding were as follows:

Statement	Agree	Disagree	Don't know
Managers spend more time in meetings	68	29	3
Managers are held accountable but lack authority to make decisions	53	46	1
Managers are clearer about other functions' roles and responsibilities	53	44	3

Source: Are Managers Getting the Message? An Institute of Management Report on Communications in the Flat Organisation by Aspen Business Communications, 1993

■ *Are senior managers communicating more effectively?*

Once again, views were mixed (figures are percentages):

Statement	Agree	Disagree	Don't know
Senior management are better at communicating short-term objectives	53	43	4
Senior management are better at communicating long-term objectives	42	54	4
Senior management have become more visible	54	44	2
Senior management make more effort to keep in touch with employees	52	44	4

Source: Are Managers Getting the Message? An Institute of Management Report on Communications in the Flat Organisation by Aspen Business Communications, 1993

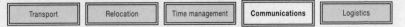

■ *Have communications improved?*

The majority thought that they had (again, the figures are percentages):

Statement	Agree	Disagree	Don't know
Communications have improved in the last few years	62	35	3
Our internal communications strategy is clearer	42	50	8

Source: Are Managers Getting the Message? An Institute of Management Report on Communications in the Flat Organisation by Aspen Business Communications, 1993

■ *Which means of communications are most effective?*

Almost 6 out of 10 thought that the most effective form was face-to-face communication:

Means of communication	Effective	Not effective
Face to face	58%	38%
Paper	33%	44%
Audio-visual	18%	40%
Information technology	34%	25%

Source: Are Managers Getting the Message? An Institute of Management Report on Communications in the Flat Organisation by Aspen Business Communications, 1993

■ *Is there still too much paper?*

The answer to this is basically 'Yes'.

- 43% thought there had been an increase in the use of memos/circulars.
- Around a third thought there had been an increase in newsletters/employee papers and reports.
- A quarter said that the use of noticeboards had risen.

Source: Are Managers Getting the Message? An Institute of Management Report on Communications in the Flat Organisation by Aspen Business Communications, 1993

■ Has information technology (IT) improved internal communications?

- Respondents thought that IT had speeded up the process, but that there had not been a parallel improvement in the targeting of information.

Source: Are Managers Getting the Message? An Institute of Management Report on Communications in the Flat Organisation by Aspen Business Communications, 1993

LOGISTICS

Logistics, or the management of the entire supply chain, is a multi-disciplinary field, encompassing the handling, transport and storage of goods from the place of manufacture to the point where they are to be used.

PURCHASING

All businesses have suppliers, if only for office stationery. The Small Business Research Trust undertook a survey which found that respondents emphasised the importance of working closely with suppliers, actively managing the relationship.

■ How does your company learn about new suppliers?

Most businesses are at both ends of the supply business – they are both supplier and purchaser. If you are seeking to supply, it helps to know the best ways to approach other companies. And if you are purchasing, it is worth looking at how other companies learn about new suppliers.

How do you learn about your suppliers? Word of mouth, through advertising, or by direct mail? Bear in mind the breadth of supplies that the average business requires. Supply proves to be a people business – the most common sources of information are personal recommendation and contact by salespeople:

Source of information	Percentage
Personal recommendation	51
Salesmen visiting/telephoning	49
Media advertising	19
Direct mail	18
Other	9

- Other methods includes trade shows and reference books.
- Retailers and wholesalers rely more than other sectors on visits by salespeople (65%).
- Business services and manufacturing are more likely to rely on personal recommendation.
- Business services seemed to be the most receptive sector to direct mail approaches.

Source: Quarterly Small Business Management Report, No.1, Vol.2. 1994. Lloyds Bank/Small Business Research Trust

■ *Does your company check the financial status of its new suppliers?*

If you do, you are unusual. While a supplier's failure can have a drastic negative effect on a firm, few firms seem to take the trouble to vet their suppliers' financial status by, for example, using a credit reference agency.

- Only 16% of respondents said they checked supplier status.

Source: Quarterly Small Business Management Report, No.1, Vol.2. 1994. Lloyds Bank/Small Business Research Trust

■ *How many suppliers does your firm have?*

The average small firm seems to have a surprisingly large number of suppliers – perhaps as high as 80. Broken down into categories, these are:

Supplier type	Average number
Goods/services for resale	31
Components/raw materials	21
Transport and storage	4
Office suppliers/equipment	3
Other equipment/capital goods	5
Financial services	3
Other	11

Source: Quarterly Small Business Management Report, No.1, Vol.2. 1994. Lloyds Bank/Small Business Research Trust

■ *How many years do firms stick with the same suppliers?*

If you are an established supplier, can you begin to feel secure? Or do firms chop and change fairly frequently? Overall, the average length of time with a supplier is about 6 years. Larger, older firms stay with their suppliers for much longer:

Supplier type	Average number of years
Goods/services for resale	6.3
Components/raw materials	6.2
Transport and storage	5.5
Office suppliers/equipment	4.9
Other equipment/capital goods	5.1
Financial services	8.2
Other	8.2

Source: Quarterly Small Business Management Report, No.1, Vol.2. 1994. Lloyds Bank/Small Business Research Trust

■ *What are relationships like with suppliers?*

An overwhelming 83% of respondents believe in having close relationships with their suppliers. Yet 79% agreed that 'there is plenty of choice of supplier'. So why does this happen? Obviously it is easier to

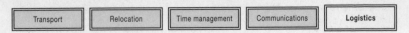

work with the known than the unknown, but is this the only reason? There appears to be a two-way flow of information between companies and their suppliers:

- 61% agreed that 'my suppliers are an important source of information/advice to my business'.

- Only 32% thought it was the other way around – 'on balance, I provide help and guidance to my suppliers'.

Source: Quarterly Small Business Management Report, No.1, Vol.2. 1994. Lloyds Bank/Small Business Research Trust

■ *Do suppliers give good value?*

Judging by the percentage of respondents rating their suppliers as 'very good' and 'good', firms think they get best value from office supplies and goods for resale, and least from components and raw materials. If you are in financial services, then you may need to take positive action to counter your sector's reputation – this type of supplier attracted the highest number of 'poor' and 'very poor' grades.

Supplier type	Percentage of 'good' and 'very good'
Goods/services for resale	13
Components/raw materials	11
Transport and storage	14
Office suppliers/equipment	15
Other equipment/capital goods	9
Financial services	16

Source: Quarterly Small Business Management Report, No.1, Vol.2. 1994. Lloyds Bank/Small Business Research Trust

■ *If suppliers give 'average' or worse value for money, why do companies stay with them?*

About half of respondents had at least one supplier which they rated as 'average' or worse. The reasons given for keeping such suppliers were:

Lack of competing alternatives	48%
Good quality	32%
Geographical proximity	32%
Good credit terms	14%
No time to find an alternative	9%

This suggests that while, overall, firms think that there is plenty of competition amongst suppliers, the main reason why firms will stick with a supplier they perceive as giving poor value is because of lack of competition.

Source: Quarterly Small Business Management Report, No.1, Vol.2. 1994. Lloyds Bank/Small Business Research Trust

SUPPLY CHAIN PARTNERSHIPS

In supply chain partnerships, 'might is right' and the customer is usually the mightier partner. There are significant cost and service benefits from supply chain integration, but they are not shared equally. Obvious losers will be those suppliers who are winnowed out in the process of supply chain rationalisation.

■ *What do supply chain relationships require?*

The wide scale of the reduction in management resources in recent years makes the establishment and monitoring of partnerships more difficult to achieve. Partnerships require:

Requirements for building a supply chain partnership
1. Information sharing
2. Regular meetings
3. Monitoring of the perceived benefits
4. Feedback to all concerned
5. The involvement of senior management

Source: Supply Chain Partnerships – Who Wins? A survey into the opportunities and threats from supply chain relationships. PE International Logistics Consulting Services, in association with the Institute of Logistics, 1994

■ *Who drives outbound supply chains?*

Nearly all companies believe it is their customers rather than themselves who drive their outbound supply chains:

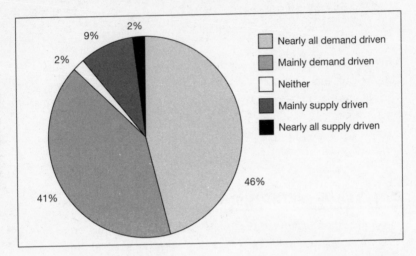

It is clear that the movement towards customer domination will, if anything, intensify in the future:

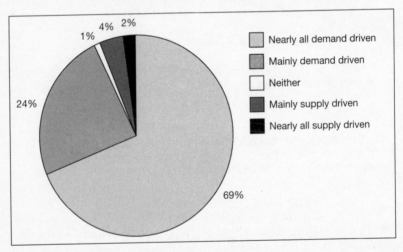

Source: Supply Chain Partnerships – Who Wins? A survey into the opportunities and threats from supply chain relationships. PE International Logistics Consulting Services, in association with the Institute of Logistics, 1994

■ Who drives inbound supply chains?

Most companies believe that they drive relationships with their suppliers and that this will become more pronounced over the three years from 1994:

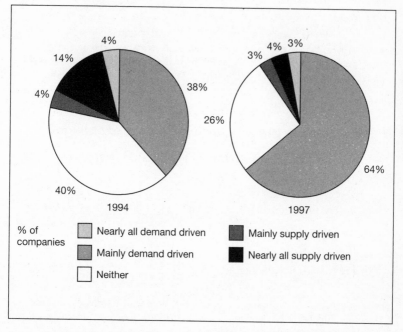

Source: *Supply Chain Partnerships – Who Wins?* A survey into the opportunities and threats from supply chain relationships. PE International Logistics Consulting Services, in association with the Institute of Logistics, 1994

■ Do companies think that ideas about integrating supply chains will become more important?

Although chains are typically demand driven, one of the key factors is the relative power of the businesses and the extent to which a business is dependent on the other members of the chain. However, irrespective of the balance of power, companies believed in 1994 that the concepts of integration would become more important over the coming 3 years, both with customers and suppliers:

	With customers	With suppliers
Critical	41%	43%
Important	41%	41%
Limited importance	14%	14%
Not important	4%	2%

Source: Supply Chain Partnerships – Who Wins? A survey into the opportunities and threats from supply chain relationships. PE International Logistics Consulting Services, in association with the Institute of Logistics, 1994

■ *What are the triggers for information exchange?*

By far the most important factor is the perceived benefits to the companies themselves:

Perceived benefits for ourselves	87%
Technology became available	43%
Pressure from customers	42%
Pressure from suppliers	22%

Source: Supply Chain Partnerships – Who Wins? A survey into the opportunities and threats from supply chain relationships. PE International Logistics Consulting Services, in association with the Institute of Logistics, 1994

ENVIRONMENTAL CONSIDERATIONS

The environmental pressures on industry are substantial and increasing almost daily. Excellence in environmental management is now recognised not as a passing fad, but as a critical area of company performance.

■ *Are companies really under increasing environmental pressures?*

Is your company having to change procedures, products or processes to meet environmental regulations? If so, you are in good company.

70% of all companies surveyed said that they were under increasing environmental pressure. Companies with large turnovers are feeling the pressure more than smaller ones:

Turnover	Percentage
0-£5m	50
£5-£25m	64
£25-£100m	69
£100-£250m	84
Over £250m	88
All companies	70

Source: Going Green, the Logistics Dilemma. A Survey into the Impact on the Environment of Environmental Issues on Logistics Operations. PE International plc in association with The Institute of Logistics and Distribution Management and David Bellamy Associates

■ *What are the major logistics environmental issues?*

Respondents were asked what issues were causing them most concern. The two issues most often cited are the disposal of waste and noise and emission levels:

Waste and packaging disposal	25%
Noise and emission levels	23%
Public perception of HGVs	15%
Fuel resources and utilisation	12%
Road congestion and vehicle utilisation	11%
Cost of environmental measures	5%
Modal selection	2%

Source: Going Green, the Logistics Dilemma. A Survey into the Impact on the Environment of Environmental Issues on Logistics Operations. PE International plc in association with The Institute of Logistics and Distribution Management and David Bellamy Associates

■ *What are the sources of environmental pressure?*

The clearest single source of environmental pressure on company operations is EU legislation. Respondents acknowledge that legislation is the main factor influencing their position on environmental matters. Other factors are far behind:

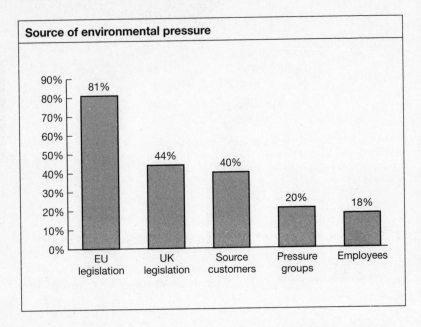

Source of environmental pressure

- Larger companies are more concerned to respond to pressures from EU legislation.
- Small companies feel no pressure at all from either their employees or lobby groups.

Source: Going Green, the Logistics Dilemma. A Survey into the Impact on the Environment of Environmental Issues on Logistics Operations. PE International plc in association with The Institute of Logistics and Distribution Management and David Bellamy Associates

■ Will environmental policies increase operating costs?

Overall, 71% of companies surveyed feel that they will. Smaller companies expect to be hardest hit:

Turnover	Percentage
0-£5million	75
£5-£25million	85
£25-£100million	60
£100-£250million	68
Over £250million	65
All companies	**71**

Source: Going Green, the Logistics Dilemma. A Survey into the Impact on the Environment of Environmental Issues on Logistics Operations. PE International plc in association with The Institute of Logistics and Distribution Management and David Bellamy Associates

■ Does your company have a specific environmental policy?

If you have not yet developed a specific environmental policy, then you are certainly not alone. Larger companies are more likely to have undertaken policy work than other companies as shown in the diagram overleaf.

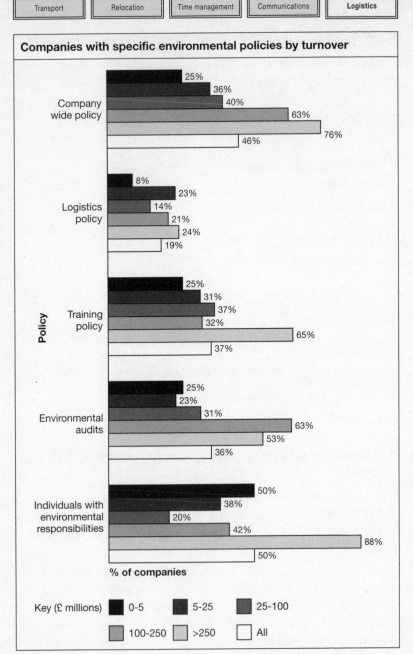

Companies with specific environmental policies by turnover

Source: *Going Green, the Logistics Dilemma.* A Survey into the Impact on the Environment of Environmental Issues on Logistics Operations. PE International plc in association with The Institute of Logistics and Distribution Management and David Bellamy Associates

■ Does your company have a specific transport policy?

● Only 19% of companies said they have specific policies.

Source: Going Green, the Logistics Dilemma. A Survey into the Impact on the Environment of Environmental Issues on Logistics Operations. PE International plc in association with The Institute of Logistics and Distribution Management and David Bellamy Associates.

■ What policy does your company have for its road vehicles?

Although most companies had not had time – or inclination – to develop a specific transport policy, a large number of companies did have policies for their road vehicles. Which issues they covered varied quite substantially:

Life of vehicles	81%
Minimise travel distance	69%
Minimise travel time	67%
Avoid congestion	62%
Minimise noise pollution	38%
Avoid peak hours	33%
Avoid residential travel	30%

Source: Going Green, the Logistics Dilemma. A Survey into the Impact on the Environment of Environmental Issues on Logistics Operations. PE International plc in association with The Institute of Logistics and Distribution Management and David Bellamy Associates

■ Does your company have a specific fuel efficiency related policy?

Fuel usually accounts for 20% of the operating cost of a large commercial vehicle, so even if environmental considerations did not figure, distribution managers would remain keen on obtaining the best levels of fuel consumption for cost reasons. Respondents were asked which measures they took to ensure fuel efficiency; multiple answers were allowed:

	For at least some vehicles	For all vehicles
Preventative maintenance	96%	91%
Correct vehicle/load selection	87%	69%
Route rationalisation	81%	52%
Backloads	68%	28%
Aerodynamic body kits	67%	14%
Driver training	64%	46%
Speed limiters	51%	14%
Reduce unladen weight	18%	33%
Fuel additives	33%	13%
Driver incentives	26%	17%

Source: Going Green, the Logistics Dilemma. A Survey into the Impact on the Environment of Environmental Issues on Logistics Operations. PE International plc in association with The Institute of Logistics and Distribution Management and David Bellamy Associates

■ *Does your company have specific emission reduction policies?*

There is considerable debate over the environmental impact of diesel and petrol engines and catalytic converters. Catalytic converters reduce the noxious gases but increase the emission of carbon dioxide which contributes further to the greenhouse effect. So if you are uncertain as to how to react to this issue, it may help to know what other companies do.

	For at least some vehicles	For all vehicles
Regular engine tuning	87%	71%
Low asbestos brakes	68%	26%
Catalytic converters	59%	6%
Fuel additives	33%	13%
Low sulphur diesel	25%	7%
Vapour recovery units	8%	1%

Source: Going Green, the Logistics Dilemma. A Survey into the Impact on the Environment of Environmental Issues on Logistics Operations. PE International plc in association with The Institute of Logistics and Distribution Management and David Bellamy Associates

MANAGING RESOURCES

■ Does your company have specific policies in the office?

Almost 70% of respondents try to reduce or recycle paper:

Policy	Percentage adopting policy
Paper reduction/recycling	69
Environmentally sound cleaning materials	46
Green purchasing policy	41
Environmentally friendly fixtures/fittings	35
Recycling of toner cartridge/ribbons	18

Source: Going Green, the Logistics Dilemma. A Survey into the Impact on the Environment of Environmental Issues on Logistics Operations. PE International plc in association with The Institute of Logistics and Distribution Management and David Bellamy Associates

■ *Does your company have specific packaging policies?*

The most common policy is one of minimising packaging levels:

Policy	Percentage adopting policy
Minimisation	70
Choice of materials	62
Re-use	56
Recyclability	54
Returnability	37

Source: Going Green, the Logistics Dilemma. A Survey into the Impact on the Environment of Environmental Issues on Logistics Operations. PE International plc in association with The Institute of Logistics and Distribution Management and David Bellamy Associates

COSTS

Cutting logistics costs is largely about building relationships – closer co-operation or better information exchange should bring the costs down. Is your logistics department running a tight ship? How well does it co-operate with its partners? One way to benchmark its activities is to find out what other companies do.

■ *How willing are companies to discuss logistics costs openly with their partners?*

Only about 1 in 4 companies discuss costs with their suppliers and only about 1 in 8 with their customers:

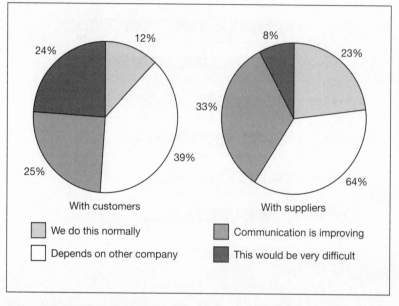

Source: Supply Chain Partnerships – Who Wins? A survey into the opportunities and threats from supply chain relationships. PE International Logistics Consulting Services, in association with the Institute of Logistics, 1994

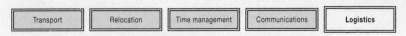

■ *What are the cost benefits of closer co-operation?*

Inventory and transport were seen as the most important areas for cost saving:

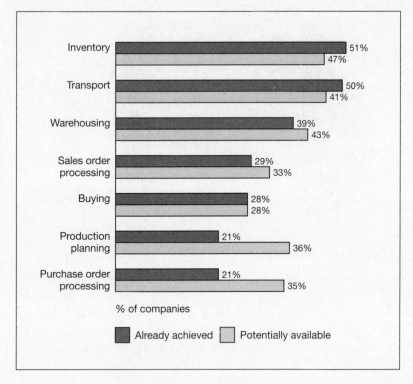

% of companies

■ Already achieved   ☐ Potentially available

Source: Supply Chain Partnerships – Who Wins? A survey into the opportunities and threats from supply chain relationships. PE International Logistics Consulting Services, in association with the Institute of Logistics, 1994

■ Does your company expect a reduction in the number of suppliers over the next few years?

If you do, then you are not alone. Manufacturers who were interviewed certainly expected the three years from 1994 to bring a reduction in suppliers. The largest reductions expected were by public sector organisations. The figures are broken down by the sectors of the respondents:

Consumer product manufacturers	32%
Industrial product manufacturers	31%
Wholesalers and distributors	22%
Distribution companies	28%
Retailers	25%
Public sector organisations	42%

Source: Supply Chain Partnerships – Who Wins? A survey into the opportunities and threats from supply chain relationships. PE International Logistics Consulting Services, in association with the Institute of Logistics, 1994

■ What will be the effect on physical distribution?

The issues on which there was the greatest unanimity in 1994 were that trans-shipment will increase at the expense of storage locations, that the number of deliveries will increase and that inventory will be pushed back up the chain:

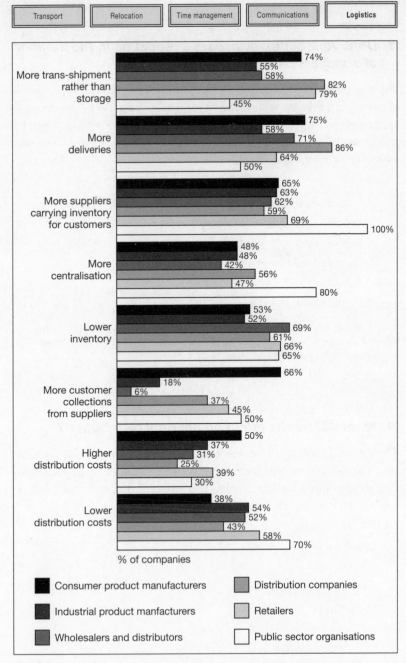

Source: Supply Chain Partnerships – Who Wins? A survey into the opportunities and threats from supply chain relationships. PE International Logistics Consulting Services, in association with the Institute of Logistics, 1994

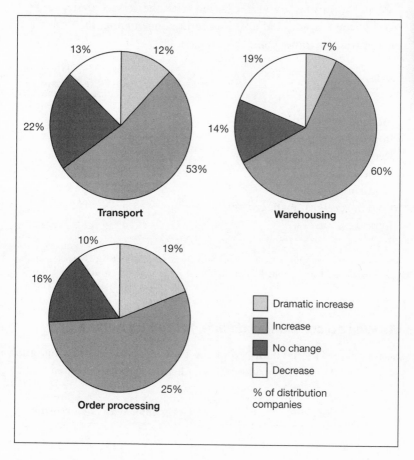

■ What are the expectations of third party distribution companies?

In transport, their expectations are similar to the average for their prospective customers, but in warehousing and order processing, their expectations are substantially higher. In order processing, the proportion of distribution companies expecting their business to increase is twice the proportion of their potential customers who expect this to happen:

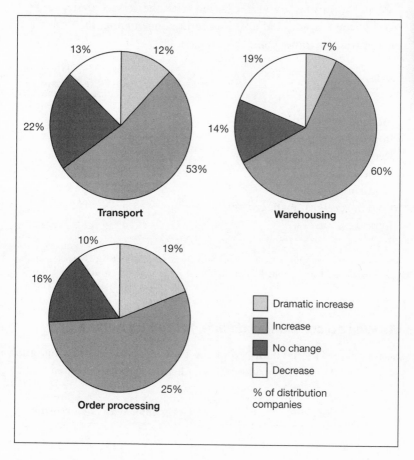

Source: Supply Chain Partnerships – Who Wins? A survey into the opportunities and threats from supply chain relationships. PE International Logistics Consulting Services, in association with the Institute of Logistics, 1994

103

OUTSOURCING DISTRIBUTION

Providers of third-party services have played a significant role in the development of distribution in the past decade. During this time their market share of the total distribution market has significantly increased.

■ Why do companies outsource?

If you are currently meeting your distribution requirements within your organisation, are you satisfied with the service that you provide? If you are not, and are considering outsourcing, then these are the reasons why other companies outsource:

Reason	Companies who cited reason
Increase flexibility	69%
Improve service	57%
Reduce cost	55%
Avoid investment	45%
Non-core activity	40%
Obtain specialist management	33%
Improve control	30%

Source: Contracting Out or Selling Out? Survey into the current issues concerning the outsourcing of distribution. PE International in association with the Institute of Logistics, 1993

■ Why do companies decide not to outsource?

Some companies have looked at the possibility of outsourcing, and rejected it. If you have, you may well identify with these reasons:

Reason	Companies who cited reason
Poorer service	83%
Reduced flexibility	76%
No cost benefits	67%
Less control	67%

- Just over half of the companies surveyed who have decided not to outsource believe outsourcing could be a serious option in the future.

Source: Contracting Out or Selling Out? Survey into the current issues concerning the outsourcing of distribution. PE International in association with the Institute of Logistics, 1993

■ *How many contractors does your company use?*

If the answer is one, then you are in the minority. About 60% of companies in the survey use more than one contractor. Companies which only contract out transport use on average more contractors, though the difference is not as great as might be expected:

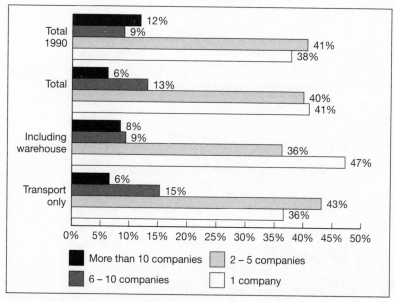

Source: Contracting Out or Selling Out? Survey into the current issues concerning the outsourcing of distribution. PE International in association with the Institute of Logistics, 1993

■ *How long are contracts with the third-party service providers?*

If you are new to outsourcing, then you may want to know what contractual arrangements with service providers are normal. About 1 in 4 companies have no formal contractual arrangements, but of those that do, most have contracts of between 1 and 3 years:

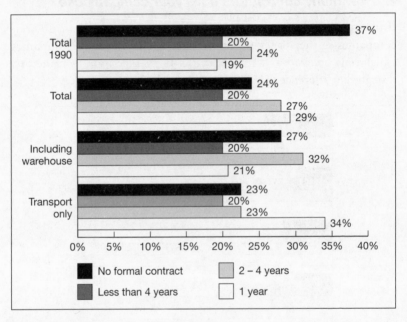

Source: Contracting Out or Selling Out? Survey into the current issues concerning the outsourcing of distribution. PE International in association with the Institute of Logistics, 1993

■ *How are charges structured?*

Do you renegotiate rate annually, or more or less frequently? What about the structure of charges? And payments for damages/losses? Again, it may help to know what other companies do. Three-quarters of the companies surveyed renegotiate rates annually:

Annual renegotiation of rates	75%
Payment for damages/losses	56%
Fixed plus variable	41%
Single cost per unit	33%
Fuel surcharge	27%
Penalties for failure	26%
Open book or cost plus	25%
Variable cost per unit	24%
RPI or cost index	21%
Shared savings (rebates)	21%

Source: Contracting Out or Selling Out? Survey into the current issues concerning the outsourcing of distribution. PE International in association with the Institute of Logistics, 1993

■ *Are you satisfied with your contractors?*

If you are outsourcing, and are experiencing problems with a contractor, have you hit the worst of the bunch, or are other companies also dissatisfied? And if you are considering outsourcing, it is vital to know what quality of service you can expect.

The majority of companies surveyed were satisfied:

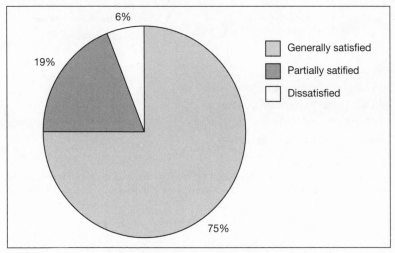

Source: Contracting Out or Selling Out? Survey into the current issues concerning the outsourcing of distribution. PE International in association with the Institute of Logistics, 1993

■ *What are the main problem areas?*

You may well be generally satisfied with your contractors, but experiencing some problems. So what are these problems likely to be? Companies were asked to identify the main problem areas:

Problem area	Proportion of companies experiencing problem
Insufficient management information	27%
Management issues	23%
Level of cost	20%
Service failures	17%
Lack of flexibility	13%

Source: Contracting Out or Selling Out? Survey into the current issues concerning the outsourcing of distribution. PE International in association with the Institute of Logistics, 1993

■ *What are the causes of these problems?*

Companies were honest enough to admit their share of the blame:

Cause of problem	Proportion of companies citing cause
Insufficient controls	36%
Poor contractor management	32%
Inadequately specified contracts	20%
Insufficient information supplied	20%
Failure of client management	18%

Source: Contracting Out or Selling Out? Survey into the current issues concerning the outsourcing of distribution. PE International in association with the Institute of Logistics, 1993

■ Has the number of contractors used by your company decreased?

If you have recently cut down on the number of contractors you use, then you will not be alone – a third of companies surveyed had also done so in the period covered by the survey. Yet half the respondents said there was no change between 1990 and 1993:

- Only 18% of companies had increased the number of contractors they were using.

- Between 1990 and 1993, 32% of companies decreased the number of contractors they were using.

- In the same period, 50% of companies said that the number of contractors they were using had remained constant.

Source: Contracting Out or Selling Out? Survey into the current issues concerning the outsourcing of distribution. PE International in association with the Institute of Logistics, 1993

LOGISTICS ACROSS EUROPE

■ What changes are taking place in the European logistics market?

If you are transporting goods across Europe, or receiving goods from European firms, you will probably already be aware of the various changes which are occurring. However, if you are newly 'into Europe', then it may help to know:

- New pan-European transport infrastructures are being encouraged by central funding.

- Cabotage[1] is rapidly being liberalised.

- Proposals for equalisation of fuel and vehicle duties are progressing.

- Road charging is being introduced.

- New regulations on maximum vehicle heights, working hours and hauliers' qualifications are in train.

Source: European Logistics, Comparative Costs and Practice, Deloitte & Touche/The Institute of Logistics/European Logistics Association, 1995

---

[1] For the uninitiated, cabotage is the practice of hauliers from one country doing internal haulage work in other countries.

■ *What changes are predicted?*

With many large businesses developing pan-European logistics operations, the following changes are predicted:

- The restructuring of manufacturing and distribution, whether by rationalisation or relocation.
- The introduction of pan-European distribution services.
- Increasing legal and fiscal pressures to transfer from road to rail and water.
- Recycling and reduction in the use of packaging will increasingly affect handling, storing and distributing methods.

Source: European Logistics, Comparative Costs and Practice, Deloitte & Touche/The Institute of Logistics/European Logistics Association, 1995

■ *What are logistics costs in Europe? Which country is the most expensive?*

Although you cannot choose your European trading partners simply by logistics costs, it helps to know what those costs are likely to be. So which country has the highest logistics costs? And what are the costs likely to be?

Spain has the highest overall costs and France follows closely behind. Since both these countries have widely dispersed populations, their higher overall costs are to be expected. Costs in Holland are higher than might be expected given the greater population density:

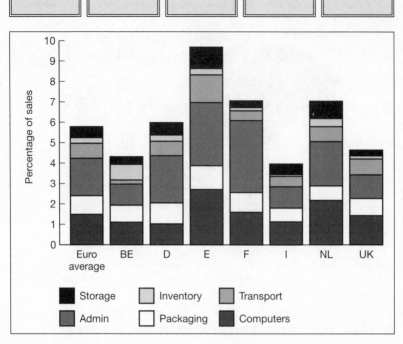

- The European average for logistics costs as a percentage of sales has remained at around 5.8% since the 1992 survey.

Key to countries:
BE=Belgium D=Germany E=Spain F=France I=Italy
NL=Netherlands UK=United Kingdom.

Source: *European Logistics, Comparative Costs and Practice*, Deloitte & Touche/The Institute of Logistics/European Logistics Association, 1995.

■ *How do logistics costs break down overall?*

The survey broke down overall European logistics costs, in order to understand which factors were proving expensive. Transport, storage and inventory make up 73% of logistics costs:

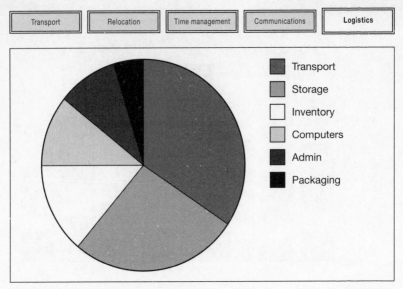

Source: European Logistics, Comparative Costs and Practice, Deloitte & Touche/The Institute of Logistics/European Logistics Association, 1995.

■ *How much does storage cost across Europe?*

In order to find a fair way of comparing costs, it was decided to represent all figures as a percentage of sales. Spain has the highest storage costs as a percentage of sales, at just over 2.5%:

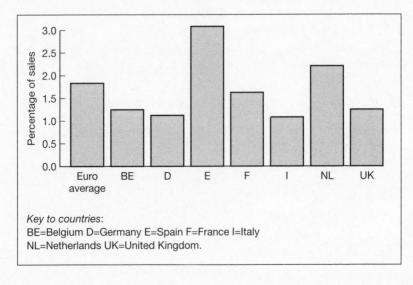

- The performance of large firms, those with a turnover in excess of 12 million ECU, is generally better than that of small and medium firms.

Source: European Logistics, Comparative Costs and Practice, Deloitte & Touche/The Institute of Logistics/European Logistics Association, 1995

■ *How much does inventory cost across Europe?*

Again, the figures are in percentages of sales. And once again, Spain has the highest cost, at 1.2% of sales:

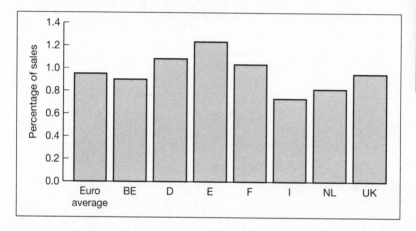

Key to countries:
BE=Belgium D=Germany E=Spain F=France I=Italy
NL=Netherlands UK=United Kingdom.

Source: European Logistics, Comparative Costs and Practice, Deloitte & Touche/The Institute of Logistics/European Logistics Association, 1995

■ *How much does transport cost across Europe?*

France has unexpectedly high costs; this may be due to the highly regionalised haulage operations there:

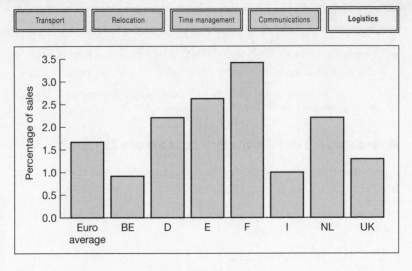

| Transport | Relocation | Time management | Communications | **Logistics** |

Key to countries:
BE=Belgium D=Germany E=Spain F=France I=Italy
NL=Netherlands UK=United Kingdom.

Source: European Logistics, Comparative Costs and Practice, Deloitte & Touche/The
Institute of Logistics/European Logistics Association, 1995

■ *How much does administration cost across Europe?*

Administration is a major cost for any logistics operation, but is difficult to identify in detail. The average across Europe is 0.75% of
sales, or 13% of total logistics costs.

Source: European Logistics, Comparative Costs and Practice, Deloitte & Touche/The
Institute of Logistics/European Logistics Association, 1995

■ *How much does packaging cost across Europe?*

Overall, packaging accounts for 0.31% of sales. In Belgium, it has
been reported that additional packaging costs are incurred as a result
of considerable damage within the supply chain:

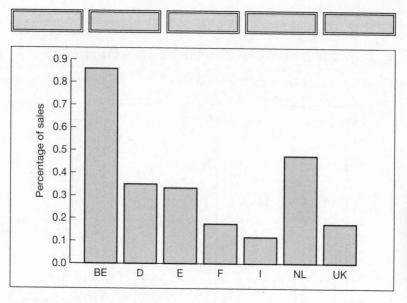

Key to countries:
BE=Belgium D=Germany E=Spain F=France I=Italy
NL=Netherlands UK=United Kingdom.

Source: European Logistics, Comparative Costs and Practice, Deloitte & Touche/The
Institute of Logistics/European Logistics Association, 1995

■ *How much do computers cost across Europe?*

The UK has the lowest computing costs:

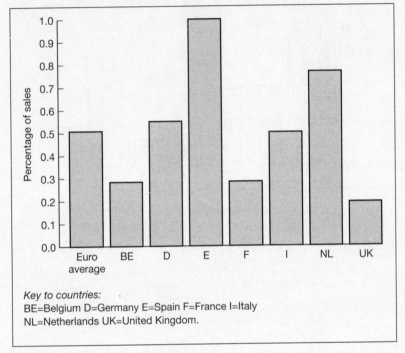

Key to countries:
BE=Belgium D=Germany E=Spain F=France I=Italy
NL=Netherlands UK=United Kingdom.

Source: European Logistics, Comparative Costs and Practice, Deloitte & Touche/The Institute of Logistics/European Logistics Association, 1995

EXECUTIVE MANAGEMENT

Non-executive directors (NEDS)   118
Becoming a NED ■ The role of the NED ■ Chairs and
NEDs ■ Terms of office

Executive remuneration   129
Performance targets ■ Share schemes

Management buy-outs and buy-ins   138
Success and failure

NON-EXECUTIVE DIRECTORS (NEDS)

BECOMING A NED

■ *Are there any guidelines for NEDs?*

The Institute of Management recently undertook a survey of non-executive directors (NEDs), entitled appropriately *Coming on Board*. It made some general comments which you may well find helpful if you are, or are thinking of becoming, a NED.

- A more thorough conduct of boardroom business and the 'good chemistry' of boardroom relationships are the most significant contributions NEDs can bring to boards of all sizes.
- The processes and criteria by which men and women are selected for NED appointments shows growing objectivity in selection, in terms of an individual's past achievements. But even with new methods of selection, 'personality fit' is as crucial as ever.
- There is not enough recognition of the role of NEDs in small and medium enterprises (SMEs).
- The research reveals a very strong consensus in favour of the training/continuing professional development of all directors, not only NEDs. Around 80% agree that training is increasingly valuable for directors appointed for the first time, while around 66% accept that 'conversion' training from executive director to NED is necessary.

Source: Coming on Board. The Non-executive Director's Role in Strengthening Boardroom Leadership, Institute of Management

■ *Do you hold too many NED appointments?*

How many appointments is it possible to hold without all of those appointments suffering? Obviously, the answer will depend partly on what your other commitments are.

118

A KPMG Peat Marwick survey found that the press comment that NEDs have 'too many appointments' may be unfair; it argued that the cross fertilisation of ideas and experience can be advantageous. Anyway, here are the proportions of NEDs who hold each number of non-executive directorships:

1 non-executive directorship	19%
2 non-executive directorships	20%
3 – 5 non-executive directorships	43%
More than 5 non-executive directorships	18%

Perhaps you are already an executive director of one company, and have now been approached by another (non-competing) company to be a non-executive director. Can you do justice to the second appointment? On average, NEDs claimed to spend around 20 days per annum in their role as a NED of a single company. Just as many NEDs hold more than one NED appointment, so many hold executive positions:

No executive directorships	56%
1 executive directorship	32%
2 executive directorships	5%
3 – 5 executive directorships	7%

Source: Survey of Non-executive Directors, KPMG Peat Marwick, 1994

■ How are NEDs approached and appointed?

Perhaps you feel that life is getting slightly easier, and that you now have enough experience to be useful to a company as a non-executive director. Would you be unusual if you approached a selection agency and flagged that fact to them? No – but you would be in a minority. By far the most common method of appointing a NED is by direct contact:

Method of appointing NED	Percentage of companies using method
By direct contact	55
Introduced by stockholder/interest group	24
By placement/selection agency	15
As owner/substantial stockholder already	10
As former employee of company	7
Other reasons	5
Other family connection	1

(Percentages exceed 100% since there is often more than one reason for such appointments.)

Source: Coming on Board. The Non-executive Director's Role in Strengthening Boardroom Leadership, Institute of Management

■ *What makes life difficult for NEDs?*

Are you experiencing difficulties? Then it may be of some comfort to know you are not alone. The NEDs surveyed found it particularly difficult to influence boards when:

1. Other directors line up behind a vested interest, when the interest was not apparent at the time.
2. The information presented is insufficient or very difficult to interpret.
3. Other directors 'bounce' or 'ambush' the NED(s) over an issue. A deferral is the only course open to the NED(s), which may or may not work.

Source: Coming on Board. The Non-executive Director's Role in Strengthening Boardroom Leadership, Institute of Management

■ *Do NEDs' interventions affect the speed and quality of decisions?*

How fulfilling is the role of the NED? If you are still toying with the idea of becoming one, then this is a very important question, given the time commitment. Respondents said that:

- On occasions, particularly in crisis, NEDs can slow down decision-making.
- In crisis, the executives may bypass NEDs.
- NEDs can raise the quality of decisions by preventing impulsive decision-making.
- Poorly selected and less than competent NEDs can reduce the quality of decisions.
- A NED's best contribution is to help reduce the possibility of crisis and the urgent need to take directorial/management decisions quickly.

Source: Coming on Board. The Non-executive Director's Role in Strengthening Boardroom Leadership, Institute of Management

■ What formal induction did you experience when becoming a NED?

If you are newly appointed, can you expect a formal induction? What other help can you expect to be given when you take up the appointment? The survey reported that the following proportions of respondents had experienced:

Introductions	73%
Internal visits	65%
Briefing papers	17%
External visits	15%
No induction	13%

Source: Coming on Board. The Non-executive Director's Role in Strengthening Boardroom Leadership, Institute of Management

THE ROLE OF THE NED

■ What do NEDs regard as their key roles?

If you are uncertain as to what the role of an NED includes – or feel that you could make a better contribution if you had more experience of the role – then help is at hand. KPMG Peat Marwick asked a

sample of NEDs what they felt their key contributions were, and how important they considered each to be. The chart below shows how they answered.

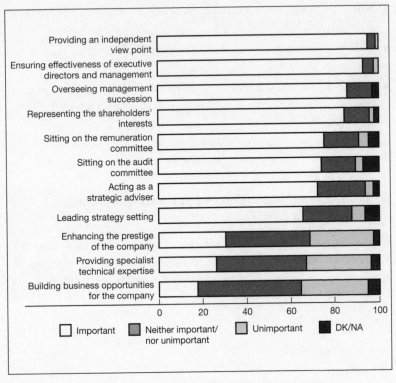

Source: Survey of Non-executive Directors, KPMG Peat Marwick, 1994

■ *What are the principal concerns of NEDs?*

The issue raised by the greatest number was that of managing the executive management. Remuneration did not seem to be a major issue, despite press coverage of large salaries for directors – it was only raised by 11%:

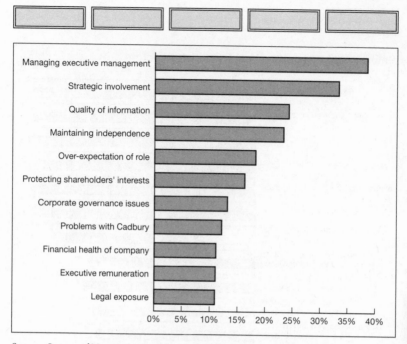

Managing executive management	
Strategic involvement	
Quality of information	
Maintaining independence	
Over-expectation of role	
Protecting shareholders' interests	
Corporate governance issues	
Problems with Cadbury	
Financial health of company	
Executive remuneration	
Legal exposure	

0% 5% 10% 15% 20% 25% 30% 35% 40%

Source: Survey of Non-executive Directors, KPMG Peat Marwick, 1994

■ *What information do NEDs need?*

If the information you receive as an NED is biased towards financial indicators, that is almost always the case. There is also a bias towards internal issues. So do you feel that the information you are given gives you only a narrow view of the business? Or that you are provided with insufficient information on many non-financial and external factors?

In the KPMG survey, 72% of respondents saw senior management performance appraisals as important. Yet less than half actually received such information:

Information required by Non-Executive Directors

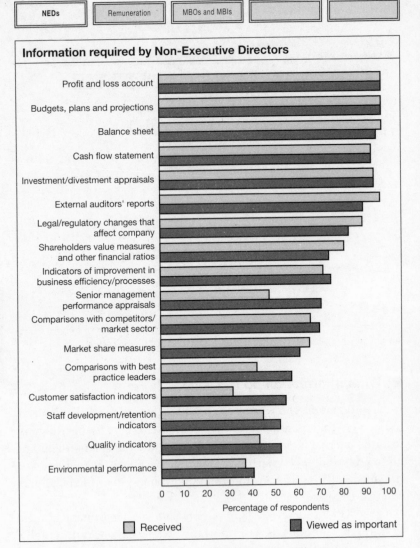

Profit and loss account

Budgets, plans and projections

Balance sheet

Cash flow statement

Investment/divestment appraisals

External auditors' reports

Legal/regulatory changes that affect company

Shareholders value measures and other financial ratios

Indicators of improvement in business efficiency/processes

Senior management performance appraisals

Comparisons with competitors/ market sector

Market share measures

Comparisons with best practice leaders

Customer satisfaction indicators

Staff development/retention indicators

Quality indicators

Environmental performance

Percentage of respondents

☐ Received   ■ Viewed as important

Source: Survey of Non-executive Directors, KPMG Peat Marwick, 1994

◼ Is there an 'information gap'?

A 'gap' exists if demand outstrips supply. The figures above suggest that NEDs' 'demand' for information (as expressed by their assessment of its relative importance) outstrips the 'supply' (as expressed by the percentage of respondents who receive the particular type of information).

If you feel that you are experiencing an 'information gap', then where is it most likely to be felt? The gap is only noticeable with regard to non-financial information and particularly external information. According to respondents, the largest gaps exist for:

Senior management performance appraisal	-24%
Customer satisfaction indicators	-23%
Comparisons with best practice leaders	-16%
Quality indicators	-11%
Staff development/retention indicators	-8%
Comparisons with competitors/market sector	-7%

Source: Survey of Non-executive Directors, KPMG Peat Marwick, 1994

◼ Does your company have a formal written strategic plan?

If you are already on a board, and are trying to talk your company into writing a formal strategic plan, then it may help to know what general practice is. 44% of respondents said their boards do not plan much more than one year ahead. The Institute of Management felt that this is a cause for concern:

No formal strategic plan	15%
Plan covering only 1 year	29%
Plan covering more than 2 years	56%

Source: Coming on Board. The Non-executive Director's Role in Strengthening Boardroom Leadership, Institute of Management

CHAIRS AND NEDS

■ Is the proportion of NEDs increasing or decreasing?

Over the last six years, there has been an increase in the proportion of non-executive directors on the board. Whilst total board sizes have decreased (from an average of 8.5 down to 7.6 directors), the average number of non-executives on the board remained constant at 3.5.

Source: Chairmen and Non-executive Directors: Fees, Facts and Attitudes – 1994. PRO NED Ltd/ Board for Chartered Accountants in Business/Institute of Chartered Accountants in England and Wales

■ What is the average size of a board of directors?

If the board on which you sit seems rather large and cumbersome, is it unusual? Yes, it is. Life must have passed your board by a bit – total board sizes have been decreasing. Overall, the average is 7.6 members, with 3.5 NEDs, but the numbers grow with the size of the company:

Size of company by turnover	NEDs	Total board
Up to £25 million	2.8	5.9
£26 – £100 million	2.8	6.7
£101 – £200 million	3.4	7.5
£201 – £500 million	4.1	8.3
£501 million – £2 billion	4.7	9.2
More than £2 billion	5.6	11.9
Total	3.5	7.6

Source: Chairmen and Non-executive Directors: Fees, Facts and Attitudes – 1994. PRO NED Ltd/ Board for Chartered Accountants in Business/Institute of Chartered Accountants in England and Wales

■ How are NEDs involved in companies?

So what can you realistically expect your role to be? What level of NED involvement is normal? And has the pattern changed recently – are NEDs becoming more, or less, involved?

| | | Percentage point shift 92-94 | |
	1992	1994	<£50m	£200m+
Audit committee	55%	89%	+50	+22
Remuneration committee	77%	89%	+21	+7
Strategy meetings/ awaydays	60%	71%	+11	+12

Source: Chairmen and Non-executive Directors: Fees, Facts and Attitudes – 1994.
PRO NED Ltd/ Board for Chartered Accountants in Business/Institute of Chartered Accountants in England and Wales

■ *How involved are Chairs in their companies?*

In 53% of the companies researched, the position of the chair is part-time, in nearly a third (30%) it is full-time and in the remaining 17%, the role of chairman and chief executive is combined.

Part time chairs devote, on average, 76 days a year to the company which they chair. Not surprisingly, the larger the company, the more time the chairman is likely to devote, ranging from 61 days per annum for companies below £25 million turnover to 116 days for companies over £500 million.

Source: Chairmen and Non-executive Directors: Fees, Facts and Attitudes – 1994.
PRO NED Ltd/ Board for Chartered Accountants in Business/Institute of Chartered Accountants in England and Wales

TERMS OF OFFICE

■ *How long is a NED's term of office?*

The most widely adopted practice is to serve for a set term, typically three years and then, subject to review, to be invited to serve another term. Other practices include:

• Retirement after an unspecified number of terms.

• Retirement on reaching a specific age. The preferred age is 65 or 70 years old.

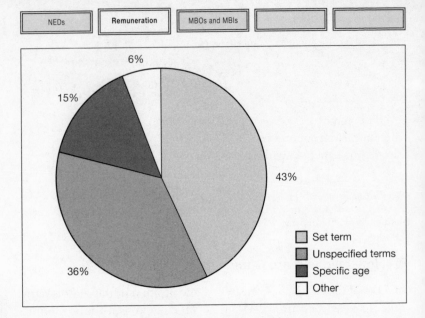

- The largest companies have adopted the most specific practices. In only 7% of the £2 billion plus companies did NEDs serve for an unspecified term, compared with 49% of companies of £25 million turnover and below.

Source: Chairmen and Non-executive Directors: Fees, Facts and Attitudes – 1994. PRO NED Ltd/ Board for Chartered Accountants in Business/Institute of Chartered Accountants in England and Wales

■ *What are NEDs' fees?*

If you are receiving, say, £1,000 a day for your services, is this about average? Not surprisingly, the level of fees paid to NEDs rises as the size of company increases. Thus, the average fee for a NED devoting 10 – 20 days to a company with a turnover of £25 million or less is £11,200, compared with £20,900 for those devoting the same amount of time to a £2 billion turnover company. There are a few chairs and NEDs whose fees are well above or well below the norm.

- Taking into account the amount of time spent on company business by the director or chair, annual fees equate to a daily rate of between £600 – £1200.

Source: Chairmen and Non-executive Directors: Fees, Facts and Attitudes – 1994. PRO NED Ltd/ Board for Chartered Accountants in Business/Institute of Chartered Accountants in England and Wales

EXECUTIVE REMUNERATION

PERFORMANCE TARGETS

Is your company thinking of introducing a performance target scheme? Certainly, schemes with performance targets are on the increase. The most popular form of performance target is earnings per share, measured against the retail price index. Performance targets are usually measured at the beginning and end of a three year period, ignoring the performance in the interim period. Although in many companies the schemes only extend to senior executives, larger companies are now beginning to extend their schemes to lower levels of management.

■ *How many companies have performance target schemes? Is there a difference between large and small companies?*

If you have not yet introduced a scheme with performance targets, are you missing out on an important way of incentivising your senior executives?

- Over 80% of small companies introduced schemes without performance targets from 1988 as against 45% of larger companies.
- In the case of small companies, the lack of performance targets may be explained by the fact that where a company has only one or two institutional investors, the influence of those investors may be limited and so the ABI guidelines may be less significant:

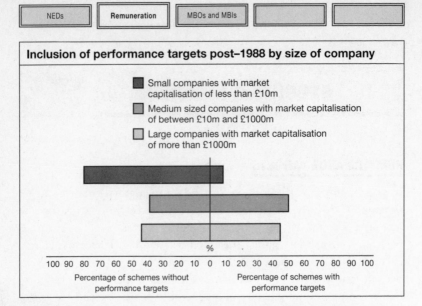

Inclusion of performance targets post–1988 by size of company

■ Small companies with market capitalisation of less than £10m

■ Medium sized companies with market capitalisation of between £10m and £1000m

□ Large companies with market capitalisation of more than £1000m

%

100 90 80 70 60 50 40 30 20 10 0 10 20 30 40 50 60 70 80 90 100

Percentage of schemes without performance targets   Percentage of schemes with performance targets

Source: Executive Share Options and Performance Targets, KPMG Tax Advisers, 1994

■ *What is the difference between performance target and share option schemes? Are there various different types of schemes?*

The only way to answer these questions is to provide a 'glossary' of schemes. Fortunately, the KPMG survey does just that:

Executive share option schemes

Executives are given rights to acquire shares in the future, usually at a price based on the market value of the company's shares at the date of grant. Schemes can be approved by the Inland Revenue (in which case they are subject to detailed legislative requirements) or not approved; the tax treatment of each type is different.

SAYE share option scheme

All the employees of the company (subject to certain permitted exceptions) are invited to apply for options in the scheme. Employees enter savings contracts and are simultaneously granted options. The participant saves during the life of the option, and the savings contract matures when the option becomes exercisable, so that the participant has funds to pay the exercise price.

Profit sharing scheme

All the employees of the company (subject to certain permitted exceptions) are allocated free shares by the trustees of this type of scheme. The shares are then held in trust for the benefit of the participants for a minimum of two years, during which time the participants are normally unable to dispose of them.

Employee share ownership trusts (ESOTs)

These are discretionary trusts, set up by companies to benefit their employees. The majority of these trusts are not regulated by the Inland Revenue, and therefore there is a great deal of flexibility in the manner in which they can be used. For example: the trust can be used to operate a share scheme (such an arrangement is known as an 'ESOP') so that shares can be transferred to employees in a tax efficient manner.

Performance targets

Performance targets are imposed at the time the option is granted, on the terms that the option is granted on. The option cannot be exercised until the performance has been satisfied. Where options are granted under an Inland Revenue approved executive share option scheme, the performance targets must be objective and, if amended, must be no more difficult to satisfy than the original performance target.

Earnings per share (EPS)

Earnings per share is calculated by dividing the after tax profit attributable to equity shareholders by the number of equity shares in issue, and ranking for dividend. In other words, the figure attempts to calculate the profit attributable to each share.

Source: Executive Share Options and Performance Targets, KPMG Tax Advisers, 1994

■ *What sorts of performance targets do companies use?*

Part of the decision about performance target schemes is which type to use. The most common type of performance targets used by companies is earnings per share (EPS):

Type of performance target used	Percentage of companies using it
Earnings per share	74
Share price	9
Total shareholder return	6
Other	9
No reply	2

Source: Executive Share Options and Performance Targets, KPMG Tax Advisers, 1994

■ *Are larger companies more likely to use different performance targets?*

- Only 53% of larger companies operating schemes with performance targets use EPS (compared with 74% of all companies).
- 27% use shareholder returns (compared with 6% of all companies).
- Larger companies have the resources available to devote to share incentive schemes, and so tend to be more innovative in developing schemes.

Source: Executive Share Options and Performance Targets, KPMG Tax Advisers, 1994

■ *What do you measure performance targets against?*

- The most common kind of benchmark for performance targets in existing executive schemes is an RPI measure.
- In new schemes, the use of RPI is declining and alternative benchmarks are being introduced.
- Popular benchmarks are the RPI, the FTSE All Share Index or the FTSE 100 Share Index or a sector of the FTSE All Share Index:

Benchmark	Percentage of companies using it
RPI	77
FT Indices	9
Other	10
No reply	4

Source: Executive Share Options and Performance Targets, KPMG Tax Advisers, 1994

■ *If you use share price as a measure of performance, what do you use as a benchmark?*

Companies using share price as a measure of performance target are more likely to use a relative index such as the FTSE All Share Index or the FTSE 100 as a benchmark (these figures relate to companies using share price as a measure of performance only):

Benchmark	Percentage of companies using it
RPI	18
FT Indices	48
Other	27
No reply	9

Source: Executive Share Options and Performance Targets, KPMG Tax Advisers, 1994

■ *If you use total shareholder return as a measure of performance, what do you use as a benchmark?*

Companies using total shareholder return were equally likely to measure achievement of the target against one of the RPI, the FTSE 100, the FTSE All Share Index or a FTSE sub-sector.

Source: Executive Share Options and Performance Targets, KPMG Tax Advisers, 1994

■ *Over what period do you measure performance targets?*

If you are considering adopting a performance target scheme, then it will help to know over what period targets are measured, and how. The KPMG survey found that options can usually be exercised after three years, and that most three year periods ignore fluctuations between the beginning and the end of the period.

There are three common structures to the three year period:

Structure	Proportion of companies adopting it
Straight 3 year period	20%
Rolling 3 year period	43%
Extending 3 year period	14%
Other	16%
No reply	7%

- The KPMG survey recommended that companies consider setting targets on a year-by-year basis, to encourage sustained growth throughout the three year period.

Source: Executive Share Options and Performance Targets, KPMG Tax Advisers, 1994

■ *Who sets performance targets?*

The answer is, increasingly, remuneration committees. 85% of schemes introduced in 1994 had performance targets set by remuneration committees, as compared to 38% in the period 1988-1991. Of all companies operating schemes with performance targets in 1994, 62% of them were set by remuneration committees.

Source: Executive Share Options and Performance Targets, KPMG Tax Advisers, 1994

■ *Why did your company choose the performance target it currently uses in its scheme?*

When asked why they chose the performance targets they currently use in their schemes, the companies' responses were split between positive responses and the need to comply.

> **Reasons for choosing current performance target**
>
> **Positive reasons**
> - Best measure of company performance/growth
> - Reflects shareholder value
> - Aligns management and shareholder interests
> - Best indicator of management performance
>
> **Compliance with regulatory requirements or the market norm**
> - Easy to monitor and understand
> - Complies with the ABI guidelines
> - Because they were advised to
> - The measures are the most commonly used

Source: Executive Share Options and Performance Targets, KPMG Tax Advisers, 1994

■ *What should performance targets achieve?*

If you are not clear about the aims of the exercise, there will be little point in introducing a performance target scheme into your company. So what should performance targets achieve?

Respondents were asked a series of questions to establish their views on the effectiveness of performance targets:

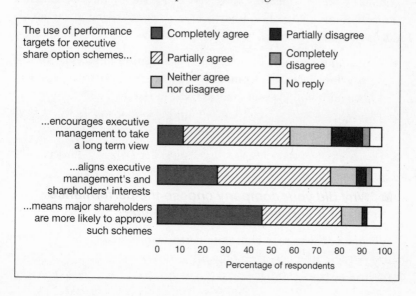

135

- Respondents agree most strongly with the statement that performance targets encourage shareholders to approve schemes.

- There was less support for the idea that performance targets align management and shareholder interests.

- There was least support for the idea that performance targets encourage management to take a long term view.

Source: Executive Share Options and Performance Targets, KPMG Tax Advisers, 1994

SHARE SCHEMES

Your company may well be uncomfortable with the idea of performance targets, but perfectly happy with the idea of share schemes. The same KPMG survey looked at share schemes in some detail. If you are thinking of introducing a share scheme, or want to benchmark your current scheme against other companies', then you may well be interested in these findings.

■ *Are share schemes popular?*

After an initial surge of schemes when Inland Revenue approved schemes were introduced, there has been a steady flow of schemes introduced each year. There has been a recent upswing in the introduction of share schemes, but is likely to be due to scheme renewals.

- Larger companies tend to confine participation in schemes to top management; smaller companies are more likely to extend the scheme to lower levels of management.

- The most popular type of all-employee scheme is the SAYE scheme.

- Few companies have ESOTs[2] (Executive Share Option Targets).

Source: Executive Share Options and Performance Targets, KPMG Tax Advisers, 1994

---

[2] For definitions of the different sorts of schemes see "What is the difference between performance target and share option schemes? Are there various different types of schemes?", pp. 132–133

Who participates in executive schemes?

Although executive share option schemes are discretionary in nature, there is nothing to prevent them being extended to employees at all levels. Executive schemes are, however, usually viewed as being used exclusively for top management:

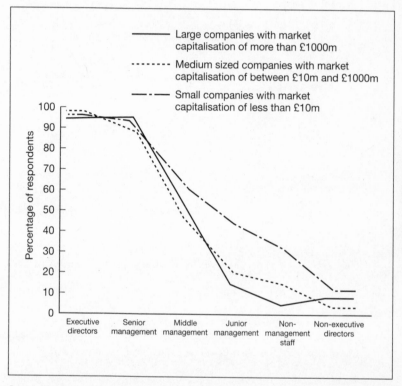

Source: Executive Share Options and Performance Targets, KPMG Tax Advisers, 1994

■ What other schemes does your company operate?

Although most listed companies responding to the survey had executive schemes, many also had some type of all-employee scheme or other share participation scheme:

Other share incentive schemes operated by size of company

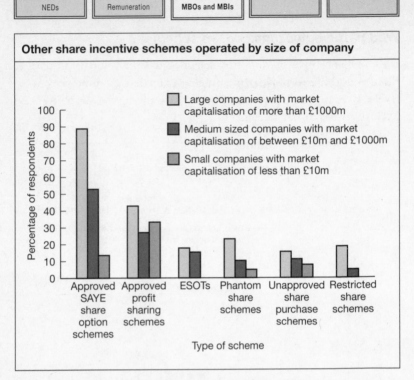

Base = All respondents with executive share option schemes (374)
Source: Executive Share Options and Performance Targets, KPMG Tax Advisers, 1994

MANAGEMENT BUY-OUTS AND BUY-INS

Throughout the 1980s, management buy-outs developed rapidly as a new form of organisation, with deals becoming increasingly large and more highly leveraged. However, in the early 1990s, a much lower number of large buy-outs were completed in either of the two largest buy-out markets, the US and the UK. Nevertheless, such transactions have increased their share of the market for corporate assets, accounting for over half of the number of enterprise ownership transfers in this period in the UK.

SUCCESS AND FAILURE

■ How many buy-outs and buy-ins fail?

In the early 1990s, failures and restructurings of buy-outs and buy-ins in the UK have so far outweighed stock market flotations and sales to third parties, although failures are now less important.

- From the beginning of 1990 to end 1993, 381 buy-outs and 127 buy-ins entered receivership according to the CMBOR database.

- In the same period, 443 buy-outs and 85 buy-ins were either floated on the stock market or sold to a non-management third party.

- 1989 is the year with the highest failure rate, with some 13.1% of buy-outs at the top of the market failing by the end of 1995:

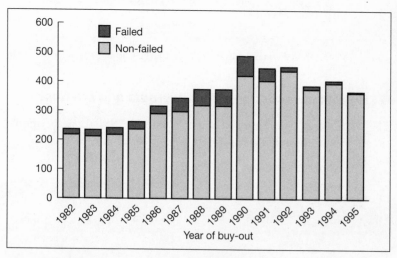

Source: CMBOR/BZW Private Equity/Deloitte & Touche Corporate Finance

■ Why are buy-ins more susceptible to problems than buy-outs?

Buy-ins seem to be more susceptible to problems than buy-outs, not least because incoming management are often not fully aware of the true extent of problems until they have effected the transaction. A far higher proportion of buy-ins in the peak years of 1988-1990 failed than is the case for buy-outs:

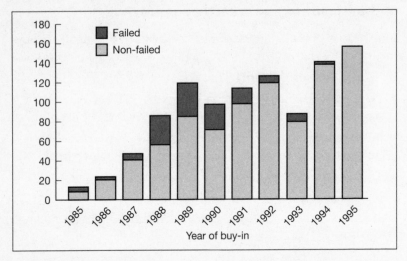

Source: CMBOR/BZW Private Equity/Deloitte & Touche Corporate Finance

■ *How does recession affect buy-outs and buy-ins?*

The rate of buy-out failure in the recession of 1990-1993 is significantly greater than that during the buoyant conditions of 1986-1989:

Period of buy-out failure by period of buy-out					
Period of failure:	1981-85	1986-89	1990-93	1994–95	Total buy-outs
Period of buy-out:					
1981–85	n/a	2.2%	4.9%	0.6%	1,117
1986–89	n/a	1.5%	10.2%	1.7%	1,410
1990–93	n/a	n/a	5.2%	2.4%	1,770
1994–95	n/a	n/a	n/a	1.2%	782

Source: CMBOR/BZW Private Equity/Deloitte & Touche Corporate Finance

So the share of buy-outs completed in the late 1980s, which failed in the recession of the 1990s, is considerably greater than for those transactions completed in the recession of the early 1980s.

Source: Restructuring and Failure in Buy-out and Buy-ins, Mike Wright, Nick Wilson, Ken Robbie and Chris Ennew, *Business Strategy Review, Summer 1994*

■ *What are the advantages of buy-outs?*

- Most buy-outs, and particularly smaller ones, do not involve massive amounts of debt finance, nor require asset disposals as part of the financial engineering of the transaction.

- Buy-outs can help the process of shedding labour – being able to restructure and therefore shed labour early in the life cycle.

- The greater levels of restructuring undertaken at buy-outs are associated with survival. The timing of restructuring is a major factor in avoiding failure.

Source: Restructuring and Failure in Buy-out and Buy-ins, Mike Wright, Nick Wilson, Ken Robbie and Chris Ennew, *Business Strategy Review, Summer 1994*

EXPORT MANAGEMENT

Why export?   144

Markets   148

Strategy   150
Recommendations

Credit, currencies and payment methods   155
Credit control ■ Exporting to the EU ■ Exporting to
the rest of Europe ■ Exporting to North America
■ Exporting to Asia ■ Credit and country risk

Financing exports   169

Exporting and the small business   171

The single market   173
...and cross-border trading ■ ...and VAT ■ Reporting

Sales chains   181

WHY EXPORT?

■ *What are the most common reasons for starting to export?*

Why should you export? Why not just sit at home and carry on as you always have? If you're just considering going into exports, you might find it useful to know why other people make this decision. This survey was about overseas business in general. About a quarter of the respondents were involved in importing, either as well as exporting, or without exporting at all. The results below reflect this.

Very important

Expansion into new markets

Personal experience of a particular country

Visit overseas by a director or manager of the business

Personal contacts

Improving quality

Reducing costs

Approach from a potential customer

Word of mouth opportunity

Approach from a potential supplier

Unsolicited overseas order

Reaction to competitor moves

Suggestion from government or trade organisation

Not at all important   Strategy of vertical integration

Source: Internationalisation for World Class Business Strategies, Association of British Chambers of Commerce, 1995

■ How do you find out about overseas business opportunities?

For all you know, there are customers in Portugal or Peru just crying out for your product. So how can you find out who – and where – they are? The following table shows where other businesses go to gather information about overseas business opportunities.

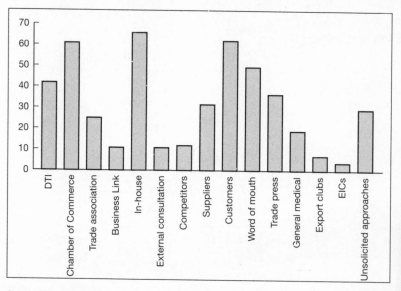

Source: *Internationalisation for World Class Business Strategies*, Association of British Chambers of Commerce, 1995

■ Which regulatory factors influence your decision on which countries to do business with?

Sometimes you may move into a particular foreign market for a specific reason – perhaps you know the area, or an agent has approached you asking to sell your products there. But if you have a more generalised wish to expand overseas, how do you decide which country to do business in? Among the most important factors to take into account are the regulatory factors, such as trade barriers. Which ones do businesses take into account when selecting a suitable country to trade in?

EXPORT MANAGEMENT

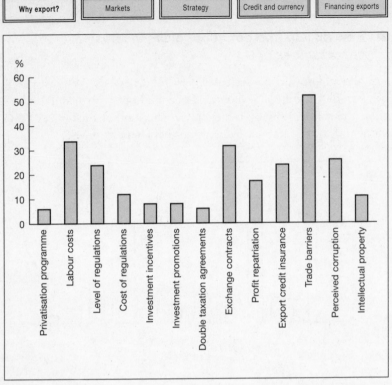

%

Privatisation programme
Labour costs
Level of regulations
Cost of regulations
Investment incentives
Investment promotions
Double taxation agreements
Exchange contracts
Profit repatriation
Export credit insurance
Trade barriers
Perceived corruption
Intellectual property

Source: Internationalisation for World Class Business Strategies, Association of British Chambers of Commerce, 1995

■ *Which other factors influence your decision?*

Once you've checked out the regulatory factors, there are other things you will want to consider as well. Is the country in question on the verge of a military coup, for example? Or is it physically inaccessible? The following table shows how many businesses in the survey took each factor into account.

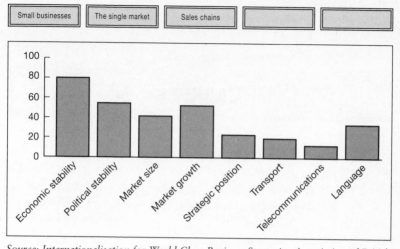

Source: *Internationalisation for World Class Business Strategies*, Association of British Chambers of Commerce, 1995

■ *If you don't export, why not?*

Of all the firms that choose not to export, over 80% have considered it at some time. So why have they rejected the idea? If you have decided against exporting, do any of these reasons apply to you?

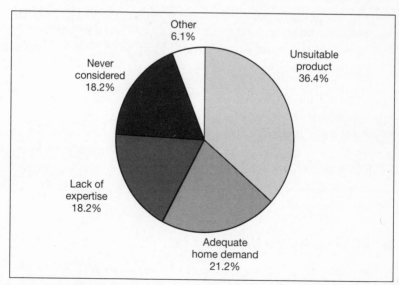

Source: *Internationalisation for World Class Business Strategies*, Association of British Chambers of Commerce, 1995

MARKETS

World trade has been growing at an average annual rate of 5.7% since 1989, driven in part by the rapid growth of new markets and new consumers in the Asia Pacific Region, South Asia and Latin America. The OECD has estimated that, within 15 years, some 700 million people in China, India and Indonesia – roughly equivalent to the combined populations of America, the European Union and Japan – will have an average income equivalent to that in Spain today. So the burning question is – which markets have most potential?

■ *What export markets worth less than £1 billion have significant potential?*

The UK currently exports over £1 billion of goods to each of 23 different countries – but only three of these, Hong Kong, Singapore and India, are rapidly growing markets according to both Government and business. Ernst & Young recently prepared a report for the CBI National Manufacturing Council which identified 11 markets under £1 billion which had significant potential. These are:

Asia Pacific: China; Korea; Taiwan; Malaysia; Thailand; Indonesia

South Asia: Pakistan, Sri Lanka

Latin America: Argentina, Brazil, Mexico

Source: Winning the Export Race, a report prepared by Ernst & Young for the CBI National Manufacturing Council

■ *Where does the UK export to?*

If you're new to exporting, then it will help to know what the present situation is. The patterns of UK exports are changing. While the EU will remain the UK's largest market, Asia represents the biggest growth opportunity for the rest of the 1990s – the Asia Pacific region constitutes over half the developing country export market, and imports almost as many goods as North America:

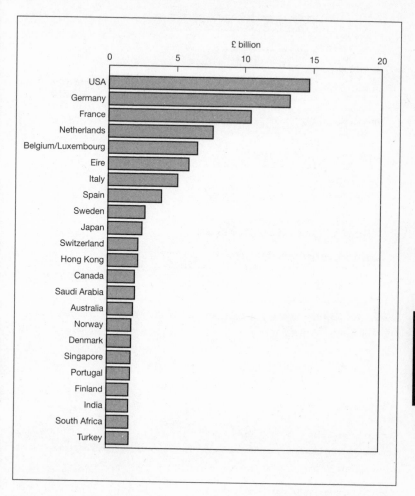

Source: Winning the Export Race, a report prepared by Ernst & Young for the CBI National Manufacturing Council

■ *Which export markets are growing fastest?*

UK exports to Eastern Europe and to Latin America have also grown at a higher than average rate, but together take only £4.5 billion worth of UK goods:

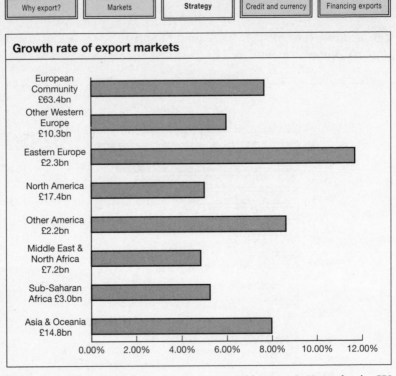

Growth rate of export markets

Source: Winning the Export Race, a report prepared by Ernst & Young for the CBI National Manufacturing Council

STRATEGY

RECOMMENDATIONS

The market opportunities may be there – but without a well planned and well executed strategy, their potential will not be realised. The Ernst & Young report for the CBI made one thing startlingly clear – that improved UK export performance will be driven by the actions of individual companies.

150

So if you are hoping to enter new markets, or increase your export drive, what is the best way to go about it? The report made four recommendations:

1. Implement a strong, self-determined business strategy, based on the core competencies.
2. Ensure 'state of the art' competitiveness in process, technology and people.
3. Apply a rigorous, professional, international approach to customer interfaces.
4. Work in partnership with government to create internationally competitive policy.

The following section looks in more detail at each of these recommendations.

Source: Winning the Export Race, a report prepared by Ernst & Young for the CBI National Manufacturing Council

■ *What are the core competencies?*

The first recommendation was to implement a strong self-determined business strategy, based on core competencies – selection, evaluation, benchmarking, capability, innovation:

- Select the right markets and products.
- Evaluate strategic alliances, or local presence, for competitive advantage.
- Benchmark against competitors.
- Ensure global supply chain capability.
- Develop innovative products that people want to buy.

Source: Winning the Export Race, a report prepared by Ernst & Young for the CBI National Manufacturing Council

■ *How do you ensure 'state of the art' competitiveness in process, technology and people?*

The report made the following recommendations:

- Establish low cost manufacturing.
- Develop internationally focused business processes.

- Implement dynamic operational measures of performance.
- Implement innovative recruitment and reward policies.
- Become expert at managing change.

Source: Winning the Export Race, a report prepared by Ernst & Young for the CBI National Manufacturing Council

■ *How do you apply a rigorous, professional, international approach to customer interfaces?*

Again, the report had the following advice for exporters:

- Build confidence and an international market.
- Invest in excellent marketing.
- Focus on sales.
- Ensure effective distribution and merchandising.

Source: Winning the Export Race, a report prepared by Ernst & Young for the CBI National Manufacturing Council

■ *Where does a partnership with government help?*

A partnership with government should make it easier to:

- Create the environment for international success.
- Maintain core technologies.
- Invest in fundamental research and development.
- Maintain and measure ministerial involvement.
- Maintain competitive export credit insurance cover.
- Continue to promote exports.
- Provide market information and export support.
- Support UK exports.

Source: Winning the Export Race, a report prepared by Ernst & Young for the CBI National Manufacturing Council

■ *Who do you rely on for expertise in conducting your overseas business?*

If you do a lot of business abroad, you will doubtless have some kind of in-house expertise. But supposing you don't have much overseas trade, or you're just starting out, or entering a new market or activity. Where can you go for advice? One survey of companies with up to 99 employees found that the main options that businesses seem to use are the DTI, Chamber of Commerce, Business Link, or outside consultants, as the table below shows. (It's worth noting that the survey was conducted among members of Chambers of Commerce.)

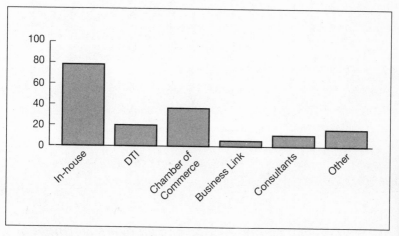

Source: *Internationalisation for World Class Business Strategies*, Association of British Chambers of Commerce, 1995

■ *What are the greatest barriers to overseas business?*

Many business people hold out against doing business overseas because they don't have a clue how to go about it. Fear of the unknown is a significant barrier for 45% of businesses with fewer than 100 employees. One of the best ways to counter this is to know what you're up against, and then you can prepare. The chart below shows the factors that respondents considered to be the greatest barriers.

EXPORT
MANAGEMENT

153

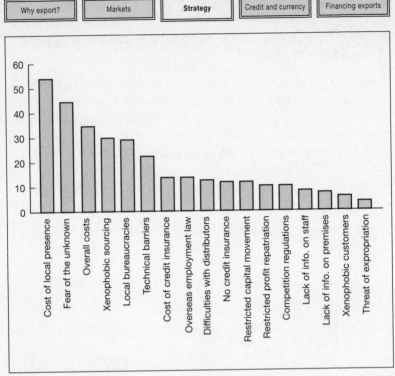

Source: Internationalisation for World Class Business Strategies, Association of British Chambers of Commerce, 1995

■ *How do you go about choosing an overseas agent or distributor?*

If you decide to sell overseas through a third party, you are putting your future success in the region into their hands. But are they safe hands? The best (and most popular) way to find an agent or distributor is by personal recommendation, but this isn't always available. So if you're investigating or interviewing several agents or distributors, what are the most important qualifications they should possess? The following table shows how one sample of UK exporters said they ranked the key criteria for selecting agents and distributors.

The top 14 criteria for selecting agents

1. Knowledge of market
2. Market coverage
3. Enthusiasm for the product
4. Knowledge of the product
5. Good reputation
6. Number and quality of sales staff
7. Previous success
8. Good connections
9. Frequency of sales calls
10. Service and stocking facilities
11. Costs involved
12. Quality of service staff
13. Dealings with competitors
14. Executive career histories

Source: A Profile of UK Exporting Companies – An Empirical Study, by Richard A Moore, from Journal of Marketing Management

CREDIT, CURRENCIES AND PAYMENT METHODS

CREDIT CONTROL

■ How do you assess the creditworthiness of new overseas customers?

Some businesses avoid the need to check their customers' creditworthiness by using letters of credit, or they use credit insurance agencies or factoring companies. But if you don't go for these options, how can you be sure that they'll pay up? This is how one survey's respondents check on their new overseas buyers.

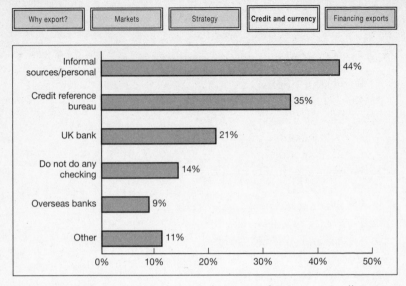

Source: Royal Bank of Scotland Quarterly Survey of Exporters, Small Business Research Trust, June 1995

■ *How do you ensure payments from your overseas buyers?*

Even assuming you've made thorough checks on your customers' creditworthiness, you still can't be sure they'll pay up unless you take other steps. What do other exporters do to ensure payments from their overseas customers? 70% of them in this survey do at least some business with no formal method of protection at all.

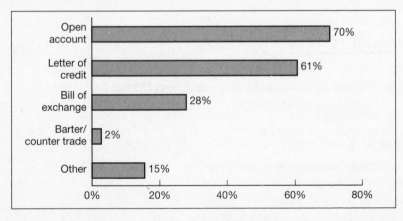

Source: Royal Bank of Scotland Quarterly Survey of Exporters, Small Business Research Trust, June 1995

156

■ How serious is the problem of late payment by export customers?

Late payment of course can be catastrophic for businesses. But if you're exporting, do you tend to find ways of avoiding these problems, or do they give you serious grief? This table shows how serious other exporters find the problem; it suggests that most of them are employing the credit control methods above to good effect.

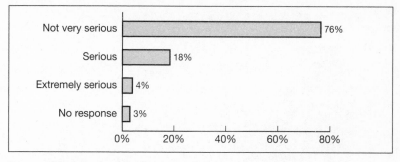

Source: *Royal Bank of Scotland Quarterly Survey of Exporters*, Small Business Research Trust, June 1995

EXPORTING TO THE EU

If you are an exporter, the chances are that you are trading with the EU. So have you experienced currency problems? Or problems with late payment and bad debt? It may help you to know which countries are the best and worst payers, and what the standard credit periods are. The Institute of Export and NCM Insurance Ltd commissioned a study of exporting which answers these questions – and more. Some of its findings are reproduced below.

■ How many exporters trade within the EU?

The UK's main export market remains the enlarged EU.

● 82% of respondents trade in the EU.

Source: *The Third Survey of International Services Provided to Exporters 1995.* Commissioned by the Institute of Export and NCM Credit Insurance Ltd.

157

■ *Which currency is most often used?*

- The number trading in sterling is falling – 47% in 1995, compared with 60% in 1994; the 1995 figures represent a fall of 13% from 1994 and a fall of 28% since 1993.

- There is a marked switch from sterling to the buyer's currency or a third currency, demonstrating a generally more flexible attitude.

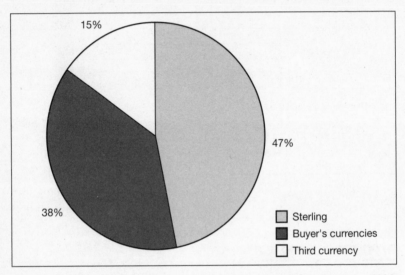

Source: The Third Survey of International Services Provided to Exporters 1995. Commissioned by the Institute of Export and NCM Credit Insurance Ltd.

■ *What credit period is standard?*

Credit period	Proportion of companies giving it
30 days' credit	44%
60 days' credit	37%
90 days' credit	10%
More than 90 days' credit	3%

- Sight payment terms have increased from 2% in 1994 to 6% in 1995.

Source: The Third Survey of International Services Provided to Exporters 1995. Commissioned by the Institute of Export and NCM Credit Insurance Ltd.

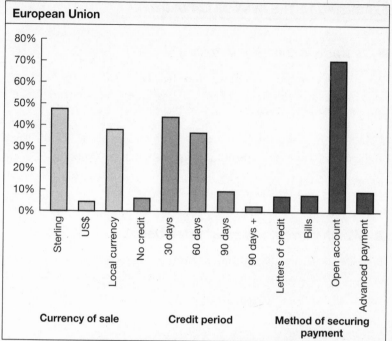

Source: *The Third Survey of International Services Provided to Exporters 1995.* Commissioned by the Institute of Export and NCM Credit Insurance Ltd.

■ *What payment methods are used?*

- Open account trading is used by 72%, increased from 69% in 1994.

- The use of letters of credit as a payment method fell by 6% to 8% this year. The use of letters of credit appears connected to specific industry sectors, irrespective of country.

- The use of bills for collection showed a significant increase from 2.5% to 9% in 1995. This reflects the increase in sales to Southern European countries and a more formal trading method linked to a reduction in credit periods. More companies are now demanding either payment in advance or sight payment.

- Despite open account trading remaining the preferred method, credit periods have been reduced and more formality appears to have been introduced by exporters selling into the European Union.

Source: *The Third Survey of International Services Provided to Exporters 1995.* Commissioned by the Institute of Export and NCM Credit Insurance Ltd

159

EXPORTING TO THE REST OF EUROPE

■ *Is trade in this region falling?*

1994/5 has seen more countries join the EU, so the number of countries included in the 'rest of Europe' has fallen. So has trade in this region taken a commensurate cut?

- 66% of respondents who trade in this region show a fall of 6% from last year – perhaps not as large as might be expected.

Source: The Third Survey of International Services Provided to Exporters 1995. Commissioned by the Institute of Export and NCM Credit Insurance Ltd.

■ *Which currency is most often used?*

The picture is somewhat different from the European Union:

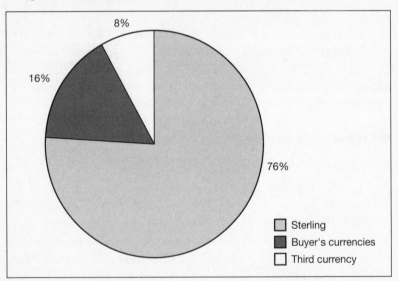

- The 8% using a third currency all trade in US dollars.

Source: The Third Survey of International Services Provided to Exporters 1995. Commissioned by the Institute of Export and NCM Credit Insurance Ltd.

160

■ *What credit period is standard?*

Credit period	Proportion of companies giving it
No credit	18%
30 days' credit	37%
60 days' credit	35%
90 days' credit	9%
More than 90 days' credit	1%

- Many companies use a variety of credit periods depending on the individual country and the buyer.

Source: The Third Survey of International Services Provided to Exporters 1995. Commissioned by the Institute of Export and NCM Credit Insurance Ltd.

■ *What payment methods are used?*

The composition of the countries in this region has resulted in a significant change in the payment methods used when compared to previous years. Over half (52%) of business is now conducted on credit terms, which demonstrates both the large increase in business in this region (particularly to Central Europe and CIS countries) and the exporter's desire for more secure methods of trading. However, the greater use of letters of credit places more demand on banks to 'confirm' letters of credit, i.e. to accept both country and credit risk of banks in these developing markets.

EXPORT
MANAGEMENT

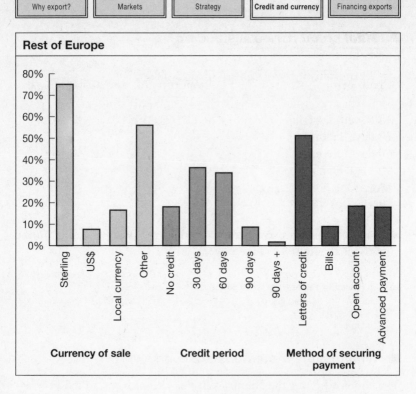

Rest of Europe

- Only 19% of exports are sold on open account terms, with 10% on bills for collection. 19% of exporters preferring payment in advance.

- The normal trading method used by respondents selling into this region is letters of credit, in sterling with a normal credit period of between 30 and 60 days.

- Banks are facing increasing pressure to accept more country and bank risks in this region, especially in the CIS and Central Europe. Not all banks will take these risks. So exporters need to ascertain which banks will accept risks, and on which overseas banks, prior to undertaking contracts.

Source: The Third Survey of International Services Provided to Exporters 1995. Commissioned by the Institute of Export and NCM Credit Insurance Ltd.

EXPORTING TO NORTH AMERICA

■ *Which currency is most often used?*

57% of exporters trade with North America. For the purposes of this chart, 'buyer's currency' is assumed to be US dollars – with apologies to our Canadian friends. No third currency is used:

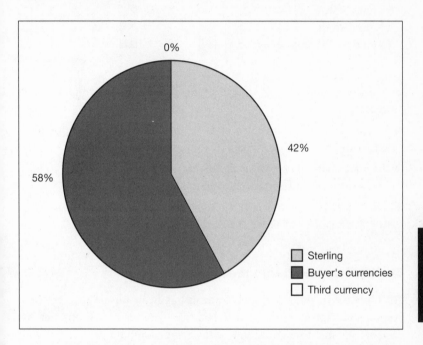

- So 58% of companies trade in US dollars, and 42% trade in sterling. This is a significant change from previous years, when at least 56% of sales were made in sterling. Many companies appear to be taking advantage of the dollar's weakness and are switching the trading currency to US dollars.

Source: The Third Survey of International Services Provided to Exporters 1995. Commissioned by the Institute of Export and NCM Credit Insurance Ltd.

EXPORT
MANAGEMENT

163

■ *What credit period is standard?*

Credit period	Proportion of companies giving it
No credit	9%
30 days' credit	37%
60 days' credit	45%
90 days' credit	8%
More than 90 days' credit	1%

- The percentage giving 30 days' credit is the same percentage as last year.
- There has been an increase of 10% in the number of respondents who offer 60 days' credit since the previous survey.
- To match this, there was a significant fall in the number of companies giving credit beyond 90 days.

Source: The Third Survey of International Services Provided to Exporters 1995. Commissioned by the Institute of Export and NCM Credit Insurance Ltd.

■ *What payment methods are used?*

An increase in open account trading has been observed, yet some respondents appear to have switched from less restrictive practices to advance payment when trading with certain companies.

- 70% of companies trade on open account terms compared with 66% in 1994.
- 10% trade on letter of credit terms, similar to last year.
- 8% sell on bills for collection terms, an increase of 4% over the previous year.
- Payment in advance is used by 12% of companies.

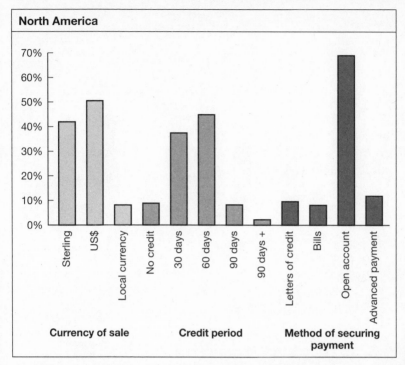

Source: The Third Survey of International Services Provided to Exporters 1995.
Commissioned by the Institute of Export and NCM Credit Insurance Ltd.

EXPORTING TO ASIA

■ *What currency, credit terms and payment methods are most often used?*

The majority of trade with Asia is conducted in sterling using letters of credit, payable at the time of shipment. However, nearly one in four exporters is using open account and providing credit for up to 60 days. The trading terms are dependent upon the buyer and the stability both politically and economically of the buyer's country.

165

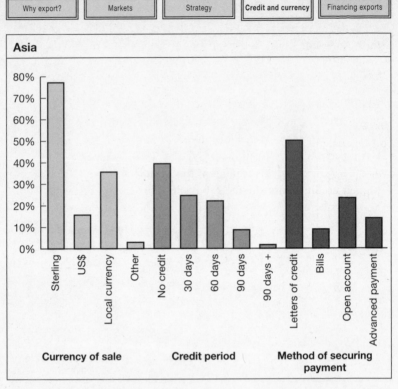

Asia

Currency of sale — Sterling, US$, Local currency, Other

Credit period — No credit, 30 days, 60 days, 90 days, 90 days +

Method of securing payment — Letters of credit, Bills, Open account, Advanced payment

Source: The Third Survey of International Services Provided to Exporters 1995. Commissioned by the Institute of Export and NCM Credit Insurance Ltd.

CREDIT AND COUNTRY RISK

■ *What credit protection measures do you use?*

If you have experienced, or are experiencing, problems with late payment and bad debts, then credit protection is an obvious answer. Credit insurance is popular – 53% of companies hold credit insurance policies, although credit insurance needs may vary according to region.

- 45% of exporters using credit insurance use brokers for advice, although the majority deal directly with underwriters.

- Nearly 33% of exporters are seeking more insurance cover for buyers, which may be currently limited due to insufficient financial information on the buyers or difficult trading conditions within a country, including late payments.

166

- 20% of respondents wish to see an increased availability of credit insurance in the Middle and Far East, whilst only 10% of companies consider they require more insurance in the remaining markets.

Many companies use letters of credit as a method of credit protection. According to the survey, these companies appear to be more content with their overall credit strategy than those exporters who rely solely on credit insurance.

20% of respondents trading in the Middle and Far East are seeking higher credit limits on their buyers. This compares with 10% of exporters who are seeking additional credit insurance in Africa and Asia.

Source: The Third Survey of International Services Provided to Exporters 1995. Commissioned by the Institute of Export and NCM Credit Insurance Ltd.

■ *How many exporters use letters of credit?*

Just as the credit risk varies from area to area, so do credit terms. The following proportion of companies used letters of credit in the following regions:

Latin America	85%
Asia	82%
Africa	79%
Middle East	73%

This trading strategy highlights a key requirement of exporters who require financial institutions to protect sellers' credit risks by confirming letters of credit. Unfortunately, it is often difficult for financial institutions to provide confirmation lines, in all cases, due to heavy demand often outstripping supply.

Many companies experience difficulties and delays in identifying banks that will 'confirm' letters of credit issued in the more difficult markets. Exporters should plan ahead before entering into contracts, ensuring that the selected advising bank will be prepared to accept both the country and the risk.

Source: The Third Survey of International Services Provided to Exporters 1995. Commissioned by the Institute of Export and NCM Credit Insurance Ltd.

EXPORT MANAGEMENT

■ *Which are the slow paying markets in the EU?*

A third of respondents exporting to the EU are experiencing payment delays. The countries identified as 'slow payers' are:

Italy	Germany	France
Spain	Greece	

Increasing payment delays are being encountered in Germany and France, whilst Italian companies 'take 60 days when 30 days are given and 120 days on 60 days trading terms'.

Source: The Third Survey of International Services Provided to Exporters 1995. Commissioned by the Institute of Export and NCM Credit Insurance Ltd.

■ *Which are the slow payers in other regions?*

The Middle East was cited for its payment delays by 1 in 8 companies trading in the region. Latin America was also identified by 1 in 5 companies for slow payment, with Brazil and Mexico signalled as the countries most often associated with delaying remittances. The CIS countries and Nigeria have the poorest payment records in the rest of Europe and Africa.

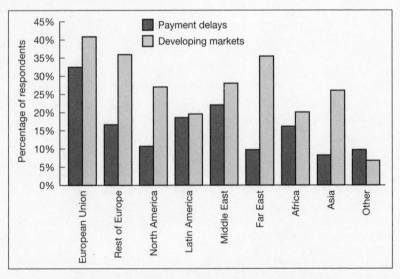

Source: The Third Survey of International Services Provided to Exporters 1995. Commissioned by the Institute of Export and NCM Credit Insurance Ltd.

■ *Who are the best payers?*

Asia, the Far East and North America appear to be the markets with the best payment records. Only 1 in 10 companies experience payment delays in these markets – compared with 1 in 3 in the EU.

Source: The Third Survey of International Services Provided to Exporters 1995. Commissioned by the Institute of Export and NCM Credit Insurance Ltd.

FINANCING EXPORTS

If your product(s) are popular in the domestic market, then you have probably built a substantial customer base in the UK – and with it, the profit to fund most of your exporting. The initial outlay on exports is usually greater than that on domestic sales – so if your product is specifically for the export market, you may need help with the start-up costs. Or you may wish to undertake a substantial export drive, and simply need finance to tide you over until your overseas customers pay. So how do other companies finance their exports?

■ *What methods of financing do you use for exports?*

Many more companies are using their company's own funds to finance international trade – 41% of respondents in 1995, compared with 24% in 1994.

- Overdrafts are used by 30% of companies compared with 64% in 1994. Many respondents commented on their reluctance to use overdrafts to finance exports.

- The trend of the use of stage payments continues to grow. This sales strategy is now adopted by many manufacturing companies who believe that buyers are less likely to withdraw from the purchase contract if stage payments are provided.

EXPORT MANAGEMENT

169

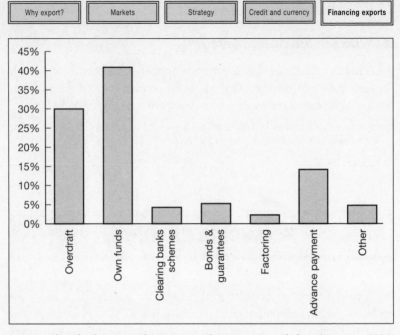

Source: The Third Survey of International Services Provided to Exporters 1995.
Commissioned by the Institute of Export and NCM Credit Insurance Ltd.

■ *What is your foreign exchange strategy?*

With a continuing trend of more companies seeking to protect their foreign exchange exposure, there is a need for banks to provide facilities which incorporate a foreign exchange line. Interestingly, though, only 9% of companies believe that their bank facilities prevent or restrict them from maintaining an active foreign exchange strategy.

Forward contracts	32%
Trade in sterling only	23%
Currency accounts	27%
No action	14%
Currency options	4%

Source: The Third Survey of International Services Provided to Exporters 1995.
Commissioned by the Institute of Export and NCM Credit Insurance Ltd.

170

■ *Do you use credit insurance?*

Some respondents claim that they have allowed their policies to lapse due to cost and availability of cover. This may prove a false economy given the reports of payment delays in the EU and other well-developed regions. Anyway, the chart below shows what proportion of companies use credit insurance:

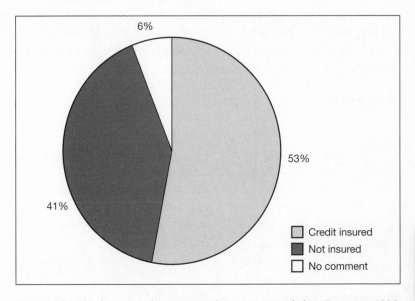

Source: *The Third Survey of International Services Provided to Exporters 1995.* Commissioned by the Institute of Export and NCM Credit Insurance Ltd.

EXPORTING AND THE SMALL BUSINESS

Small and medium sized companies that export remain very confident about export prospects, according to a Royal Bank of Scotland survey. The optimism is a result not of a recovery in one particular region, but because most companies hold the view that gains in some markets will outnumber losses in others.

If you run one of this highly adaptable band of companies, what are your main concerns? Your competitors, probably – and your sources of support. So how are other small firms faring in the export market?

■ Did your sales rise or fall in the 12 months to January 1995?

If the size of your overseas sales has remained fairly constant for the last few years, are you failing to take advantage of a growing trend? Yes and no – nearly a quarter of respondents report little change, but over half say their sales are increasing:

By size of business

	Number of people who work in the business			
	1-4	5-14	15-49	50+
Rise	49%	55%	59%	70%
Fall	24%	21%	15%	10%
Same	26%	25%	26%	19%
No response	1%	–	–	1%

By business activity

	Rise	Fall	Same	No response
Consumer goods	66%	14%	21%	–
Capital goods	56%	19%	25%	–
Intermediate goods (N.B. all the above are manufacturers)	66%	9%	25%	1%
Export houses	55%	23%	21%	1%
Other services	50%	21%	29%	[1]

Source: The Royal Bank of Scotland Quarterly Survey of Exporters, Royal Bank of Scotland and the Small Business Research Trust, 1995

---

[1] These figures relate to companies with under 100 employees only.

■ If you face competition in your export markets from any other exporters, which ONE country provides the most competition?

Exporters from Germany	34%
Exporters from Italy	18%
Exporters from France	11%
Exporters from Netherlands	7%
Exporters from Spain	3%
No response	27%

Source: The Royal Bank of Scotland Quarterly Survey of Exporters, Royal Bank of Scotland and the Small Business Research Trust, 1995

THE SINGLE MARKET

...AND CROSS-BORDER TRADING

■ How much trade is there between member states?

Perhaps you only dispatch goods to member states, and do not purchase directly from foreign sources. In which case, are you alone?

Overall, 63% of respondents both dispatch and acquire goods from member states, while 15% acquire only, and 13% dispatch only:

Undertake dispatch and acquisition of goods	63%
Undertake acquisition only	15%
Undertake dispatch only	13%
Undertake neither	8%

Source: VAT and the Single Market '95 Report, KPMG Tax Advisers

■ *From which country do exporters most regularly acquire goods?*

Most goods are obtained from Germany. This is most apparent in transportation companies (82%), but the small size of the sample may mean that this figure is not representative:

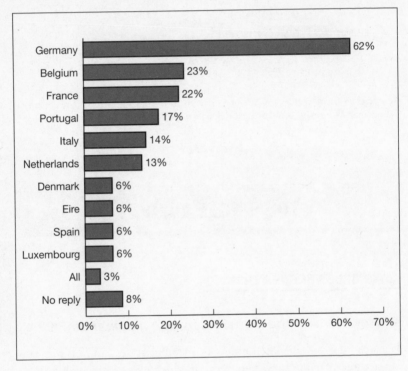

Source: VAT and the Single Market '95 Report, KPMG Tax Advisers

■ *To which country do exporters most regularly dispatch goods?*

Dispatching of goods appears to be less biased to one particular country. The results accurately reflect not only the geographical closeness of the countries involved (hence intra-EU trade is more convenient) but also their economic power as industrial nations:

174

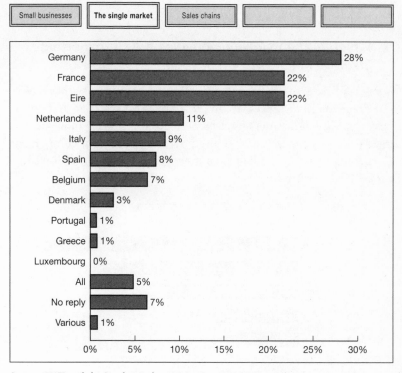

Source: *VAT and the Single Market '95 Report*, KPMG Tax Advisers

...AND VAT

■ *Do the Single Market Rules put a strain on your company?*

Not a popular subject, this. If Intrastat and EU Sales Lists (EU reporting requirements) are dirty words in your company, it may not be any consolation to know you are not alone. More than half of UK exporters (56%) agree that EU reporting requirements put a strain on their company.

- Each company spends on average 19 man hours reporting per month. This times increases dramatically according to the size of the company.

- 80% of companies have not adjusted their pattern of trade to fit Single Market Rules.

Source: *VAT and the Single Market '95 Report*, KPMG Tax Advisers

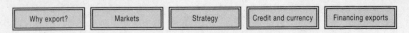
■ *Which of the following activities are UK exporters involved in?*

Some trading areas have experienced more problems with EU VAT requirements than others. It would seem, however, that despite the hassle, few manufacturers have been deterred. Intra-EU movement of goods for processing (i.e. making different goods from components or raw materials) is the most common business activity, followed by intra-EU movement for repair/modification/treatment:

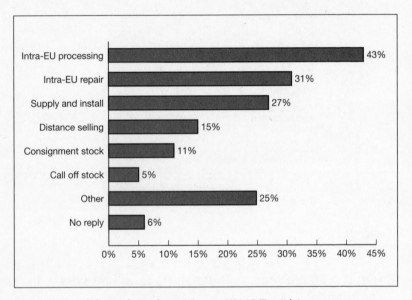

Source: VAT and the Single Market '95 Report, KPMG Tax Advisers

■ *Do exporters register for VAT in other countries?*

Are you considering registering for VAT in other countries? It can, of course, have cost advantages. France and Germany are the most common European member states in which UK companies have also registered for VAT (13% and 12% respectively). However, the most favoured country for VAT registration varies according to the size of the industry (in this case, by turnover) :

176

	Percentage registering in:	
	France	Germany
Over £500 million	47	47
£100 – 500 million	21	21
£50 – 100 million	4	7
£10 – 50 million	11	12
£1 – 10 million	5	6
less than £1 million	4	0

Source: VAT and the Single Market '95 Report, KPMG Tax Advisers

■ Why do exporters register?

Although the figures of the preceding table echo those below, which
show member states with which the UK most often trades, they also
indicate the burden of multiple registrations that businesses involved
in these activities can endure. Supply and install contracts, for example, continue to present difficulties for VAT purposes, due to the
absence of common EU wide treatment. So why do people register
for VAT abroad?

Main reason for VAT registration by country

Reason	France	Germany	Eire	Netherlands
Supply & install contracts	36	36	40	26
Intra-EU movement for processing	50	51	28	32
Intra-EU movement for repair/modification/work on goods	32	30	30	24
Distance selling	16	15	15	18
Consignment stock	18	13	15	26
Call of stock	6	11	0	3
Other	22	28	30	29

177

The high number of registrations in France is unsurprising, since it has no simplification procedure enabling non-resident suppliers to avoid registration. Similar numbers in Germany and Eire, however, where simplifications do exist for supply and install, perhaps indicate more complex arrangements, or cases where a local registration has been preferred as a means of speedier recovery of local VAT costs.

A high number of multiple registrations are in connection with processing supplies (where goods finished by a processor are delivered directly to the owner's customers in a country where the owner is not registered, thus constituting supplies of goods by the owner in the processor's country). Such operations do not benefit from the simplification introduced last year, which allowed the owners to avoid registration in the processor's countries if processed goods were shipped to any member state where the processor is registered.

Source: VAT and the Single Market '95 Report, KPMG Tax Advisers

■ *Have you experienced problems with VAT in the EU?*

If you are trading abroad, you will have your own stories of the problems you have encountered. But in case there are still some issues waiting to surprise you, respondents to the KPMG survey mentioned the following problems:

Distance selling. EU based operations need to register in their customers' countries and charge local VAT, something which non-EU based organisations can avoid and thus trade at a competitive advantage.

Stock-holding operations. Whether for call-off by one customer or on consignment for sale to many, stock holding operations pose problems due to the absence of common EU-wide treatment.

Fiscal representation. In all cases, businesses face difficulties surrounding the appointment of fiscal representatives (where required) and any directly related tax concerns.

Source: VAT and the Single Market '95 Report, KPMG Tax Advisers

REPORTING

■ *Do you find VAT reporting manageable?*

Do you find your VAT reporting takes up too much time and is a major headache? On the whole, respondents found general VAT reporting manageable (53%). Nearly a quarter described reporting as easy.

Source: VAT and the Single Market '95 Report, KPMG Tax Advisers

■ *Do you find EU sales lists easy to complete?*

Easy or otherwise, this also seems to be a manageable exercise; 20% find completion easy and 40% find it manageable across all industry groups.

Source: VAT and the Single Market '95 Report, KPMG Tax Advisers

■ *What is the average reporting commitment?*

If you seem to be spending hours each month meeting EU reporting requirements, are you alone? The picture varies by industry sector. The average number of hours spent on EU reporting requirements each month are

Sector	Hours
Transport	103
Retailing	38
Manufacturing	17
Leisure/tourism	10
Wholesaling	9
Construction/property	6
Other	15
No reply	1

Source: VAT and the Single Market '95 Report, KPMG Tax Advisers

EXPORT MANAGEMENT

■ *Do you find reporting requirements a burden or a benefit?*

There is a general agreement that companies feel that reporting requirements put a strain on their company (56%):

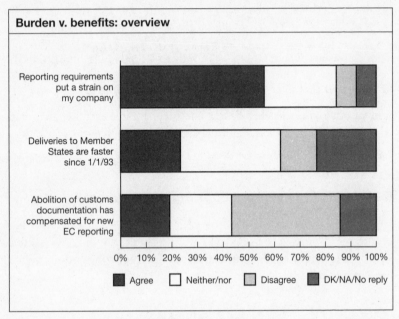

It appears that this strain increases the larger the company. Larger firms are the most likely to experience faster delivery times since the introduction of the Single Market. However

- 42% of respondents disagree that the abolition of customs documentation has compensated for the introduction of EU reporting requirements.

Source: VAT and the Single Market '95 Report, KPMG Tax Advisers

SALES CHAINS

■ What are sales chains?

Sales chains are where Company A sells to Company B, and B sells to Company C, all in different countries (this is called 'triangulation' when only 3 companies are involved).

Source: VAT and the Single Market '95 Report, KPMG Tax Advisers

■ How much trade is in this form?

If you are involved in a sales chain, you may well want to know how much trade takes this form. A surprising amount of trade is in the form of triangulation and sales chains – nearly 30% of respondents are involved:

Types of sales 'chains'	Percentage
None	55
Triangulation	25
Chains of 4 or more parties	5
No reply	3
Don't know/no answer	12

Source: VAT and the Single Market '95 Report, KPMG Tax Advisers

■ Have the triangulation simplification measures made trade easier for you?

Recent measures relating to triangulation were brought in with the specific intent of making it easier for traders. Have they worked? The respondents felt that things were now:

EXPORT MANAGEMENT

Easier	27%
No different	44%
More difficult	21%
Don't know/no answer	8%

Source: VAT and the Single Market '95 Report, KPMG Tax Advisers

■ *Have you been able to reduce your VAT compliance burden on sales chains?*

If you are involved in a sales chain and are struggling with your VAT compliance burden, you are certainly not alone. Only 4% of exporters involved in sales chains have been able to reduce their VAT compliance burdens:

Yes	4%
No	33%
No reply	20%
Don't know/no answer	43%

At present, it would appear the burdens for intermediate principals related to chain transactions can only be reduced by changing role from principal to that of an agent, or using VAT grouping rules, or replacing non-resident principals with resident associated companies.

Source: VAT and the Single Market '95 Report, KPMG Tax Advisers

■ *Have Customs and Excise reviewed exporters' single market trade, ESL and intrastate returns?*

The answer to this varied by the company; only 67% recorded that they have:

Yes	67%
No	24%
Don't know/no answer/no reply	9%

Source: VAT and the Single Market '95 Report, KPMG Tax Advisers

■ How do you feel about the review by Customs and Excise?

If you have experienced a Customs and Excise review of single
market trade, ESL and intrastate returns, did you find it helpful? It
seems that the majority of companies appreciate the review:

Found review:	Percentage of companies
Helpful	51
Neutral	41
Unhelpful	7
Don't know/no answer	1

Source: VAT and the Single Market '95 Report, KPMG Tax Advisers

CURRENT MANAGEMENT ISSUES

Ethics in management 186
Ethical standards ■ Management and ethics
■ Ethical codes

Managers and the millennium 194
Main challenges

Office and locations 197
Offices ■ Relocation within the UK ■ International
business locations

Managing information technology (IT) 209
IT directors ■ Development ■ Outsourcing IT
■ Budgets and costs ■ Benefits and problems
■ Scope of IT ■ Emerging technologies

Fraud 232
Extent ■ Detection ■ Prevention and cure

ETHICS IN MANAGEMENT

ETHICAL STANDARDS

The Institute of Management published a survey on ethics in 1994 entitled *Walking the Tightrope*. The survey defines 'ethics' as being the 'norms of conduct in society'. The current interest in business ethics is probably a reaction to widespread unethical business behaviour in the 1980s. So how ethical is business? Can we rely on the ethical standards of managers to avoid a pensions swindle or fraud, or to protect our environment? Or does corporate governance need to be further regulated, and the environment protected by tighter laws? If you are interested in any of these questions, then the survey makes interesting reading; its key findings are shown below.

■ *Do you adopt an ethical approach to management?*

Around 90% of respondents say that they adopt an ethical perspective towards management and are prepared to speak out on ethical issues at their places of work, particularly on issues close to the organisation, such as financial conduct, treatment of workers and control of information.

- When asked about leadership, 96% agree that, as managers, they should give ethical leadership.
- Over 80% use their own moral values to decide on ethical issues.
- Yet a frightening 30% of respondents identify senior management as the main obstacle to ethical management in their organisations.

The ethical tensions which seem to arise for these respondents are a reminder of the harsher competitive pressures which affect certain sections of management and types of organisation.

Source: Walking the Tightrope. A Survey of Ethics in Management, Stephen Brigley, Institute of Management (sponsored by the University of Bath), 1994.

186

■ Do your views on ethical issues differ from your organisation's?

Perceived differences between individual managers' views and their organisations' views of what constitutes an ethical issue suggest that a minority of managers do experience an ethical mismatch. This is more pronounced on issues relating to salary and pay, and may be reflected in the reluctance of a small minority to express their views openly.

- Just over three-quarters believe that the ethical issues which concern them are also seen as ethical by their own organisations.

Source: Walking the Tightrope. A Survey of Ethics in Management, Stephen Brigley, Institute of Management (sponsored by the University of Bath), 1994.

■ Which ethical issues concern most organisations?

Ethical consideration of the environment receives general support from the respondents, and is widely seen as a prominent ethical concern of their organisations.

A large majority of respondents report that their organisations have strong expectations of them as managers, particularly their performance relating to internally set standards of conduct, public morals, the quality of their product or service, and the use of professional discretion.

Source: Walking the Tightrope. A Survey of Ethics in Management, Stephen Brigley, Institute of Management (sponsored by the University of Bath), 1994.

■ How ethically responsible is your organisation?

About 50% of the respondents' organisations have codes of ethics in place. These are generally well received and supported, and are seen to signal organisations' social responsibility. However, their value in allowing free and open discussion of ethical problems and in the day to day running of the organisations seems less certain.

- More organisations are believed to be ethically 'blind' on issues which could affect external relationships and their freedom to adopt competitive business tactics.

Source: Walking the Tightrope. A Survey of Ethics in Management, Stephen Brigley, Institute of Management (sponsored by the University of Bath), 1994.

MANAGEMENT AND ETHICS

■ *How do you regard various different ethical issues?*

If ethics matter to you, then you can probably relate stories of the times you have had to stand up and be counted. Yet there are some issues – such as incentive schemes and commission related earnings – which might be considered acceptable by one organisation, yet seen as unethical by another. So this survey presented 32 types of behaviour which could have ethical implications for organisations, covering business conduct, relationships with employees, external relationships and issues about information.

Even though managers found some issues more relevant to them than others, the level of personal ethical awareness was very high. 80% or more of respondents saw 75% of the types of behaviour as raising ethical issues for organisations.

The percentages of respondents who said they would speak out, if faced with these behaviours, were almost as high. Generally, a lower number (around 55-75%) of respondents believed the listed behaviours were viewed as ethical issues by their organisations:

Key:
1 – An ethical issue for organisations
2 – An ethical issue within their organisation
3 – An issue they would speak out on if it were taking place in their organisation

Types of behaviour	Percentage considering this behaviour		
	1	2	3
Business conduct			
Knowingly providing shoddy goods/services	95	84	96
Use of company assets for private gain	95	78	84
Padding of expense accounts	93	80	86
Use of kickbacks	93	78	85
Tax evasion	92	78	84
Insider share dealing	92	75	84
Inaccurate accounting	91	79	90
Giving/receiving excessive gifts or hospitality	89	77	82

Types of behaviour	Percentage considering this behaviour		
	1	2	3
Business conduct continued			
Lengthy delay in settling debts	89	63	79
Overcharging clients	88	66	83
Big salaries for top managers	82	46	61
Relationships with employees			
Theft from organisation	95	90	95
Unsafe working conditions	95	85	96
Personal harassment	95	83	97
Discrimination	95	83	94
Drug/alcohol abuse at work	92	84	93
Insensitive handling of redundancies	89	68	84
Depressing pay to lowest levels	80	53	74
Earnings too closely linked to commissions	51	32	44
External relationships			
Bribing to win contracts	95	83	85
Causing environmental damage	94	81	89
Wasting natural resources	86	70	80
Deviously gaining preferential treatment from central/local government	83	67	68
Financial/commercial links with repressive regimes	79	59	65
Large financial donations to political parties	72	59	61
Rejecting responsibility for local poor/unemployed	67	52	57
Information			
Ignoring confidential status of information	93	84	88
Spreading lies or untruths about a competitor's performance	92	75	79
Misrepresentation in advertising/PR	91	77	82
Withholding important information from shareholders	91	69	76
Marketing which exploits the 'weak' in society	84	69	77
Covert information gathering on competitors	52	42	41
Other	83	58	85

| Ethics | The Millennium | Offices/Locations | Info. Technology | Fraud |

These results appear to contradict the common view that in business it is the law of the jungle which prevails. It is an apparently impressive rebuttal by those in authority of the claims that business is, by its very nature, amoral, and that managers divorce ethics from business and see decision-making as a purely technical matter.

As one manager commented, however, 'What people say and what people do are very different'.

Source: Walking the Tightrope. A Survey of Ethics in Management, Stephen Brigley, Institute of Management (sponsored by the University of Bath), 1994.

■ *Do managers in financial services speak out against unethical practices?*

The last few years have seen several major scandals in financial services. So this was a particularly pertinent question – with enough people prepared to stand up and be counted, perhaps at least one of those scandals could have been avoided. Around 90% of financial services managers say they would speak out if their companies took part in insider dealing or used company assets for private gain.

● 32% of financial services managers say they would speak out if their companies were to reject responsibility for the poor or unemployed.

Source: Walking the Tightrope. A Survey of Ethics in Management, Stephen Brigley, Institute of Management (sponsored by the University of Bath), 1994.

■ *Do you feel that, as a manager, your ethical responsibilities increase towards your immediate social and business circles?*

Other managers were asked whether their ethical responsibilities increase towards their immediate social and business circle as a result of their role. A negative answer is not, of course, an abdication of responsibility – it indicates that managers have not noticed any increase in responsibility.

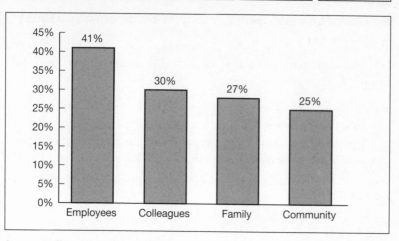

Source: Walking the Tightrope. A Survey of Ethics in Management, Stephen Brigley, Institute of Management (sponsored by the University of Bath), 1994.

■ *Do you consider withholding information from shareholders unethical?*

If you do, then you are with the majority. 89% of chairmen believe that withholding important information from shareholders is seen as an ethical issue by their organisations, compared with 68% of directors and senior managers, and 54% of middle managers.

Source: Walking the Tightrope. A Survey of Ethics in Management, Stephen Brigley, Institute of Management (sponsored by the University of Bath), 1994.

■ *What are your organisational ground rules for ethics?*

Most of the respondents agree that their organisations trust them to act professionally and use their own discretion on ethical matters.

- Being trusted as a professional is most prominent in marketing (100%) and professional, scientific or consultancy groups (91%).

- 87% of those in utilities believe they are expected to follow environmentally friendly policies by their organisations.

Source: Walking the Tightrope. A Survey of Ethics in Management, Stephen Brigley, Institute of Management (sponsored by the University of Bath), 1994.

| Ethics | The Millennium | Offices/Locations | Info. Technology | Fraud |

■ *Does the need for efficiency override ethical issues?*

Very few agree that efficiency overrides ethics, or that ethics is equated with competitive advantage in their organisations' priorities, but the level of pressure varies:

- 22% in organisations of 5,001 to 10,000 employees and 16% in public companies feel that they are only expected to show concern for ethics where it is advantageous for the organisation, compared with 6% of those in not-for-profit organisations.

Source: Walking the Tightrope. A Survey of Ethics in Management, Stephen Brigley, Institute of Management (sponsored by the University of Bath), 1994.

ETHICAL CODES

■ *Do both organisations and managers favour the introduction of ethical codes?*

Managers' commitment to professional standards is exemplified in the widely held view that they are expected to create a product or service which brings real benefit to society. Individually, almost all managers said that they favour a 'professional' approach to ethics. What about their organisations?

- The introduction of professional ethical codes is generally seen as a constructive step and meets with majority support at all levels in their organisations (43% strongly agree, 47% agree). The majority also take heed of publicly accepted moral standards (74% combined agreement).

Source: Walking the Tightrope. A Survey of Ethics in Management, Stephen Brigley, Institute of Management (sponsored by the University of Bath), 1994.

■ *How common are ethical codes?*

The number of organisations with codes of ethics (47%) and those without (48%) is roughly equal. 5% did not know whether their companies had codes, or did not answer. The breakdown by sector is quite interesting. Codes are more common in large organisations, the public sector, and public service companies.

Public administration	75%
Utilities	71%
Financial services	65%
Other services	56%
Leisure	32%
Manufacturing or production	31%
Retail	29%
Distribution and transport	29%

- Over half of all organisations with over 500 employees have codes of ethics, rising to 80% of those with over 50,000 employees.

Source: Walking the Tightrope. A Survey of Ethics in Management, Stephen Brigley, Institute of Management (sponsored by the University of Bath), 1994.

■ *How well do you know your organisation's code of ethics?*

If your company has an ethical code, are you familiar with it? Obviously, having a code in place is two steps away from it working. Managers need to know what it contains, and then carry out its provisions. So how well do managers know their organisations' codes of ethics?

Very well	44%
Quite well	50%
A little	6%

Source: Walking the Tightrope. A Survey of Ethics in Management, Stephen Brigley, Institute of Management (sponsored by the University of Bath), 1994.

■ *Are written ethical codes effective?*

If you are considering introducing a formal ethical code, then you will want to know whether the effort will prove worthwhile. Managers whose organisations have codes of ethics in place were asked this question. They mostly indicated that these have a positive impact on the professional culture of management.

Source: Walking the Tightrope. A Survey of Ethics in Management, Stephen Brigley, Institute of Management (sponsored by the University of Bath), 1994.

MANAGERS AND THE MILLENNIUM

We are fast approaching the millennium. Given the enormous changes on every level of the last 100 years – technological, social, political, economic – the only reasonable assumption is that the rate of change will increase in the next century. The Institute of Management's report, *Management Development to the Millennium. The New Priorities*, looks at the main challenges that managers will face, and how prepared they are for the challenge. So if you are trying to plan for the millennium, read on.

MAIN CHALLENGES

■ *What are the main challenges facing management in the next few years?*

The Institute of Management has identified six challenges for management development in the coming years:

The 6 challenges for management development

1. Organisations both large and small need to be educated to recognise that investment in management development contributes directly to long term competitiveness.
2. Managers must commit themselves to lifelong learning.
3. Senior managers must provide commitment and leadership.
4. Standards and qualifications must be transferable and widely acceptable.
5. Providers must recognise and respond to the diverse training needs of users.
6. A more coherent infrastructure for management development must be created.

Source: Management Development to the Millennium. The New Priorities. Institute of Management, July 1995.

■ *How are jobs changing?*

There has been a marked change in the ways in which work is organised.

- 25 years ago, 41% of men worked in manufacturing, and today it is closer to 28%.
- Part-time work has more than doubled in the last 15 years, as has self-employment.
- Temporary employment and fixed-term contracts have significantly increased.
- New working arrangements such as job sharing and annual hours contracts have become established.

As the job market becomes more varied and volatile, individuals may in future be employed on demand for periods of a year or two, followed by periods without work.

Source: Management Development to the Millennium. The New Priorities. Institute of Management, July 1995.

CURRENT
MANAGEMENT ISSUES

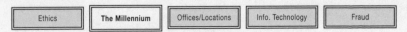

■ *How do changing work patterns affect managers?*

Do you feel threatened by changing working patterns? Or do you welcome them with open arms, as it gives you a chance to find a better balance between home and work? As firms employ fewer core staff, more people will form a contingency workforce, employed on a contract, temporary or interim basis.

- Networking between managers, both from other organisations, and from other functions, will increase in importance.
- The delayering of middle management jobs will probably continue, given the increasing power of networked computers and executive information systems.

Source: Management Development to the Millennium. The New Priorities. Institute of Management, July 1995.

■ *Are managers getting the training they need?*

Do you feel that you are getting the training you need to cope with an ever-changing world? The following pattern of training emerged from the report :

- A formal training programme for managers was provided in 8 in 10 large organisations (with 501 or more employees); 1 in 2 organisations have some formal system of management training and development.
- 40% of organisations have a management development and training policy at supervisory level.
- 31% have a formal training policy for senior managers, 35% for junior managers and 35% for middle managers. A further 1 in 10 stated that they were planning to introduce a formal training programme.
- Smaller firms, i.e. less than 10 employees, are half as likely to have any form of management training. This gap is greatest for senior management.You'll find management training covered in more detail in *The Essential Personnel Sourcebook*.

Source: Management Development to the Millennium. The New Priorities. Institute of Management, July 1995.

■ What skills will managers need in the next millennium?

Respondents felt that the following skills would be important:

Strategic thinking, e.g. longer term, broader perspective, anticipating	78%
Responding to and managing change	75%
An orientation towards total quality/customer satisfaction	67%
An orientation towards total/quality/customer satisfaction	46%
Financial management e.g. role and impact of key financial indicators	44%
Facilitating others to contribute	42%
Understanding the role of information and IT	42%
Verbal communication e.g. coherent, persuasive	38%
Organisational sensitivity e.g. cross functional understanding	37%
Risk assessment in decision-making	35%

Source: Management Development to the Millennium. The New Priorities. Institute of Management, July 1995.

OFFICES AND LOCATIONS

OFFICES

■ How do businesses choose offices to rent?

How do you choose yours? One thing is certain – tenants are better educated than they were a decade ago; they are far more demanding

| Ethics | The Millennium | Offices/Locations | Info. Technology | Fraud |

of the space they occupy, and knowledgeable about what to expect in terms of performance and value for money.

Importance of key variables in the choice of office	
(Average ranking on a 1–7 scale, 1 being top)	
Variable	**Ranking**
Location	1.98
Minimise rents	2.84
Building flexibility	3.47
Minimise non-rent property costs	3.98
Interior design	4.61
External appearance/image	4.82
Environmental issues	6.14

Source: The Good Office – Management and Staff Requirements, Healey and Baker .

■ *What are the most important factors when choosing offices?*

- Location, cost, building flexibility and interior design were the key issues for all decision makers.
- Interior design was generally seen as the occupier's chance to make the building mirror its corporate image. The need to impress and reassure clients was seen to be important.
- Design influences went further than this, with a recognition that relocation should be progressive and bring about an improvement in the working environment of all employees.

Source: The Good Office – Management and Staff Requirements, Healey and Baker.

■ ...and the least important?

Respondents felt that car parking was relatively unimportant. Proximity to international transport links and closeness to the original location also came low on the list of priorities.

Most important issues in the relocation process

Issue	Percentage considering it most important
Cost	18
Access clients/employees	17
Proximity to clients/suppliers	14
Image – right address	7
Proximity to national transport links	6
Central location	6
Proximity to competition	5
Proximity to local transport	5
Staff retention	5
Image – external environment	4
Space flexibility	3
Proximity to international transport links	2
Close to original location	2
Staff availability	1
External facilities	1
Car park	0

Source: The Good Office – Management and Staff Requirements, Healey and Baker.

■ How satisfied are managers with their office environments?

Generally respondents thought their offices to be good or satisfactory. They were asked to rate their satisfaction with the following features, looking at the property as a whole:

Satisfaction with office property

Feature	Percentage who rate feature:		
	Good	Satisfactory	Poor
Reception/entrance design	66	26	8
Lifts	68	24	8
Natural daylight	70	23	7
Artificial daylight	67	30	3
Carpet/flooring	72	24	4
Useable space	71	24	5
Ceiling design	61	33	6
Cable trunking provision	75	15	10
Kitchen/catering	61	31	8
Heating	54	35	9
Air conditioning	52	34	14
Individual heating control	45	34	21
Security systems	70	24	6
Storage space	37	43	20
Servicing provision	60	35	5
Car parking facilities	57	25	18
Toilets	73	24	3
Flexibility	65	30	5
Interior design	72	23	5
Average	63	28	9

Source: *The Good Office – Management and Staff Requirements*, Healey and Baker.

■ *What do office workers feel are essential features in their office environments?*

Clearly the priorities of staff and decision makers will be different, the former set by the comfort and efficiency offered by their surroundings, and the latter governed by the efficiency of the firm. But if you want to please your workers when choosing new offices, then these results are worth bearing in mind. Office workers were required to identify essential features; on the basis of their answers, the following features were ranked:

Ranking of essential features by office workers	
1. No smoking area	10. Staff canteen
2. Spacious	11. Parking – for all
3. Natural light	12. Parking – limited
4. Good storage	13. Double glazing
5. Attractive internal	14. Individual heating
6. Lifts	15. Open plan
7. Air conditioning	16. Attractive external
8. Flexible layout	17. Crèches
9. Rest rooms	18. Artificial light

Source: *The Good Office – Management and Staff Requirements*, Healey and Baker .

RELOCATION WITHIN THE UK

For many companies, the decision to move offices can bring major change. Healey and Baker, in their survey *The Good Office – Management and Staff Requirements*, interviewed by telephone a sample of companies about relocation. Of the sample of companies included in the telephone survey, 99% had moved within the last four years or intended to move in the next year. Consequently their views give a good feel for the current pattern for relocation.

■ *How far do most companies move?*

Most of the moves in the sample were over short distances, 44% within one mile and 73% within 5 miles. Most moves over long distances took place in the South East. In London, 96% of relocators chose to stay in London, with the greatest loyalty being in the City and West End. Likewise, 88% of new tenants to Docklands came from the London area, underlining this area's main market for tenants.

	Distance moved (miles)			Same town
	0-5	6-20	21+	
By region:				
All	73%	18%	9%	85%
London	88%	9%	3%	96%
South East	22%	50%	28%	39%
South West/Wales	50%	30%	20%	75%
Birmingham	60%	35%	5%	85%
North	75%	14%	11%	83%
Scotland	89%	8%	3%	92%
By sector:				
Computer/electronics	50%	38%	12%	71%
Manufacturing/oil	63%	21%	16%	75%
Professional/financial	88%	7%	5%	95%
Public sector	63%	22%	16%	76%
By size of office:				
<20,000 sq. ft	62%	22%	16%	76%
>20,000 sq. ft	77%	17%	6%	88%

Source: The Good Office – Management and Staff Requirements, Healey and Baker.

■ *Are some relocations more popular than others?*

Overall, 64% of moves were to city centres, 27% to edge or out of town sites and just 9% to fringe urban areas. The majority of moves to edge or out-of-town locations were in the South East and South West/Wales. Such locations proved to be most popular with computer and electronics companies. Most relocations by professional services and financial companies were to built-up areas.

Source: The Good Office – Management and Staff Requirements, Healey and Baker.

■ Why do companies move to new locations?

Most moves were motivated by the need to expand, with cost being important, particularly for smaller firms, and lease expiries also forcing a number of relocations. Image and obsolescence were also identified as significant motivators. Those companies that had moved were asked to state their main reason. Answers were ranked 1-7.

Reasons for choosing new accommodation

	1986	1989	1993
Proximity to market	2	1	1
Proximity to competition	7	6	5
Minimise rent	5	4	2
External factors	6	7	7
Staff availability	4	5	5
Image	3	3	4
Communications	1	2	3

It is not surprising that expansion has declined significantly as a motivator since the mid 1980s, nor that cost is now more important than it was in 1989. Similarly, fewer firms are motivated to move by image, or to secure an improved working environment. An increase in relocations caused by rationalisation or contraction has yet to be seen, but may emerge as profitability and investment recover after the recession.

Source: The Good Office – Management and Staff Requirements, Healey and Baker .

■ How do office workers rate locations?

If you want to keep your employees happy, you may wish to consult them about the location of new offices. These findings may help you. Employees were asked to rank the following locations from very good to very poor. The percentage ranking each location as good or very good was:

Location	Percentage who rated location good/very good
North	80
City of London	76
Scotland	72
South West/Wales	72
South East	67
West End London	60
Birmingham	60
London Docklands	58
London Mid-town	42

The moral of the story appears to be: don't locate in London.

Source: The Good Office – Management and Staff Requirements, Healey and Baker.

■ *So what factors influence employees' views about locations?*

When it comes to the choice of a more specific location for your office, local factors and personal considerations are much more important. Perhaps as a manager you are more preoccupied with contacts, and want to locate where your clients can reach you easily. With any luck, you can choose the area, and then let your employees' feelings influence the actual choice of office. Employees were asked to rank 12 different locational considerations in order:

Ranking of locational considerations
1. Within 5 minutes walk of public transport
2. In a safe area
3. Within 10 minutes' walk of public transport
4. Close to convenience shops
5. Close to main shops
6. Pleasant surroundings
7. Close to cafes/pubs
8. Close to restaurants
9. Close to leisure/entertainment facilities
10. Within 30 minutes walk of public transport
11. More than 30 minutes from public transport

Source: The Good Office – Management and Staff Requirements, Healey and Baker

INTERNATIONAL BUSINESS LOCATIONS

As well as looking at what influences the location of offices in the UK (see above), Healey and Baker have undertaken a survey of European location. Senior executives from 500 companies throughout Europe were interviewed to obtain an overview of their attitudes towards various international business locations. If you are thinking about locating a subsidiary or offices abroad, then their findings should be of use.

■ *Do some European cities dominate British choices of European location?*

The leading cities of London, Paris, Frankfurt and Brussels maintain their dominance. After the leading cities, the remainder of the top 30 are closely bunched.

- London remains the strongest city in terms of the key communication factors, and is strong too on cost grounds.

- Dublin, included in the survey for the first time. is highly placed at 14th. This is due to its perceived cost advantages. Indeed, it is seen

| Ethics | The Millennium | Offices/Locations | Info. Technology | Fraud |

to have the best climate created by government for business in Europe.

- Manchester is again seen to have the best value office space.
- Paris scores strongly all round and is seen to offer the best quality of life.
- Oslo is seen as the most pollution free of Europe's major cities.

Source: European Cities Monitor, Healey and Baker.

■ *Are some European cities 'on the up'?*

The southern cities of Barcelona, Milan and Madrid continue their advance and are established in the top 10 business cities. With the exception of Frankfurt, the German cities all slipped a little in 1995. The ex-communist bloc cities have ceased to advance.

Source: European Cities Monitor, Healey and Baker.

■ *Which cities do European companies favour?*

The table below shows how senior executives ranked European cities in 1993, 1994 and 1995. For the unmathematically minded, it might help to explain the principle of a weighted score. It works like an index – and the only important thing to grasp is that the numbers relate to each other, but that the size of the number per se is not important. The amount that London is preferred is classified as 1 – the amount of preference for the other cities is then categorised in comparison to that score of 1. If you still don't understand the principle, then Appendix 1 will help – it gives a guide to statistics for the unmathematical.

	Rank			Weighted score
	1993	1994	1995	1995
London	1	1	1	1
Paris	2	2	2	0.70
Frankfurt	3	3	3	0.49
Brussels	4	4	4	0.39
Amsterdam	5	5	5	0.26
Barcelona	10	7	6	0.18
Zurich	6	6	7	0.17
Milan	12	9	8	0.16
Madrid	16	10	9	0.14
Dusseldorf	7	8	10	0.13
Geneva	10	11	11	0.12
Munich	16	11	12	0.12
Manchester	9	11	13	0.12
Dublin	–	–	14	0.10
Berlin	14	14	15	0.09
Stockholm	12	14	16	0.09
Lisbon	15	17	17	0.09
Glasgow	7	17	18	0.08
Hamburg	16	17	19	0.07
Vienna	23	23	20	0.07
Prague	20	16	21	0.06
Lyons	21	17	22	0.05
Rome	26	27	23	0.05
Budapest	19	22	24	0.05
Copenhagen	22	24	25	0.04
Warsaw	23	17	26	0.03
Turin	25	27	27	0.03
Oslo	–	25	28	0.03
Athens	26	25	29	0.02
Moscow	26	29	30	0.02

Source: *European Cities Monitor*, Healey and Baker.

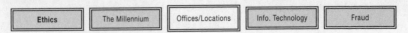

| Ethics | The Millennium | Offices/Locations | Info. Technology | Fraud |

■ *Which areas outside Europe are favoured by British companies?*

According to the survey, European companies see vigorous expansion outside Europe over the next 5 years. The most significant area of activity is south east Asia, with 7 of the top 10 locations nominated.

Source: European Cities Monitor, Healey and Baker.

■ *Which are the favourite non-European cities?*

- Singapore leads from Peking, Hong Kong and Shanghai.
- The leading non-oriental cities for expansion by European companies are all in the Americas: New York (5th), Buenos Aires (7th) and Mexico City (8th).
- Johannesburg is the African city most likely to see an influx of European companies.

Source: European Cities Monitor, Healey and Baker.

■ *What are the key factors in deciding where to locate?*

If you are trying to decide where to locate outside Europe, you are no doubt asking yourself this question. According to the survey, communication factors remain the most important, followed by cost factors. Quality of life factors are less important.

- Cost factors are, however, more significant than previously, with staff costs in particular assuming a greater significance than in previous years.
- Instability is the factor that most deters companies from locating in a city. Political instability will outweigh commercial considerations such as market potential and transport communications. Economic problems and crime also count against a city.

Source: European Cities Monitor, Healey and Baker.

MANAGING INFORMATION TECHONOLOGY (IT)

'If the motor car industry', said a management guru addressing a conference, 'had made the same rate of progress that we have made in the IT industry, a Rolls Royce would cost two dollars forty' – he paused dramatically, then, punching the air with his fists – 'And do a million miles to the gallon.'

Absolute silence fell on the audience. Suddenly a voice was heard from the back of the hall.

'Yes,' said the voice, 'But it would be very small!'

Information technology has not only brought more changes in its wake than the motor car- it also continues to change the business world dramatically. Managing IT is a unique challenge – whether it is your job to manage IT or to manage IT managers.

IT DIRECTORS

■ Why do companies appoint IT directors to their boards?

Since the 1950s, businesses have experienced difficulties in controlling their specialist IT departments, particularly in terms of cost and efficiency. If you have experienced, or are experiencing, problems with cost containment or efficiency, the following facts may throw some light on the situation.

- In 1983, 48% of computer installations had no measure of efficiency. By 1988 this had fallen to 12%.

- In 1987, 'cost containment' entered the top four in the IT executives' problems chart, mentioned by 29% of respondents.

- In 1990, 28% of IT directors gave 'cost control' as the main reason for their appointment.

Source: Managing IT at Board Level, 2nd edition, by Kit Grindley, FT/Pitman Publishing, 1995

| Ethics | The Millennium | Offices/Locations | **Info. Technology** | Fraud |

■ *How many companies have IT directors on the board?*

70% of the UK's top 500 companies have a main board director responsible for integrating IT with corporate objectives.

Source: Managing IT at Board Level, 2nd edition, by Kit Grindley, FT/Pitman Publishing, 1995

■ *What are the main roles of IT directors?*

54% of IT directors said that one of their specific remits on appointment was to demystify the IT department and integrate it with the rest of the company.

The main roles were:

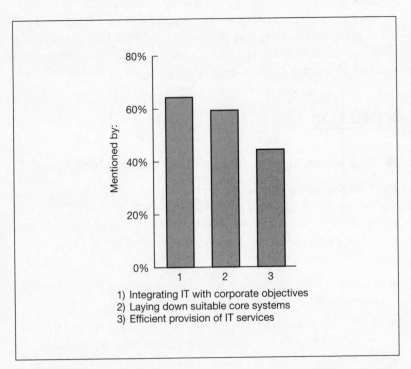

1) Integrating IT with corporate objectives
2) Laying down suitable core systems
3) Efficient provision of IT services

Source: Managing IT at Board Level, 2nd edition, by Kit Grindley, FT/Pitman Publishing, 1995

DEVELOPMENT

■ *What problems have you experienced with systems development?*

If you have watched your company invest time and money in 'home-growing' its own systems, only to discover that a cheaper and easier solution was available off the shelf, you are certainly not alone. The IT executives who were interviewed agreed that in the 1980s they might well have recruited another programmer to solve their systems development problems, but that they are now concentrating on other aspects of systems development, such as sub-contracting and using pre-written software packages.

When top management were asked this question, the whole issue appeared to be one of 'meeting project deadlines'. The figure below shows how this issue compared with rival problems:

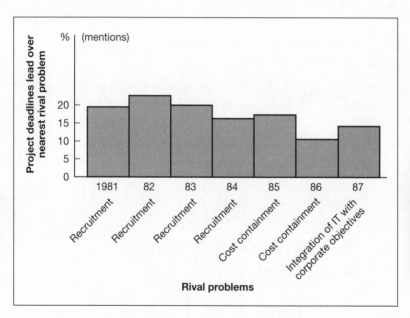

CURRENT
MANAGEMENT ISSUES

- In 1988, 36% of all programmes were estimated to have been bought in as packages

Source: Managing IT at Board Level, 2nd edition, by Kit Grindley, FT/Pitman Publishing, 1995

| Ethics | The Millennium | Offices/Locations | Info. Technology | Fraud |

■ *How has the use of software contractors grown?*

By 1990, contractors were responsible for 23% of all systems development work in Europe.

Source: Managing IT at Board Level, 2nd edition, by Kit Grindley, FT/Pitman Publishing, 1995

■ *Is there an IT 'culture gap'?*

There is a 'culture gap' if IT managers understand IT and company managers don't. You may well be experiencing one in your company. How many IT specialists think there is a culture gap?

- 62% of IT directors said it was their top problem.
- 56% of IT directors believe the culture gap is losing or seriously delaying IT opportunities for their company to gain a competitive edge.

Source: Managing IT at Board Level, 2nd edition, by Kit Grindley, FT/Pitman Publishing, 1995

■ *How long will the culture gap be a significant problem?*

Over a quarter of IT executives believe that the current generation of managers will never fully accept the role of IT in their work:

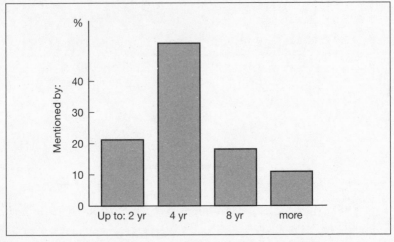

Source: Managing IT at Board Level, 2nd edition, by Kit Grindley, FT/Pitman Publishing, 1995

212

■ Do business people trust IT staff?

- 31% of IT directors say business people have difficulty understanding and appreciating the worth of IT people and absorbing
them within the organisation.

- A further 30% say business people have difficulty trusting IT staff.

Source: Managing IT at Board Level, 2nd edition, by Kit Grindley, FT/Pitman
Publishing, 1995

■ What are the remedies for the culture gap?

More than half of IT directors believe that patience is the solution.
None of them is prepared to put their jobs on the line:

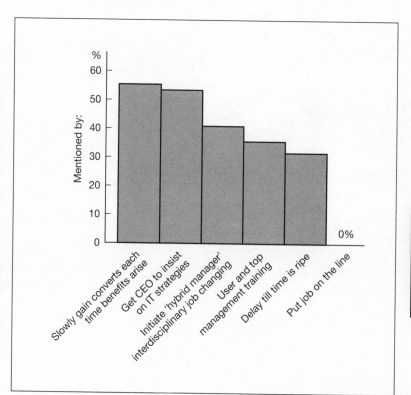

Source: Managing IT at Board Level, 2nd edition, by Kit Grindley, FT/Pitman
Publishing, 1995

■ *What are the reasons for programme maintenance?*

Programmes are hard to write. They are even harder to alter. IT directors gave the following reasons for continuing programme maintenance:

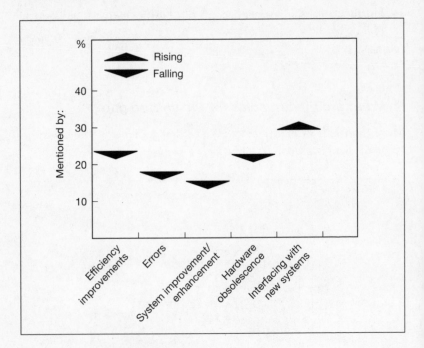

- 26% of IT directors stated their main concern was that their companies are at the mercy of badly written and fragile programmes which can no longer be altered.

Source: Managing IT at Board Level, 2nd edition, by Kit Grindley, FT/Pitman Publishing, 1995

■ *Will programme maintenance continue in the future?*

- 86% of IT directors predict that a continued need to maintain or adapt their old programmes would inhibit any new systems development by the year 2000.

- However, 16% of companies now pursue a minimal maintenance policy. By the year 2000 this figure is predicted to rise to 81%.

Source: Managing IT at Board Level, 2nd edition, by Kit Grindley, FT/Pitman Publishing, 1995

| Ethics | The Millennium | Offices/Locations | Info. Technology | Fraud |

OUTSOURCING IT

In 1980, 6% of the average systems development budget was spent on outside contractors. By 1995, this proportion had risen to 40%. 12% of IT directors now outsource all their systems development. If you are re-evaluating how much of your systems development budget to spend internally, and how much to outsource, it may help to know what other companies are currently doing.

■ Why do companies outsource IT?

During the recession, laying off contractors was a relatively painless way of cutting staff costs. Since the recession, the demand for outsiders has returned with a vengeance:

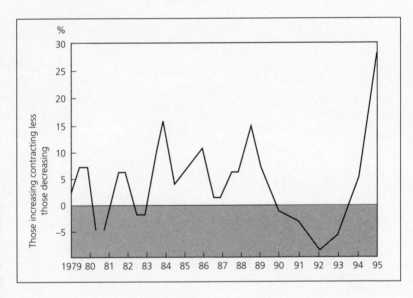

- Over a third of the world's computer systems are now developed by outside contractors.

Source: Managing IT at Board Level, 2nd edition, by Kit Grindley, FT/Pitman Publishing, 1995

216

■ Why use outside contractors?

Why use outside contractors? Do you simply use them when your staff cannot handle the workload? Or do you use them whenever you need specialist skills that your current IT staff do not possess? IT directors gave the following reasons:

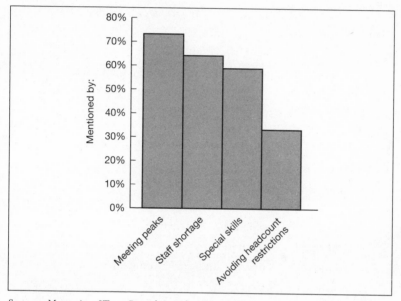

Source: Managing IT at Board Level, 2nd edition, by Kit Grindley, FT/Pitman Publishing, 1995

■ What are programmers' views on outsourcing?

It would appear from the survey that the majority of programmers would prefer everything to be outsourced, and to work as contractors!

- 36% of exiting in-house programmers have ambitions to become contractors.

- 58% of existing contractors intend to stay as contract programmers all their lives, either as individuals or working with a consultancy or software house.

- Only 16% of in-house programmers state that career opportunity in their company is a reason for staying.

Source: Managing IT at Board Level, 2nd edition, by Kit Grindley, FT/Pitman Publishing, 1995

| Ethics | The Millennium | Offices/Locations | Info. Technology | Fraud |

■ *Do more companies outsource IT now than previously?*

The savings in costs and efficiency that outsourcing can give have led to an increasing number of companies choosing this option over the past few years.

- 41% of contract programmers are employed by consultancies and software houses.
- This proportion is rising by 2% a year.

Source: Managing IT at Board Level, 2nd edition, by Kit Grindley, FT/Pitman Publishing, 1995

■ *What are IT directors' roles in outsourcing?*

Relatively few IT directors saw their main roles as managing the outsourced operation:

Formulating IT supported strategies	83%
Achieving business objectives	60%
Contractor performance and quality control	43%
Contract negotiation	37%
Specifying and designing IT infrastructure	28%
Defining core systems not to be outsourced	27%
Project management and implementation	17%

Source: Information Technology Review 1994/1995, Price Waterhouse.

■ *What are the weak points in managing outsourcing?*

Many IT managers felt their departments had weaknesses in their outsourcing management skills, particularly in handing over to contractors and in quality control and inspection. These were the problems they identified:

Weakness	Proportion of companies with weakness
Hand-over management	66%
Quality control/inspection	54%
Delivering business benefit	49%
Architecture design (esp. infrastructure)	45%
Contractor selection	44%
Project management	41%

Source: Information Technology Review 1994/1995, Price Waterhouse.

■ *What are the risks of outsourcing?*

Outsourcing can create problems between the employing company and the contractor. The main risks were seen as:

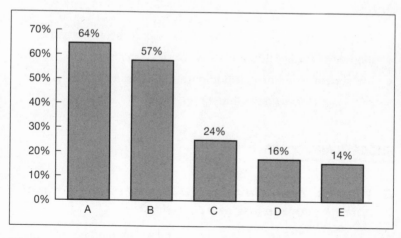

(For key see over page)

Key:

A = Conflicts of interests between contractor and employer

B = Contract is an unenforceable fiction

C = Corporate security jeopardised

D = Contractors out of control

E = Undue influence by contractors on corporate systems

Source: Information Technology Review 1994/1995, Price Waterhouse.

■ *How can you solve your outsourcing problems?*

While IT executives predict an increase in the use of outsourcing, many feel that their departments are unprepared to cope. The following are key points that IT executives felt were essential for successful outsourcing:

DO:

- Outsource for measurable benefits, not because of a general policy.
- Manage contractors using a research project management approach, using cut off points, short step objectives and frequent overview of the contract.
- Make sure you can inspect contractors' work and manage each project internally.

DON'T:

- Let contractors manage themselves or inspect their own work.
- Choose the cheapest option – pay for the system you really need.
- Give systems with long term importance to facilities managers.

Source: Information Technology Review 1994/1995, Price Waterhouse.

BUDGETS AND COSTS

■ *What has been the average IT spend by large organisations over the last few decades?*

Adjusted for inflation, the average spend on IT by data processing departments world-wide has been:

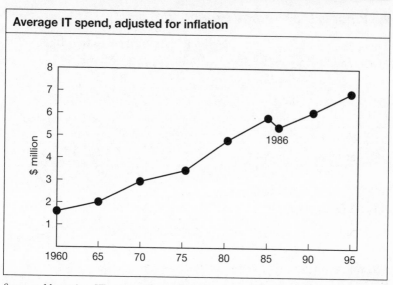

Average IT spend, adjusted for inflation

Source: *Managing IT at Board Level, 2nd edition*, by Kit Grindley, FT/Pitman Publishing, 1995

■ *What does your company spend its IT budgets on?*

If you are trying to work out whether your IT budget is appropriately spent, then these figures will help. Staff is the highest cost:

Item	Average proportion spent on item
User spend	21%
Outsourcing	10%
PCs	8%
Mainframes	12%
Maintenance	5%
Telecommunications	6%
Software	6%
System software	4%
Staff	26%

Source: *Information Technology Review 1994/1995*, Price Waterhouse.

■ *What is the average expenditure on IT?*

The 1994/95 survey found respondents reporting actual figures for 1993, and forecasts for 1994 (in £000s per installation):

	1993 actual	1994 forecast
IT hardware: Mainframe/midrange	647	565
PC/workstations	396	389
Maintenance	288	282
Total IT hardware	1331	1236
IT software: Application	288	282
System	216	212
Total IT software	504	494
Telecommunications (Networks & usage)	252	283
Staff	1259	1236
Outsourcing (FM, consultancy &c)	491	482
Total average dp department budget (A)	3837	3731
IT spend outside dp department (B)	1022	1004
TOTAL IT EXPENDITURE (A + B)	4859	4735

Source: Information Technology Review 1994/1995, Price Waterhouse.

■ *What are IT budgets by total number of employees?*

Spending on hardware exceeds that on software in all categories (figures are in £000 per installation):

Employees		1993 actual	1994 forecast
Up to 500	Hardware	470	446
	Software	161	157
	Telecommunications	86	72
	Staff	458	446
	Outsourcing	93	105
	User spend	70	54
	Total	**1338**	**1280**
500 – 5,000	Hardware	1024	981
	Software	398	433
	Telecommunications	199	202
	Staff	1023	1039
	Outsourcing	316	286
	User spend	944	948
	Total	**3904**	**3889**
Over 5,000	Hardware	3033	2679
	Software	1089	1116
	Telecommunications	700	744
	Staff	2488	2456
	Outsourcing	1944	1978
	User spend	4574	4852
	Total	**13828**	**13625**

Source: *Information Technology Review 1994/95*, Price Waterhouse

BENEFITS AND PROBLEMS

■ *What are the benefits of IT?*

83% of IT directors admit that the cost/benefit analyses supporting proposals to invest in IT are a fiction. Only 17% of IT directors consider it a valid technique to cost/justify IT investments in isolation. However, IT still seems to be justified in this way:

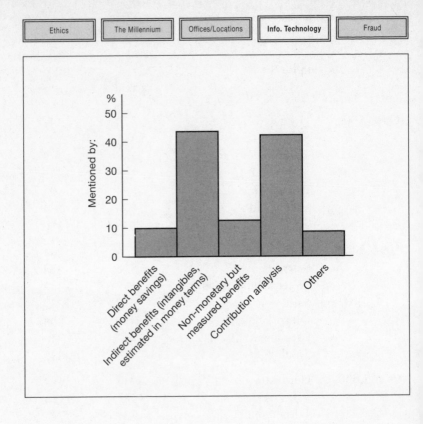

- Despite this, 30% of companies justify IT investment by the achievement of necessary performance objectives rather than financial benefits.

Source: Managing IT at Board Level, 2nd edition, by Kit Grindley, FT/Pitman Publishing, 1995

■ *Does your company suffer from a 'legacy' of obsolescent systems?*

If it does, then you are not alone. Perceived problems in previous years regarding the 'legacy' of older systems seem to be lessening, according to the survey, but only 9% of companies say they are completely satisfied with their IT systems:

Attitudes towards existing computer systems	Proportion of companies
Completely satisfies business requirements	9%
Adaptable within business planning cycle	35%
Imposes difficulties	38%
Major constraint on alignment	14%
Business requirements not known	4%

Source: Information Technology Review 1994/1995, Price Waterhouse.

■ *What are the constraints on rewriting legacy programmes?*

The average rewrite of a complete system costs £6 million and takes 97 years of programmers' time. The constraints on rewriting seem to be:

Lack of money	62%
Lack of staff	40%
Lack of perception of benefits	37%
Poor project and change management skills	22%
Out-of-date technical skills	22%
Reluctance to outsource	8%

There were also complaints that companies find themselves 'locked-in' to legacy systems, broken down as:

Locked into packages (including database)	22%
Locked into hardware	18%
Locked into language	16%
Locked into maintenance	11%

Source: Information Technology Review 1994/1995, Price Waterhouse.

■ *What are the preferred solutions to legacy problems?*

Companies were allowed more than one answer to this question. There was considerable variation in the answers given. The following were proposed as solutions to legacy problems:

Solution	Proportion of companies using solution
Flexible packages	58%
Accept limitations of existing systems	36%
Adapt business to suit inflexible packages	34%
Adopt infrastructure approach to systems development	28%
Re-write	19%
Outsource legacy	14%
Outsource replacement	14%
Outsource everything	4%
Decentralise IT	4%

The respondents offered the following advice for dealing with legacies:

DON'T:

- Replace for technological reasons only
- Neglect short-term benefits
- Expect the new system to last forever
- Expect users to welcome the change
- Replace until you have to

DO:

- Re-write programmes as part of re-engineering
- Use packages for non-critical elements
- Undertake re-engineering as part of a CEO initiative
- Use consultants

Source: Information Technology Review 1994/1995, Price Waterhouse.

SCOPE OF IT

■ How many PCs and terminals are there in large organisations?

The average number of PCs and terminals supported by IT departments grew from 969 in 1993 to 1130 in 1994.

Source: Information Technology Review 1994/1995, Price Waterhouse.

■ How effective are IT services?

One of the perennial difficulties faced by IT executives is the measurement of the value provided by IT services. A popular method is to use a form of charge-back or transfer charging system where users get a bill for predefined service or usage levels. These systems have two benefits:

1. Users become much more aware of the IT resources they are using, and

2. The IT department has a benchmark against which its performance can be measured.

The average proportion of IT budgets recovered by transfer charging is 75%.

Source: Information Technology Review 1994/1995, Price Waterhouse.

EMERGING TECHNOLOGIES

If you don't know a CDi from CD-Rom, or think that DIP is something you put raw vegetables into, then you could probably do with a glossary of emerging technologies. So here goes:

Glossary of IT terms

Client/server
An application of distributed computing, in which processing is divided between programmable workstations or PCs (clients),

primarily running end-user applications, and powerful processors (servers) which handle mainly background tasks and manage resources such as printers, database searching and network management.

Document image processing (DIP)

Through the use of scanners, imaging systems digitise and store documents, including charts, graphs, signature records, engineering drawings and other data, and provide the tools for their retrieval. Workflow software automates the flow of tasks and data through the organisation by controlling the routing and scheduling of information in identified processes, and reports on their status. Applications include insurance claim processing, credit card voucher storage and expense claim handling.

Groupware

Software which enables groups of people, who may be geographically separated, to work together on the same data and applications. An example is Lotus Notes, which provides document database management within an electronic mail system.

Knowledge-based and expert systems (KBS)

Designed to capture the knowledge or experience of one or more human experts on particular tasks, KBS typically consist of two parts – a collection of facts and relationships about the subject (the knowledge base) and an interpreter programme (the inference engine) which draws conclusions about a specific problem, often based on facts provided interactively.

Mobile computing devices

Primarily hand-held devices for the capture, storage and transmission of data, they include:

- Palmtops, which are miniature versions of notebook computers
- Pen tablets, which allow input and data capture primarily by pen
- Personal digital assistants (PDAs)
- Personal intelligent communicators (PICs) which are miniature pen tablets and may incorporate wireless communications
- Special purpose hand-held devices designed for specific data collection such as inventory and meter reading.

Multimedia

This is a catch-all term used to encompass the use in applications of some or all of the following components in combination:

- Text
- Images (both still and moving)
- Sound

This is enabled by the increasing availability and falling costs of powerful processors, high-density storage (primarily CD ROM), sound and digitised video cards, and high-resolution monitors. The main business application is in presentations.

Object-oriented tools (OOPS)

Objects are modules of a computer programme that contain not only the data type of a data structure, but also the types of operation or functions that can be applied to the data. In addition, objects may contain relationships with other objects, and may inherit characteristics from them. As a result of this modularity, programmes based on object technology are easier to modify and maintain, reusable in other applications and resilient. A widespread use at present is the construction of graphical user interfaces.

Rapid application development (RAD)

A technique first developed in the mid 1980s and typically having 5 stages:

1. Modelling
2. Prototyping
3. Integration
4. Optimisation
5. Deployment

It is claimed to be better than the old 'waterfall' approach of creating specifications and then moving to coding and testing, because it yields systems that are more flexible and have much more end-user input and feedback.

| Ethics | The Millennium | Offices/Locations | **Info. Technology** | Fraud |

Virtual reality (VR)

An outgrowth of multimedia, VR systems are based on a collection of input/output devices, graphics programmes and techniques which immerse the user or audience in an interactive environment, which at minimum provides interactivity with simulated scenery. It may also contain sound, motion, tactile feedback and scent. VR already has important applications in modelling, simulation and training.

Source: Information Technology Review 1994/1995, Price Waterhouse.

■ *Which emerging technologies are popular?*

The following technologies are coming into use:

Client/server architecture	58%
Rapid application development (RAD)	48%
Document image processing (DIP)	26%
Groupware	22%
Telecomms	20%
Mobile	17%

Source: Information Technology Review 1994/1995, Price Waterhouse.

■ *Which emerging technologies are less popular?*

The actual take-up on other new technologies is significantly lower:

Knowledge-based systems (KBS)	10%
Multimedia	10%
Object-oriented tools (OOPS)	8%
Virtual reality	2%

Source: Information Technology Review 1994/1995, Price Waterhouse.

■ *Which emerging technologies are being considered?*

The picture changes, however, when respondents say what new technologies their companies are seriously considering introducing:

230

Document image processing (DIP)	50%
Telecomms	46%
Groupware	34%
Client/server	26%
OOPS	26%
Multimedia	25%
Mobile	22%
KBS	22%
RAD	12%
Virtual reality	6%

Source: Information Technology Review 1994/1995, Price Waterhouse.

■ *Many of these developments may be very exciting for the technically-minded, but are they really going to be useful?*

A panel of experts ranked the technologies according to which offered the greatest potential benefits to their companies:

The 10 most useful emerging technologies

1. Client/server
2. DIP
3. RAD
4. Telecomms
5. Groupware
6. Multimedia
7. Mobile
8. KBS
9. OOPS
10. Virtual reality

Source: Information Technology Review 1994/1995, Price Waterhouse.

FRAUD

The 1980s may have appeared to have been a boom time for the fraudsters, but the 1990s are proving that fraud is still as hot and contentious a topic as it always has been.

EXTENT

Levels of reported fraud have continued to rise over the past few years, and although there has been a temporary fall in the value of large reported frauds in the first half of 1994, the Serious Fraud Office (SFO) alone was dealing with 57 active cases, whose aggregate value was £6 billion, as at April 1993. Despite the feelings of many commentators, that the levels of fraud would fall as the UK economy emerged from recession, there is little evidence that the relationship between the economy and fraud is quite so straightforward. For example, with heightened employee insecurity about the future, we may be witnessing a long term trend towards lower levels of trust. The position is complicated further by the series of time lags between the commencement of a fraud (which can continue for years), its detection and the formal action taken against the perpetrators by criminal justice agencies.

A large number of companies seem to be victims again and again; many appear to be confused by the whole issue of fraud. If you are in one or other of these categories, or simply want to arm yourself with information about this issue, then the Ernst & Young report *Fraud – The Unmanaged Risk* may be of interest. Ernst & Young's Fraud Investigation and Risk Management group (FIRM) surveyed senior executives at Times Top 1000 companies. They found that:

- 4 out of 10 respondents had been the victims of fraud on more than one occasion during the period January 1993 to July 1994 inclusive. It seems, therefore, that in practice companies do not, for whatever reason, learn from the incidents they suffer.

Source: Fraud – The Unmanaged Risk. 1994/5 Executive Summary. Ernst & Young, 1995.

232

■ **Have companies taken action over the worst fraud they have suffered since January 1993?**

9 out of 10 companies had taken further action following the discovery of the fraud. This action was usually some form of tightening of existing controls or the introduction of new procedures.

- 4 out of 5 respondents, however, felt that the fraud could possibly happen again. Respondents must not, therefore, have had much faith in the ability of the new procedures to prevent further frauds.

Source: Fraud – The Unmanaged Risk. 1994/5 Executive Summary. Ernst & Young, 1995.

DETECTION

■ **What kinds of fraud are the most common?**

The areas of greatest concern were purchasing, and computers and payroll, in that order of priority. The one 'big hit' fraud was the type with which respondents were most preoccupied, with a higher response than either cumulative employee frauds to the same value or catastrophic fraud which would result in the business going into liquidation.

Ernst & Young has increasingly seen examples of the 'big hits' against large companies. These frequently arise within more complex areas such as derivatives, commodities and foreign exchange, all areas that involve large sums of money and exposure to risk.

Source: Fraud – The Unmanaged Risk. 1994/5 Executive Summary. Ernst & Young, 1995.

■ **How is fraud detected?**

If you are thinking of introducing new procedures to tackle fraud, then which would be most effective? Sadly, there is no cut and dried solution – no fraud-free system that you can introduce. In both 1992 and 1994, the most common way of detecting fraud was through normal procedures, although the proportion discovered in this way was much larger in the 1994 survey (38% compared with 24%).

Ethics | The Millennium | Offices/Locations | Info. Technology | **Fraud**

- The tip-off became more significant along with the detection of fraud by new management and discovery 'by accident'.
- Internal investigation and external audit were less frequently the method of discovery for the 1994 sample.

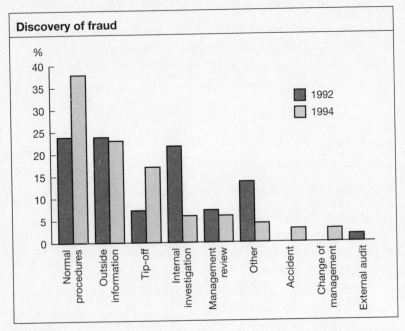

Discovery of fraud

Source: Fraud – The Unmanaged Risk. 1994/5 Executive Summary. Ernst & Young, 1995.

■ *Do companies report frauds to the authorities?*

Respondents reported a larger proportion of frauds to the authorities than did those of 1992 – this may be an indication of a tougher attitude to fraud – or simply an acknowledgement from most companies that it is better to involve the authorities.

- In 1994, 84% of companies reported the worst suspected fraud that they had suffered in the past year; two years previously, under two thirds were reported.

Source: Fraud – The Unmanaged Risk. 1994/5 Executive Summary. Ernst & Young, 1995.

234

■ So why do companies report frauds to the authorities?

The primary motive for reporting was, in the 1992 survey, 'to get the money back'. In the 1994 survey, the primary motive was 'deter(ring) others from committing fraud against your company' with 61% of respondents rating it a primary consideration.

- The most commonly cited reason for not reporting a fraud was the waste of management time involved in reporting the crime.

Source: Fraud – The Unmanaged Risk. 1994/5 Executive Summary. Ernst & Young, 1995.

■ Do companies have written fraud policies?

Within the companies surveyed, only 37% had written fraud reporting policies and an even smaller 23% had written fraud prevention polices.

Source: Fraud – The Unmanaged Risk. 1994/5 Executive Summary. Ernst & Young, 1995.

■ What are the most and least vulnerable sectors?

The banking and financial services sector had total losses, between January 1993 and July 1994, averaging nearly £4 million pounds per company, with £753,000 additional costs each, on average. The insurance sector experienced the largest individual frauds (over £1 million actually obtained).

The smallest losses were suffered by paper, printing and textiles companies, with an average of £333 per case.

Source: Fraud – The Unmanaged Risk. 1994/5 Executive Summary. Ernst & Young, 1995.

■ What types of fraud are the most common?

Cheques/transfers were the most common type:

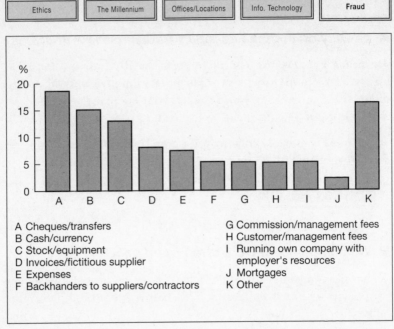

A Cheques/transfers
B Cash/currency
C Stock/equipment
D Invoices/fictitious supplier
E Expenses
F Backhanders to suppliers/contractors
G Commission/management fees
H Customer/management fees
I Running own company with employer's resources
J Mortgages
K Other

Source: Fraud – The Unmanaged Risk. 1994/5 Executive Summary. Ernst & Young, 1995.

■ *What proportion of frauds are committed by employees?*

The suspected offender, where known, was an employee on half of all occasions; collusion was a factor in one out of five frauds, meaning that there was employee involvement in 71% of cases.

Source: Fraud – The Unmanaged Risk. 1994/5 Executive Summary. Ernst & Young, 1995.

■ *What do companies see as the worst feature of frauds?*

The worst feature of the fraud and its aftermath was seen to be the waste of management time, followed by the 'degeneration of company culture and trust', which ranked second and 'psychological strain on executives', which ranked third.

Source: Fraud – The Unmanaged Risk. 1994/5 Executive Summary. Ernst & Young, 1995.

■ What proportion of frauds receive media coverage?

Only 22% of cases received media coverage. This was perceived as fair by 7 out of 10, and by 57% as making 'little difference' to the company.

Source: Fraud – The Unmanaged Risk. 1994/5 Executive Summary. Ernst & Young, 1995.

PREVENTION AND CURE

■ Can fraud be anticipated?

- 4 out of 10 companies felt that in retrospect they had anticipated that the fraud might happen.
- 8 out of 10 felt that the incident was preventable.

Source: Fraud – The Unmanaged Risk. 1994/5 Executive Summary. Ernst & Young, 1995.

■ Do companies take action to prevent similar frauds happening again?

- 9 out of 10 companies took action to reduce the risk of it happening again.
- 8 out of 10 believed that the same or similar frauds could happen again.

Source: Fraud – The Unmanaged Risk. 1994/5 Executive Summary. Ernst & Young, 1995.

■ What preventative measures can be taken?

The most commonly taken measure in this survey was to tighten existing controls:

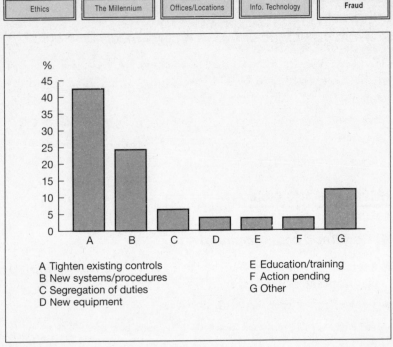

A Tighten existing controls
B New systems/procedures
C Segregation of duties
D New equipment

E Education/training
F Action pending
G Other

Source: Fraud – The Unmanaged Risk. 1994/5 Executive Summary. Ernst & Young, 1995.

■ *Is fraud on the increase?*

- In the same survey in 1992, 54% believed that fraud had become 'much more common' in the preceding two years.

- In 1994, 70% felt that levels of fraud were 'about the same'.

- 77% believed that computer and credit card fraud had increased over the preceding 5 years.

Source: Fraud – The Unmanaged Risk. 1994/5 Executive Summary. Ernst & Young, 1995.

■ *How many years of service have perpetrators of fraud given to their companies?*

Hoffman Investigations Ltd, an international firm based in Holland, analysed their corporate assignments in order to understand a possible profile of the would-be fraudster.

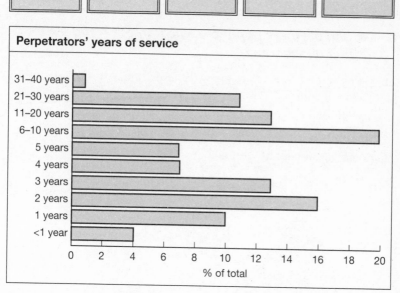

Source: Hoffman Investigations Ltd.

■ *What is the average age of perpetrators?*

Again, Hoffman Investigations Ltd give the following data, based on fraudsters involved in all the corporate frauds they have investigated:

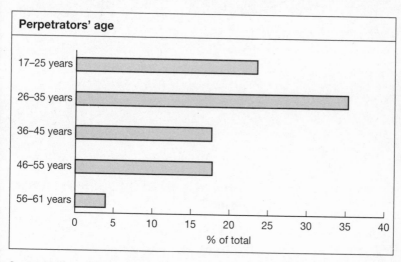

Source: Hoffman Investigations Ltd.

■ *Are the partners of people who commit fraud aware of their misconduct?*

These statistics suggest that you will never think ill of the one you love. 73% of fraudsters' partners said they were completely unaware of the fraudster's misconduct.

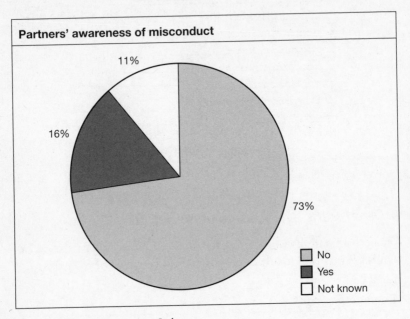

Partners' awareness of misconduct

11%

16%

73%

☐ No
■ Yes
☐ Not known

Source: Hoffman Investigations Ltd.

■ *When are investigation firms called in?*

It would seem that companies are most likely to use professional investigators when a search has to be undertaken – for possessions or witnesses. Hoffman Investigations Ltd, an international firm based in Holland, break down their corporate assignments as follows:

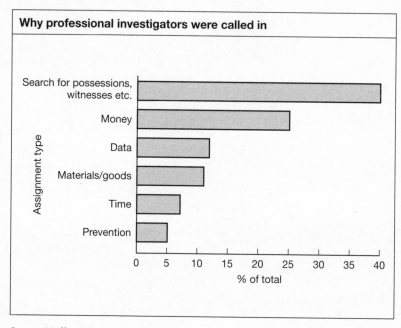

Source: Hoffman Investigations Ltd.

CURRENT FINANCIAL AND ACCOUNTING ISSUES

Banks 244
Relationships with banks ■ Quality of service
■ Credit ■ Bank charges ■ Banks and British business

Debt and company failure 263
Debt ■ Remedial action against debt ■ Factoring
and invoice discounting ■ Company failure

European country risk 268
Country risk ■ Delays in payment in Europe

Tax issues 275
Transfer pricing ■ International tax issues

Internal financial control 279
Internal audit ■ External audit ■ Outsourcing
■ Partnering

BANKS

RELATIONSHIPS WITH BANKS

■ *How many companies have a relationship with a bank, and with which banks?*

Do you remember the 'bank manager in the wardrobe' adverts? The idea was that your bank manager wanted a good relationship with you, even if you couldn't have him in your wardrobe. So how good are companies' relationships with banks? Do all companies have a relationship with a bank?

- 98% of companies retain a relationship bank.
- 77% have relationships with the big four UK clearers.
- 13% bank with Scottish banks.

Source: Bank Relationship Survey 1995, The Bank Consultancy Group/Manchester Business School

■ *Do companies stay loyal to one bank?*

According to the *Bank Relationship Survey*, almost two-thirds of respondents were dealing with more than one bank.

- Extensive switching between banks is occurring; 1 in 8 companies have changed banks in the last 2 years, and 1 in 5 are contemplating doing so.
- Larger companies are increasing the number of banks they use and are increasingly ready to reallocate work amongst their bankers.

Source: Bank Relationship Survey 1995, The Bank Consultancy Group/Manchester Business School

■ *Have relationships with banks improved?*

Companies who have moved bank are more critical than average about their new banks, and often about the same things, so a

244

high proportion of complaints are produced by a small number of customers.

- There has been a remarkable improvement in the availability of bank credit although both fees and conditions and guarantees continue to irk small business.

- Although a majority of corporate clients identified with their relationship manager rather than their bank, the figure is well down on 1992's 70%.

Source: Bank Relationship Survey 1995, The Bank Consultancy Group/Manchester Business School

■ *How much help do banks offer with currency risk and international trading?*

A record 60% of the sample of companies interviewed were active internationally; these companies overwhelmingly expect cross border business to grow. Despite this, banks give low priority to client's currency exposure or to selling risk management products. So if you have found that banks are not providing appropriate facilities to help you manage country and currency risk, you are not alone.

Source: Bank Relationship Survey 1995, The Bank Consultancy Group/Manchester Business School

■ *How good are the banks' relationships with small companies?*

Although charges to small business are now causing less acute problems, international charges are still regarded as too high. The survey also found that there was little doubt that banks have been getting tougher in the last few years, particularly with smaller companies, and the quest to increase fee income in particular is perceived by clients as a major irritant to relationships.

- Despite talk of a financing gap, financial constraints seem not to be major constraints on the growth of small and medium sized companies.

Source: Bank Relationship Survey 1995, The Bank Consultancy Group/Manchester Business School

■ *How important are different sources of strains on bank relationships?*

Companies were asked to rank the different sources of strain in order of importance. 1 was the highest strain on the relationship; 9 was the lowest. Do you identify with any of these problems?

Ranked importance of strains on bank relationship, 1995

1. Level of fees
2. Quality of service
3. Introduction of new service fees
4. Securities and guarantees required
5. Interest rates charged
6. Failure to understand business
7. Relationship with bank manager
8. Restrictions on lending
9. Incomplete/outdated range of products

Respondents who reported a recent change in bank, and those who expected to change their current bank in the next two years, provided some interesting differences in terms of relationship strain. Both groups attach higher importance to understanding their business. Restrictions on lending and their relationship with their manager (which were relatively unimportant for non-changers) were more likely to be sensitive issues with these groups.

Source: Bank Relationship Survey 1995, The Bank Consultancy Group/Manchester Business School

QUALITY OF SERVICE

■ *How do you rate your bank's quality of service?*

Respondents tended to find that foreign (European and non-European) and Scottish banks had the edge both on the major clearers, and on the smaller UK banks such as Yorkshire/Clydesdale. The latter are generally reckoned to use their smaller size to provide good service – so this is an interesting finding.

246

The Big Four UK banks typically serve the complex and more discriminating needs of multinationals, while the smaller banks are engaged with middle market customers or, in the case of foreign banks, mainly with secondary relationships. When asked to rate the quality of advice and service from corporate advisers including banks, respondents answered that:

Advisor	Quality of service		
	Weak or poor	Good or excellent	Rank–1=best
Relationship bank	19%	36%	6
Merchant bank	14%	52%	3
Solicitor	12%	55%	2
Stockbroker	16%	48%	5
Accountant	11%	55%	1
Ad/PR Agency	30%	30%	8
NEDs	18%	51%	4
Consultants	27%	32%	7

Source: Bank Relationship Survey 1995, The Bank Consultancy Group/Manchester Business School

■ *How dependable are banks?*

Respondents were asked to agree, agree strongly, disagree, or disagree strongly with eight statements about relationship banks (a neutral option was also allowed). Only 44% of respondents saw their bank as providing dependable support in a crisis. A substantial 17% were not sure that anything more than the contractual minimum was on offer from banks:

	Disagree or disagree strongly	Agree or agree strongly
1. A relationship bank provides dependable support in a crisis	25%	44%
2. A relationship bank means paying over the odds for some products	35%	25%
3. It saves money to channel most banking through one source	28%	39%
4. My relationship bank is proactive in solving my problems	38%	30%
5. A relationship bank sticks by the spirit of its commitments	18%	41%
6. Bank's customer charter resulted in noticeable improvements	41%	15%
7. My relationship is with my bank manager rather than my bank	30%	45%
8. Published tariffs have proved useful in negotiating bank charges	39%	24%

Source: Bank Relationship Survey 1995, The Bank Consultancy Group/Manchester Business School

CREDIT

■ *What are the most important factors when a bank assesses a company financially?*

If you're in the process of seeking bank finance for expansion or a major project, then you will probably want to know which factors influence the bank's decision in your favour.

The length of the banking relationship and the strength of the bank's management team were thought to be the most important factors. Surprisingly, many respondents thought that banks did not attach a high priority to foreign exchange exposure, even for companies heavily involved in foreign trade:

Priorities	Unimportant/ low importance	Important/ very important
Current year's earnings	5%	78%
Future earnings potential	11%	68%
Smooth trend in earnings	20%	47%
Cash flow performance	3%	55%
Dividend cover	55%	18%
Working capital management	10%	65%
Capital expenditure plans	25%	41%
R & D expenditures	72%	9%
Strength of management team	13%	63%
Product quality	30%	39%
Length of bank relationship	26%	44%
Growth potential of market	28%	39%
Forex exposure	46%	21%

Source: Bank Relationship Survey 1995, The Bank Consultancy Group/Manchester Business School

■ *Are banks 'short termist'?*

For 56% of bank relationships, the assessment horizon was two years or less, compared with 42% of non-bank suppliers. Only 17% of banks were thought to be interested beyond 3 years, which falls short of the needs of knowledge/skill intensive high-tech businesses, which enjoy the most favourable growth opportunities.

- Only 33% of respondents agreed that fixed rate loans were offered as an alternative to overdraft finance.

- UK companies carry only half as much finance in terms of medium- and long-term debt as their French and German counterparts.

- Mainstream banks in the UK have generally steered clear of equity positions in companies, although this type of funding is common on the Continent and goes hand in hand with higher levels of long-term debt finance.

Source: Bank Relationship Survey 1995, The Bank Consultancy Group/Manchester Business School

■ *What are the major constraints on company growth?*

High growth companies complain the most strongly about credit availability. Overall, the biggest constraint was seen as lack of market demand, with the cost and conditions of credit a distant second:

Constraint	Unimportant/ low importance	Important/ very important
Availability of bank credit	42%	42%
Availability of long term credit	39%	43%
Cost and conditions of credit	33%	42%
Lack of market demand	22%	55%
Production and operating capacity	43%	33%
Marketing and distribution	32%	37%
Loss of control	70%	15%
Forex exposure	46%	21%

Source: Bank Relationship Survey 1995, The Bank Consultancy Group/Manchester Business School

■ *What proportion of companies have changed their principal bank in the last 5 years?*

Overwhelmingly, companies believe banking is a relationship business. However, the last 5 years of economic turbulence and recession have put strains on bank arrangements. Companies have increasingly reacted by changing their banking arrangements (the figures relate to 1995):

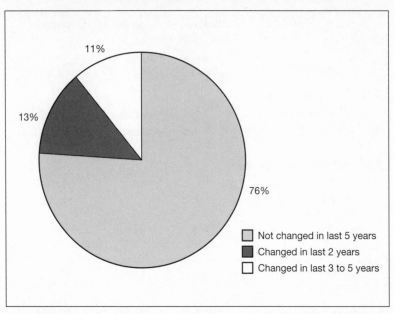

11%

13%

76%

☐ Not changed in last 5 years
■ Changed in last 2 years
☐ Changed in last 3 to 5 years

Source: Bank Relationship Survey 1995, The Bank Consultancy Group/Manchester Business School

■ *Has the availability of credit changed over the last 3 years?*

Since 1992, banks appear to be keen to lend money again, with 37% of respondents disagreeing with the proposition of banks refusing to lend for worthwhile projects and only 26% agreeing with it. This perception of increased lending is not confined to working capital finance; it extends to capital expenditure. But this increased willingness to lend is accompanied by increased requests for security and guarantees. The trend established in 1992 continues, although companies do feel banks are not so concerned as they were at the height of the recession:

Behaviour	Disagree/ disagree strongly	Agree/ agree strongly	Difference(%) 1995 1992	
Refusing credit even for worthwhile projects	37%	26%	+11	−15
Not passing on base rate cuts	27%	45%	−18	−1
Only interested in funding working capital needs	38%	27%	+11	+5
Imposing increased guarantees and security requirements	14%	61%	−47	−57

Source: Bank Relationship Survey 1995, The Bank Consultancy Group/Manchester Business School

■ *What causes most strains on companies' banking relationships?*

Banks do not get the same level of approval when it comes to the interest rates charged to the corporate sector. 17% more companies were dissatisfied than satisfied with the speed with which banks passed on the reduction in base rates that started in 1993:

	Unimportant/ low importance	Important/ very important	Difference (%) 1995 1992	
Restrictions on lending	51%	34%	17	−13
Interest rates charged	44%	31%	13	−25

Source: Bank Relationship Survey 1995, The Bank Consultancy Group/Manchester Business School

■ *Are banks refusing credit even for worthwhile projects?*

With the exception of TSB, where the sample is small, all banks are perceived to be willing to finance worthwhile projects, which is in sharp contrast to 1992 findings:

	Disagree or disagree strongly	Agree or agree strongly
Bank of Scotland	48%	27%
Barclays	31%	30%
Lloyds	35%	28%
Midland	45%	24%
NatWest	40%	25%
Royal Bank of Scotland	39%	25%
TSB	18%	27%
Yorks/Clydesdale	29%	26%
Other UK	41%	22%
European	37%	32%
Other foreign	46%	18%

Source: Bank Relationship Survey 1995, The Bank Consultancy Group/Manchester Business School

■ *Do banks pass on cuts in interest rates?*

There is a significant divergence between banks. Respondents were asked to comment on the statement 'banks have not been passing on recent cuts in interest rates'.

	Disagree or disagree strongly	Agree or agree strongly
Bank of Scotland	26%	34%
Barclays	22%	50%
Lloyds	23%	49%
Midland	29%	42%
NatWest	26%	49%
Royal Bank of Scotland	41%	28%
TSB	36%	36%
Yorks/Clydesdale	25%	50%
Other UK	40%	29%
European	42%	32%
Other foreign	36%	46%

Source: Bank Relationship Survey 1995, The Bank Consultancy Group/Manchester Business School

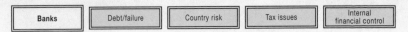

BANK CHARGES

■ *Who in your company is responsible for negotiating bank charges?*

Respondents were asked this question, and it transpired that the Financial Director negotiates bank charges in 49% of companies, but that other posts also carry that responsibility:

Financial Director	49%
Treasurer	18%
Financial Controller	17%
Company Secretary	5%
Others	11%

Source: The Bank Consultancy Group's Bank Report, 1993

■ *How do banks charge for facilities?*

There are many ways a bank can charge for its facilities. The most common methods of charging were found to be:

- Turnover basis: a percentage of the value of the total entries, both debit and credit, on the bank statement
- Per item tariff, i.e. a separate price for every type of activity
- Per entry, i.e. a charge related to the number of debits/credits only
- A fixed charge: this may vary according to the volume of transactions and is sometimes adjusted for inflation
- Interest on overdrawn accounts.

Source: The Bank Consultancy Group's Bank Report, 1993

■ *How do the types of charges vary?*

The Bank Consultancy Group's Bank Report gave the following guide to charges:

Turnover charges

Turnover charges are calculated as a percentage of the total value of all the entries on the bank statement. Unfortunately it does not give any incentive to the organisation to improve its efficiency in its banking operation.

Turnover charges		
Bank	Percentage charged	Total bank charge
Lloyds	0.48	£800,000
Clydesdale	0.13	£60,000
NatWest	2.5	£40,000
Midland	1.75*	£30,000
Nat West	5.25*	

(* = calculated on debit turnover only)

Fixed charges

This is similar to the turnover basis in that it does not give any incentive to the organisation to improve its efficiency and move towards electronic banking. Its main advantage is that the organisation can budget fairly accurately in this area.

Per entry basis

This method seems to be reserved for the small organisation. A charge is made on the number of entries on the bank statement. Charges are made on entries which debit or credit the account with bank charges or interest as well as actual debit and credit transactions.

The big four were found to charge the following per entry:

Barclays	63p
NatWest	64p
Midland	74p
Lloyds	75p

Per item tariffs

A separate charge is made for each transaction, and varies according to the nature of the transaction. Transactions can be categorised as to whether they are cash, paper (cheques, telexes, etc.) or electronic (BACS, etc.).

Source: The Bank Consultancy Group's Bank Report, 1993

■ *Are bank charges sometimes reduced or waived?*

Bank charges may be reduced or waived under the following schemes:

- Notional interest is given on credit balances and set off against bank charges
- A deposit is held in a non-interest bearing account in return for 'free' banking.
- A minimum balance is maintained in the current account in return for waived or reduced fees.
- A 'loyalty' discount on charges is given in return for an agreement to stay with the bank for a number of years.
- A limited period of free banking may be offered when a new account is opened.
- Apart from the benefits to the bank under some of the above schemes, banks also gain from 'float times', i.e. the time between the date a payer's account is debited and the payee's account is credited.

Source: The Bank Consultancy Group's Bank Report, 1993

■ *What are typical bank charges?*

If you are thinking of changing your bank, or simply want to know if what you are charged is standard, then the following figures may be of use to you. Typical charges by the Big Four were:

Transaction	Barclays	Lloyds	Nat West	Midland
Credit terms				
Cash deposited	20p	25p	21p	17.5p
Cheques deposited	8.25p	13p	8p	11p
Credit entries	26p	–	30p	11p
Debit items				
Cash withdrawn	20p	25p	21p	17.5p
Cheques drawn	12p	13p	12p	11p
Bank giro credits	4.5p	–	14p	11p
BACS	3p	–	5p	3p

Source: The Bank Consultancy Group's Bank Report, 1993

■ *What are typical charges on plastic cards?*

Typical charges and commission on plastic cards were:

Type of card	Typical charge / Commission approx.
Chargecard	3.95%
Credit card	1.5 – 2%
Debit card	5p – 60p
Store card	up to 6% commission

On a £500 sale, the following charges could be levied:

Payment method	Charge
American Express	£19.75
Access/Visa	£10.00
Cheque or cash	50p
Interest free credit (10 months)	£55.00

Source: The Bank Consultancy Group's Bank Report, 1993

■ *What costs can be expected for cash transactions?*

Generally electronic transactions are the cheapest and cash transactions are the most expensive, although this is not always the case. The results of 4 tenders received by an organisation for cash deposits of £5,200,000 p.a. were:

Bank	Charge per £100	Total charge
Girobank	5p	£2,600
RBS	19p	£9,880
Clydesdale	26p	£13,520
Bank of Scotland	27p	£14,040

Source: The Bank Consultancy Group's Bank Report, 1993

■ *What are charges for cheques paid/deposited?*

There are approximately 10 million cheques cleared each day by the Cheque and Credit Clearing Company in London. The results of the survey show that charges for a cheque paid out range from 5p to 74p, while charges for a cheque paid in range from 4p to 74p.

■ *What were the cheapest and most expensive charges for manual credits?*

The cheapest and most expensive charges made by various banks for manual credits were:

Bank	Price	Volume	Total bank charge
NatWest			
Cheapest	21p	5,000	£150,000
Most expensive	48p	5,000	£23,000
Irregular	32p	500	£6,000
Barclays			
Cheapest	16.5p	700,000	£314,000
Most expensive	69p	12,000	£84,000
Irregular	22p	1,500	£15,000
Lloyds			
Cheapest	13p	60,000	£90,000
Most expensive	52p	4,000	£307,000
Irregular	15p	8,000	£21,000
Midland			
Cheapest	11p	180,000	£88,000
Most expensive	47p	£1,000	£120,000
Irregular	11p	£160,000	£32,000
RBS			
Cheapest	16p	£80,000	£200,000
Most expensive	50p	£250,000	£148,000
Irregular	None found		

Source: The Bank Consultancy Group's Bank Report, 1993

■ ...and for automatic credits?

The cheapest and most expensive charges made by various banks for automatic credits were:

Bank	Price	Volume	Total bank charge
NatWest Most expensive	12p	20,000	£23,000
Irregular	6p	2,000	£8,000
Barclays Most expensive	15p	8,000	£360,000
Irregular	6.4p	10,000	£46,000
Lloyds Most expensive	10.5p	400,000	£307,000
Irregular	None found		
Midland Most expensive	44p	10,000	£23,000
Irregular	38p	260,000	£54,000

Source: The Bank Consultancy Group's Bank Report, 1993

■ *What charges can be expected for electronic transactions?*

Most large organisations use electronic banking in one form or another. There are four types of transferring funds and receiving payments:

- BACS (Bankers Automated Clearing Service)
- BACSTEL (BACS Telecommunication Service)
- CHAPS (Clearing House Automated Payment System)
- EFTPOS (Electronic Funds Transfer at Point of Sale)

Payments or receipts can be made by using BACS in a variety of ways:

---

1. A paper listing or magnetic tape or disc can be sent to the bank for onward despatch to BACS.

---

2. Magnetic tapes can be sent directly to BACS.

---

3. Organisations can use BACSTEL, which is a telecommunications service linked directly to BACS. BACSTEL now accounts for 68% of the volume of transactions at BACS.

---

4. In 1991 a new method using a cartridge tape input system was introduced.

Source: The Bank Consultancy Group's Bank Report, 1993

BANKS AND BRITISH BUSINESS

■ *How much European expertise do banks have?*

If you are looking for a banking partner for your European operations, will your bank fit the bill? Only 19% of respondents think that their main bank has the knowledge and facilities to deliver good service in Europe:

	Disagree or disagree strongly	Agree or agree strongly
Main bank provides good European advice	25%	37%
Main bank provides good European service	42%	19%

Source: Bank Relationship Survey 1995, The Bank Consultancy Group/Manchester Business School

■ *What role do the "big four" play in corporate banking?*

If you do not bank with one of the big four clearers (Barclays, Nat West, Lloyds and Midland), then are you out on a limb? They certainly dominate UK corporate banking. The majority of the companies listed on the Stock Exchange bank with one or more of the big four:

Bank	Top 50 Amount	%	Top 250 Amount	%
Barclays	9	18	54	22
NatWest	9	18	62	25
Lloyds	10	20	46	18
Midland	16	32	43	17
Others	6	12	45	18

Source: The Bank Consultancy Group's Bank Report, 1993

DEBT AND COMPANY FAILURE

DEBT

■ *How big a problem is late payment of commercial debt (LPCD)?*

If you are experiencing serious problems with bad payers, then you are sadly on the wrong end of a growing trend. LPCD is a significant issue for British business. More businesses appear to be pursuing short-term self interest – a strategy damaging to the business community as a whole. The damage also affects the economy.

- 95% of respondents indicated that LPCD is a significant issue.

Source: Late Payment of Commercial Debt. A response to DTI consultation by the Creditors Group Ltd. March 1994

■ *What does LPCD cost companies in interest and loss of return?*

A direct and identifiable cost to companies is interest charges on monies not received or the loss of return on funds not invested. The average company in the survey identified a cost of £5,603.40 per month (£67,241.88 per year) caused by LPCD.

Source: Late Payment of Commercial Debt. A response to DTI consultation by the Creditors Group Ltd. March 1994

■ *What does LPCD cost to administrate?*

Companies suffering LPCD have to put in place administrative systems to chase payment.

- The average cost of chasing late payment was £1,636.33 per month – £19,635.96 per year.

- The average cost of securing external services to pursue debt is £465.07 per month or £5,580.85 per year.

Thus for an average medium sized business, there is a monthly expenditure of £7,704.84 per month or £92,458.68 per year, representing approximately 1.5% of the average respondent's turnover.

Source: Late Payment of Commercial Debt. A response to DTI consultation by the Creditors Group Ltd. March 1994

■ *What is the cost of financing the VAT element of unpaid debt?*

A VAT quarter plus 30 day payment terms provides a total VAT payment period of 120 days. The survey showed that 60 days from the date of invoice, on average, only 41.9% of debt is paid; at 90 days a further 33.41% is paid; and at 120 days a further 15.21% is paid.

This, based on a quarter's trading, suggests that businesses are financing approximately 30.7% of the VAT due in each quarter, as they are having to pay the input VAT before being able to collect it from their customers. This element is a hidden cost of LPCD and very few companies would have accounted for this in estimating the cost of overdue debt.

Source: Late Payment of Commercial Debt. A response to DTI consultation by the Creditors Group Ltd. March 1994

REMEDIAL ACTION AGAINST DEBT

■ *What are the remedies?*

The current law allows a company to include in its terms of trade a 'late payment interest (LPI)' clause. However, there is a significant reluctance to enforce this clause.

Source: Late Payment of Commercial Debt. A response to DTI consultation by the Creditors Group Ltd. March 1994

■ Have you ever invoked a remedial clause?

If you haven't, then you are not alone. The survey showed that just under 47% of companies had such clauses in their Terms and Conditions of Sale. Of these, only 15% (around 7% of all companies) actually enforced this clause, and then only in a small percentage of cases. The clause is usually only enforced when the business relationship has already ended, and when litigation is being undertaken for recovery of the debt.

- The survey concludes that remedies currently available are voluntary and impractical, even where they are legally enforceable, and that the costs/time involved in litigation militate against the pursuit of financial redress.

Source: Late Payment of Commercial Debt. A response to DTI consultation by the Creditors Group Ltd. March 1994

FACTORING AND INVOICE DISCOUNTING

■ What are factoring and invoice discounting?

Factoring and invoice discounting are financial services designed to improve cash flow, primarily by providing finance secured against the outstanding invoices of a business. They offer companies a flexible means of growth, by allowing them to make maximum use of their assets.

Source: Association of British Factors and Discounters Annual Review 1995.

■ What are the advantages of factoring and discounting?

This form of financing can enable companies to make better use of management time and the money tied up in trade credit to customers.

- Companies which do not use factors or discounters wait on average for about 75 days before invoices are paid.
- At any one time, there are £57 billion of payments due to small businesses tied up in unpaid invoices.

Source: Association of British Factors and Discounters Annual Review 1995.

■ *What could a factoring or discounting company offer you?*

A factoring or discounting company:

---

1. Buys the unpaid invoices due to you as they arise.

---

2. Provides immediate finance of up to 80% of the value of your invoices, with the balance (less administration and finance charges) payable after a set period, or when the invoice is paid.

---

3. Advises on your credit risks.

---

4. Can protect you against bad debts.

Businesses using factors and discounters get paid 80% of the value immediately, with the balance paid on average only 58 days later.

Source: Association of British Factors and Discounters Annual Review 1995.

■ *What is the cost of factoring?*

So if you are now actively considering using a factoring company, how much will it cost? The factoring and invoice discounting companies claim that they are providing a cost effective service, which would otherwise be paid for in increased staff and overhead costs. The charges for factoring are made in two ways:

- Service fees, typically of between 0.5% and 3% of gross annual turnover. A company with a £500,000 turnover could pay a service fee of around £6,000.

- A separate charge, geared to current base rates, for the finance made available against sales often comparable to overdraft rates.

Source: Association of British Factors and Discounters Annual Review 1995.

■ *What is the cost of invoice discounting?*

If factoring appears expensive, is invoice discounting any cheaper? In most cases, a fee is charged to cover the administration of the agreement, which is normally between 0.2% and 0.5% of turnover. The principal cost is the finance charge which, like factoring, is linked to established base rates and is comparable with overdraft rates.

Source: Association of British Factors and Discounters Annual Review 1995.

COMPANY FAILURE

■ *What are the causes of company failure?*

Does late payment cause company failure? The obvious way to find out is to look at why companies fail. The Society of Practitioners in Insolvency indicate a marked increase in 'loss of market' as a cause of company failure, but about an eighth of companies fail because of bad debts, and another eighth because of financing:

Cause of failure	Percentage		
	March 1992	Sept 1992	June 1993
Poor management	31	34	10
Loss of market	28	31	46
Bad debts	11	9	12
Financing	15	12	9
Other	15	14	21

Source: Payment Procedures and Late Payments in Italy and Europe, Dun & Bradstreet Kosmos.

EUROPEAN COUNTRY RISK

COUNTRY RISK

■ *How do you assess country risk?*

If you are experiencing problems assessing country risk, then help is at hand. Dun and Bradstreet's 'DB' risk indicator provides a comparative, cross-border assessment of the risk of doing business in a country. Essentially, the indicator seeks to examine the broader commercial environment in respect of transactions costs and transfer risks over a time horizon of two years.

The 'DB' risk indicator is a composite index of three over-arching country risk categories; economic, socio-political and commercial. Variables within each group are comprehensively assessed, scored and weighted by regional analysts before an indicator is assigned.

Source: The Dun and Bradstreet Country Risk User Guide

■ *How do risk indicators work?*

In principle, the indicator seeks to assess such key issues as

- The ability of a country to generate sufficient foreign exchange to service its payment obligations.
- The willingness of the country to create an enabling environment for trade and foreign investment.
- The resilience of an economy to withstand domestic and external shocks.

The Dun and Bradstreet DB risk indicator has seven categories:

DB1	Highest creditworthiness
DB2	Good creditworthiness
DB3	Creditworthy
DB4	Adequate credit risk
DB5	Questionable creditworthiness
DB6	Poor creditworthiness
DB7	Lowest creditworthiness

Each indicator is sub-divided by quartiles (a–d). For example, within the DB1 banding, DB1a represents slightly less risk than DB1b. This does not apply to the DB7 indicator.

Source: The Dun and Bradstreet Country Risk User Guide

■ *So how do you rate European countries for risk?*

If you have never systematically rated one European country as more of a risk than another, but wonder why you find trading with Turkey difficult, then Dun and Bradstreet's indicators may help. If you find the '1' in the indicator for most European countries surprising, bear in mind that the indicators are used to assess country risk throughout the world (*see* Table overleaf).

Country	Indicator
Denmark	DB1b
Switzerland	DB1b
France	DB1c
Netherlands	DB1c
Luxembourg	DB1c
Germany	DB1c
UK	DB1c
Austria	DB1c
Eire	DB1c
Belgium	DB1c
Norway	DB1c
Finland	DB1d
Italy	DB1d
Sweden	DB1d
Portugal	DB2a
Spain	DB2a
Iceland	DB2a
Malta	DB2a
Greece	DB2c
Cyprus	DB2d
Turkey	DB3b

Source: The Dun and Bradstreet Country Risk User Guide

DELAYS IN PAYMENT IN EUROPE

■ *How long does it take you to collect an invoice in Europe?*

If you find that, when it comes to your European customer, your 30 days is their 60 and your 60 is their 90, then you are not alone. Invoices seem always to take longer to collect than credit terms allow. The average number of days before receiving payment for 30 and 90 day credit periods in each country is given below:

Country	Credit terms	
	30 days	90 days
Germany	40	100
UK	47	77
Holland	49	79
Italy	54	114
France	80	110
Belgium	81	111

Source: Payment Procedures and Late Payments in Italy and Europe, Dun & Bradstreet Kosmos.

■ *What proportion of payments do you receive at the due date or with a maximum delay of 15 days?*

So if your European customers are paying up and looking pretty, are you particularly lucky? Do you receive a reasonable proportion of payments on or just after the due date? Companies in each country were asked to assess how many invoices were settled within this time period. The UK is only slightly below the European average.

European average	59%
Germany	80%
United Kingdom	57%
France	56%
Italy	53%
Holland	51%
Belgium	49%

Source: Payment Procedures and Late Payments in Italy and Europe, Dun & Bradstreet Kosmos.

■ What credit period do you offer your customers?

When it comes to extending the credit period for your European customers, you could argue the point either way. Making your current credit period longer might encourage your customers to pay within it. Or shortening it might mean that you can start chivvying them for payment sooner. The most frequent terms of payment in each country are:

Country	Number of days
UK	30 – 60
Holland	30 – 60
Germany	30 – 90
Italy	30 – 90
France	60 – 90
Belgium	60 – 90

Source: Payment Procedures and Late Payments in Italy and Europe, Dun & Bradstreet Kosmos.

■ What are the average delays in payments in Europe? (1994)

So how long do you normally wait to be paid? Does the problem lie with a few very bad payers, or do all your customers keep you waiting for months? Only Germany has a lower delay rate than the UK:

Country	Average delays (days)
Italy	30
Belgium	21
France	20
Holland	19
UK	17
Germany	10

Source: Payment Procedures and Late Payments in Italy and Europe, Dun & Bradstreet Kosmos.

■ How do you assess the creditworthiness of new overseas customers?

Some businesses avoid the need to check their customers' creditworthiness by using letters of credit, or they use credit insurance agencies or factoring companies. But if you don't go for these options, how can you be sure that they'll pay up? This is how one survey's respondents check on their new overseas buyers.

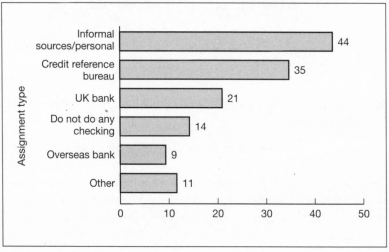

Source: *Royal Bank of Scotland Quarterly Survey of Exporters*, Small Business Research Trust, June 1995

■ How do you ensure payments from your overseas buyers?

Even assuming you've made thorough checks on your customers' creditworthiness, you still can't be sure they'll pay up unless you take other steps. What do other exporters do to ensure payments from their overseas customers? 70% of them in this survey do at least some business with no formal method of protection at all.

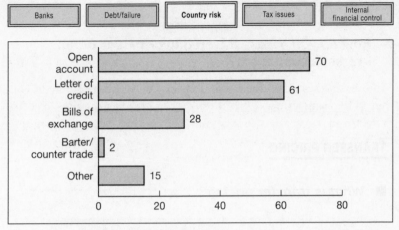

Source: *Royal Bank of Scotland Quarterly Survey of Exporters*, Small Business Research Trust, June 1995

■ *How serious is the problem of late payment by export customers?*

Late payment of course can be catastrophic for businesses. But if you're exporting, do you tend to find ways of avoiding these problems, or do they give you serious grief? This table shows how serious other exporters find the problem; it suggests that most of them are employing the credit control methods above to good effect.

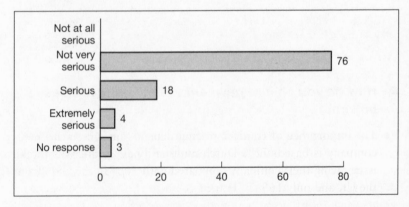

Source: *Royal Bank of Scotland Quarterly Survey of Exporters*, Small Business Research Trust, June 1995

TAX ISSUES

TRANSFER PRICING

■ *What is transfer pricing?*

Transfer pricing is what affiliated members of a multinational corpo-
ration (MNC) charge one another for transfers of goods, intellectual
property or loans, as well as providing services.

Source: Transfer Pricing: Risk Reductions and Advance Pricing Agreements, Ernst & Young

■ *Is transfer pricing a major tax issue?*

This is probably the most important tax issue facing multinationals.
With the explosive growth in world trade, MNCs' transfer pricing activities have come under increased scrutiny by tax authorities in many
countries – this is explained by the fact that almost 50% of all trade
between the advanced nations takes place between related companies.

■ *Is transfer pricing an important issue to you?*

If you hadn't heard of transfer pricing before today, or you feel this
issue has passed you by, then you are not alone. Financial companies
(40%) are less likely to regard transfer pricing as the major tax issue
they face than non-financial companies (51%).

- The importance of transfer pricing depends on where the parent
  company is based: 72% Dutch multinationals said it was the key
  issue facing their company compared with 50% in the US, 40% in
  the UK and only 16% in France.

Source: Transfer Pricing: Risk Reductions and Advance Pricing Agreements, Ernst & Young

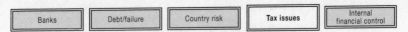

■ *How does the threat of investigation affect your company's policy on transfer pricing?*

If your company is part of a MNC, how do you react to the threat of investigation? Just under a third of multinationals tailor transfer pricing policies to the requirements of local revenue authorities:

Policy on transfer pricing	Percentage
Set defensible policy with adequate documentation	34
Adopt policies in different countries according to practice of the local authority	29
Set arm's-length, market level prices	25
General caution	12
No conservative policy in particular jurisdictions	11

Source: Transfer Pricing: Risk Reductions and Advance Pricing Agreements, Ernst & Young

■ *What form have transfer pricing enquiries taken?*

Nearly 2/3rds of multinationals who have faced an enquiry in a subsidiary country did so through a greater than normal degree of concentration on transfer pricing issues during an annual tax audit:

Form of enquiry	Proportion of companies
Questions of an information gathering nature	17%
Greater than normal concentration on transfer pricing issues during annual tax audit	61%
One-off transfer pricing enquiries	18%

Of those companies who faced enquiries in their home countries, half experienced greater than normal concentration on transfer pricing during an audit, and one in four faced questions of an information-gathering nature.

Source: *Transfer Pricing: Risk Reductions and Advance Pricing Agreements*, Ernst & Young

INTERNATIONAL TAX ISSUES

■ *What do you consider are the main international tax issues?*

You will probably have a picture of which international tax issues figure large for your company. Utilisation of foreign credits, perhaps – or simply the time commitment in coping with the sheer range of rates and regimes in the different countries. Companies throughout Europe were surveyed to discover which international tax issues concerned them. Overall, transfer pricing[1] is clearly the most important issue and is expected to continue to be so in the near future:

Transfer pricing	82%
Rates/regimes in different countries	13%
Allocation of costs/overheads	12%
Utilisation of foreign tax credits	10%
Withholding taxes	9%
Repatriation of dividends	8%
Double taxation	7%
Controlled Foreign Corporation regulations	5%

Source: *Transfer Pricing: Risk Reductions and Advance Pricing Agreements*, Ernst & Young

CURRENT FINANCIAL AND ACCOUNTING ISSUES

---

[1] See above– 'What is transfer pricing?', p.277

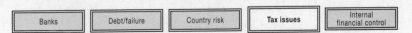

■ *What are the most important international tax issues to multinationals?*

Were these answers weighted by a large number of multinationals amongst the respondents? Transfer pricing is largely a multinational issue. By a wide margin, multinationals identify transfer pricing as the most important issue facing their own particular companies, but they also were concerned by other issues:

Transfer pricing	48%
Rates/regimes in different countries	8%
Utilisation of foreign tax credits	7%
Controlled Foreign Corporation regulations	5%
Risk of double taxation	4%
Hostile attitude/protectionism of US revenue authority	4%

Source: Transfer Pricing: Risk Reductions and Advance Pricing Agreements, Ernst & Young

■ *Which cross-border transactions do you find are susceptible to disputes with revenue authorities?*

When an international survey of companies was undertaken by Ernst & Young, they found that the picture varied between other countries and the UK. In the US, royalties for intangible rights are identified as the most problematic area. Internal charges for administration or managerial services are described as most susceptible to disputes by Australian, Dutch and UK multinationals.

Ernst & Young's experience in the UK is that charges for administration/managerial services are more susceptible to dispute there because they are more visible to the revenue authority than transfer of goods:

Transaction	Percentage of companies experiencing problems with revenue authorities
Charges for administrative/ managerial services	54
Royalties for intangible rights	44
Transfer of finished goods for resale	43
Intercompany financing	38
Charges for technical services	34
Sales of raw materials or components	29
Technology cost-sharing arrangements	25

Source: *Transfer Pricing: Risk Reductions and Advance Pricing Agreements,* Ernst & Young

INTERNAL FINANCIAL CONTROL

INTERNAL AUDIT

■ *Does your organisation use internal financial controls? Does it work?*

Are you in a position to monitor internal financial controls? If you have yet to sort out an efficient system of internal audit, or have chosen to use external auditors, then you are not alone. An Ernst and Young Survey found that:

- Almost 40% of top companies have no internal audit service.
- Less than 50% of companies with an internal audit service are confident that their monitoring will be an adequate input to the directors' report on internal control under the Cadbury framework.

- 66% of finance directors believe that the skills of their internal audit service need to be strengthened.

Source: Is Your Organisation in a Position to Monitor Internal Control? Ernst & Young Internal Audit Services

■ How many companies have internal audit departments? How big are they?

The same survey found that 61% of the organisations interviewed currently have an internal audit department. The size of these departments varies greatly.

Source: Is Your Organisation in a Position to Monitor Internal Control? Ernst & Young Internal Audit Services

■ What role do internal audit departments play in your organisation?

Of course, you may not have an internal audit department (IAD). But the Finance Directors and Audit committee chairmen of companies which had internal auditing agreed that the principal role of the IAD is to provide assurance on internal financial control and, to a lesser extent, to aid fraud investigation.

Source: Is Your Organisation in a Position to Monitor Internal Control? Ernst & Young Internal Audit Services

■ How effective are internal audit departments?

Almost all the respondents look to their IAD to provide assurance on internal financial control. Yet less than 50% of Finance Directors and Audit Committee Chairmen claim to be 'very confident' that their IAD provides the requisite assurance to enable compliance with Cadbury.

Respondents were even less confident in their IAD's ability to provide assurance on wider operational controls (i.e. beyond financial controls). Only 27% of Finance Directors and 11% of Audit Committee Chairmen are 'very confident' in this respect.

Source: Is Your Organisation in a Position to Monitor Internal Control? Ernst & Young Internal Audit Services

■ Does your internal audit department need strengthening?

When asked this question, 66% of Finance Directors of companies with IADs say that areas exist where the IAD's skills require strengthening, either at present or in the future.

Source: Is Your Organisation in a Position to Monitor Internal Control? Ernst & Young Internal Audit Services

■ Do you rely on external auditing?

If you are amongst these 40% of companies, and have not introduced internal auditing, do you rely on external auditing? There is a widely held view among Finance Directors that external auditors and line management confirmation procedures provide an adequate basis for assurance on internal control. Ernst & Young, however, believes this is unlikely to be true.

Source: Is Your Organisation in a Position to Monitor Internal Control? Ernst & Young Internal Audit Services

■ Are you envisaging introducing internal audit? If so, why?

In the same survey, the main reasons companies gave for introducing internal audit in the future were growth of the company, the influence of the Cadbury Code and the role of non-executive directors:

- Over half the Finance Directors of these companies considered the current or potential growth of their organisation, either organically or through mergers and acquisitions, to be the most significant factor encouraging the establishment of an IAD.

- 3 in 10 of organisations without an internal audit function believe that the contribution of the Cadbury Code and the expectations of the non-executive directors make it more likely that an IAD will be established in their organisation.

Source: Is Your Organisation in a Position to Monitor Internal Control? Ernst & Young Internal Audit Services

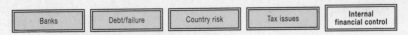

| Banks | Debt/failure | Country risk | Tax issues | Internal financial control |

OUTSOURCING OF INTERNAL AUDIT

■ *If you have an internal department, do you outsource part of your internal audit function?*

If you do, you are not alone. Almost 23% of organisations interviewed, whether currently possessing an IAD or not, currently outsource some element of their internal audit function.

- A further 7% of companies are currently considering outsourcing some of their internal audit function, and a further 25% say they are likely to do so in the future.
- 19% have considered the above option in the past but have rejected it.

Source: Is Your Organisation in a Position to Monitor Internal Control? Ernst & Young Internal Audit Services

■ *Which areas of internal audit do companies need most help with?*

External assistance is currently most sought for computer/IT systems issues.

Source: Is Your Organisation in a Position to Monitor Internal Control? Ernst & Young Internal Audit Services

■ Why do companies outsource and what are the major objections to outsourcing?

The principal reason for outsourcing is to address a lack of in-house resources in a particular area, followed by cost reduction opportunities.

The major barriers to outsourcing have been:

- Perceived cost implications.
- Fears over an external organisation's depth of understanding of the business.
- The potential loss of an in-house capability.
- The potential lack of continuity in auditing personnel.
- The lack of direct control over external consultants.

Source: Is Your Organisation in a Position to Monitor Internal Control? Ernst & Young Internal Audit Services

■ How receptive are managers to the idea of outsourcing?

- Over 25% of Audit Committee Chairmen are immediately receptive to the concept of outsourcing, seeing it as a means of handling special project requirements and providing access to a large range of skills.

- 23% of Finance Directors and 20% of Audit Committee Chairmen currently operating an IAD believe that outsourcing can lead to a cost saving for an organisation.

Source: Is Your Organisation in a Position to Monitor Internal Control? Ernst & Young Internal Audit Services

INTERNAL AUDIT PARTNERING

■ What is internal audit partnering?

Partnering is an arrangement whereby a department works together with an external supplier who can provide additional skills and resources to supplement the in-house resource.

Source: Is Your Organisation in a Position to Monitor Internal Control? Ernst & Young Internal Audit Services

■ *Do companies prefer partnering to outsourcing?*

64% of Finance Directors with IADs and 48% of Audit Committee Chairmen see partnering as a more attractive option than outsourcing with regard to internal skills. Partnering is also seen to address many of the concerns held about outsourcing.

- The appeal of partnering lies in its ability to provide additional skills and experience to supplement the in-house resource base in a more flexible manner. By so doing, it enables the organisation to maintain control and continuity.

Source: Is Your Organisation in a Position to Monitor Internal Control? Ernst & Young Internal Audit Services

APPENDIX 1
HOW TO READ STATISTICS

This book is packed with statistical figures – percentages, average marks out of ten, tables, graphs, charts – and after a while it can become hard to take in so much information in this form. There are also various conventions and standard formulae that are used to analyse and present such statistics. It seemed worthwhile to give brief descriptions and explanations of these in case you haven't come across them before, or not for a long time, and might benefit from some clarification of what it all actually means.

This appendix, then, is intended to clarify some of the types of statistical data that can be found in *The Essential Personnel Sourcebook, The Essential Management And Finance Sourcebook*, and *The Essential Marketing Sourcebook*. Of course, it may come in handy any time that you are presented with some statistics and would like to refresh your memory of what exactly they are telling you, or not telling you. It is also intended to clear up some of the confusions that can easily be caused by the use of technical terms, particular formats and so on.

CHARTS, GRAPHS AND MATRICES

There are many charts included in this book, and each has been picked to present the data in the most convenient way. It is therefore worth mentioning the particular properties and uses of each chart, so that you will know at a glance what is being presented. The easiest way to do this is to go through the different types of chart and give a brief explanation of each one.

285

Bar Chart

This is one of the most common types of chart. It shows figures (usually quantity or percentage) for various different items. For example, it might show what percentage of people in an office have each of the following items of fruit in their fruit bowl at home:

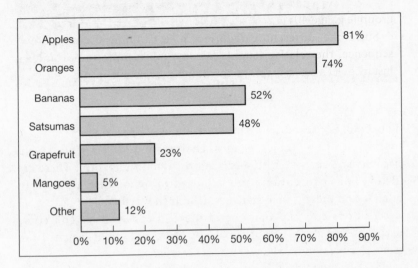

As with this chart, the highest number (and hence longest bar) should come at the top, with the others decreasing in order. Certain categories are exceptions to this rule, by always coming at the end. The most common of these are 'other' and 'none' (which may occur, for instance, in a survey of what the people in the office had for breakfast). The figures in this example do not add up to 100%, of course, since many people have more than one type of fruit in their fruit bowl.

Column chart

This looks very similar to a bar chart, but the blocks go up rather than across. Despite this similarity, it is used in a significantly different way from a Bar Chart. It is used in instances where the different columns progress along a sequence. Typical examples of this are when the figures apply to different times (1990, 1991, 1992, etc), different scores (strongly agree, agree, not sure, disagree, strongly disagree), and different age groups (16-19, 20-23, 24-35, 36-39).

This last example is important since the groupings given are not equal. The column for people age 24-35 is likely to be much larger than for the other groupings, since it covers a much wider range of people. This sort of distortion is worth looking out for in general (although in this series we have avoided it wherever possible), and has a certain amount of effect every time there is an open-ended group (e.g. age 40+).

Since the different categories in a Column Chart follow a sequence, the relative heights become much more important. For instance, let's see a graph of the number of people in the office with apples in their fruit bowls for each of the last 4 weeks.

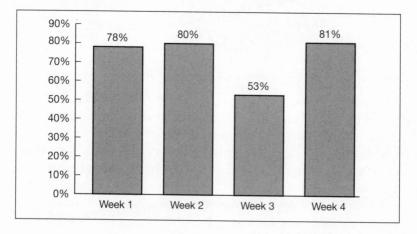

Perhaps there was a major deadline at work at the end of Week 3 and no-one had time to go shopping. It is variations like this that are the main point of information in most Column Charts.

Pie chart

A Pie Chart is used in similar cases to a Bar Chart, but there is one special property of a Pie Chart. This is that the figures in it must add up to 100%. Of course, the figures may be given as quantities rather than percentages, but there are no overlaps or omissions – the total sample is divided up completely between the various sections of the chart. For example, let's look at one fruit bowl, and see how many pieces of each type of fruit there are in it:

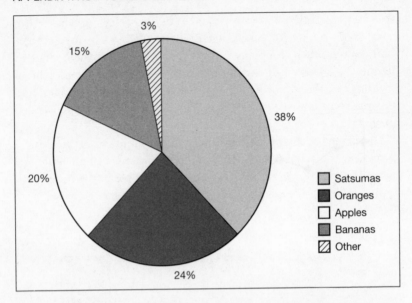

The largest segment should start at 12 o'clock and be measured clockwise from there, with subsequent segments being progressively smaller. In this way, the chart not only shows which figure is largest, but also visually conveys the relative sizes of the sections very effectively. Of course, it can be confusing if you try to fit 18 segments into a Pie Chart, so these are generally only used when there are 6 sections or fewer. Also, since the main strength of a Pie Chart is to convey relative sizes, there may be times when a Bar Chart is used instead, since this is not the main significance of the figures.

Line graph

These are used almost exclusively to show changes over time, and also sometimes to show changes according to age group. As we have seen, Column Charts can also be used for this purpose. The main differences between these two charts are:

- Column Charts are only useful when there are relatively few figures – otherwise you end up with too many columns and it is hard to read.

- Column Charts tend to be used to show specific variations rather than general trends.

So a Line Graph is used for time-series comparisons when there are many figures, and usually when there is a general trend rather than a horizontal line with a few kinks in it. An example would be an analysis of the number of apples I have eaten each week for the last 3 months.

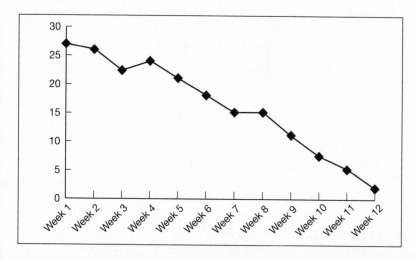

I am now completely sick of apples. What this chart conveys most effectively is the rapid decline in my apple addiction, rather than the number of apples that I ate in any given week.

Scatter chart

Scatter Charts are used to show correlation – that is, the relationship between two factors. In this way, they could be used to show the relationship between the value of the pound and my tendency to eat apples. There is unlikely to be any real relationship here – both of these factors will vary without having any effect on each other. However, the relationship between the number of apples I eat and the number of bananas I eat may be very strong.

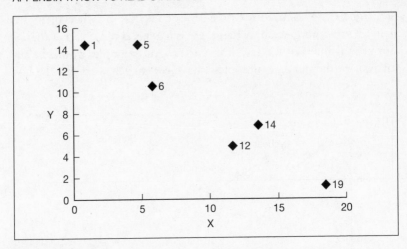

This shows that as my consumption of apples decreased (as shown by the values on the vertical Y-axis) my consumption of bananas increased (as shown by the value on the horizontal X-axis). So when I eat 15 apples, I eat one banana; when I eat one apple I eat 19 bananas. This can be seen from the fact that the points on the graph go in something approximating to a straight line from the top left to bottom right of the chart. If there were no correlation then they would not form any noticeable line. Scatter Charts are quite uncommon, but are the most appropriate chart for showing this sort of correlation.

Matrix

Matrices vary from the other charts described here in that they are not necessarily dependent on numerical figures. The axes are normally shown crossed, giving a dead centre at the point where they cross. This divides the chart into four quarters, and the main information given is which quarter each item is in. In some Matrices, items are not positioned any more specifically than this, while in others they are given a precise place on the chart.

Suppose, for instance, that I generally eat fruit either because it tastes nice, or because it is filling, and I want to know how well each type of fruit fills each of these criteria. If I were only interested in taste then I might give marks out of ten and show the results on a Bar Chart, but I want a chart that will show me both figures at once. The chart I want is this one:

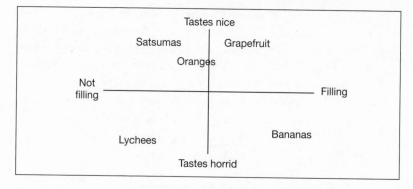

This chart tells me that if I want something filling, and I don't care about the taste, I should have a banana (the most filling item), or if I want it to taste nice as well, then I should have a grapefruit (not as filling, but much nicer). It also tells everyone exactly what I think of lychees. I could have given marks out of ten on each axis, which would have given each fruit a precise point on the graph, or I could have simply put each fruit in one of the four quarters and not been any more specific than this. The Matrix above is a compromise between the two.

So Matrices are useful for showing how a variety of items rate according to two different variables (e.g. taste and fillingness).

INDEXING

One particular statistical convention that may be used occasionally in these books is indexing. This is a relatively uncommon way of quantifying information, so it is probably worth giving a brief explanation of it for anyone who may not have come across it before.

Indexing is used when there are no absolute figures, only relative ones. The information therefore shows the relationships between these figures. However, this cannot be done with percentages or quantities. So how can the information be presented? The solution is to take an arbitrary figure as the standard, or as the maximum, and then rate other figures relative to this.

Suppose I want to rate how much Alice, Bruce, Cynthia and David enjoy eating apples. I am not asking for scores out of ten from each of them, I am trying to measure their actual enjoyment, so there is no absolute measurement that I can apply. However, I may still have meaningful and useful information to give on this topic. One way that I can present this is to say that Cynthia seems to be fairly ambivalent about eating apples, while the others have stronger feelings one way or the other. So I take 100 as the amount of pleasure Cynthia experiences from eating an apple. Using this, I now have a scale on which to judge the pleasure of my four subjects.

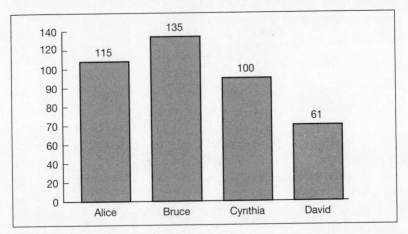

Note that the '100' here does not measure anything specific such as the volume of 'Mmmm' noises or number of endorphins released in the brain. And rather than having 100 as the most neutral point, I could have had it as the maximum enjoyment. This choice was entirely arbitrary, it was simply necessary to provide a way of presenting the data, and the data itself shows only the relationship between these four people's enjoyment of eating apples, and cannot be related to anything beyond this.

AVERAGES

Most of us can remember from school that there are three different kinds of average, even if we can't quite recall what all of them are. Since they are used in these books, it might be wise to recap them. Imagine that 35 of us have fruit bowls, and I want to know the average number of apples in each bowl. My three options are:

1. Mean average: the total number of apples divided by the total number of fruit bowls (this is the most commonly used type of average, and the one that we generally mean when we don't specify which sort of average we are talking about).

2. Median average: the half way point between the highest (9) and lowest (0) number of apples.
3. Mode average: the single number of apples that occurs more frequently than any other.

I'll give you an example. The following line chart shows the number of fruit bowls containing each quantity of apples; 5 bowls have no apples in them, one contains one apple and so on.

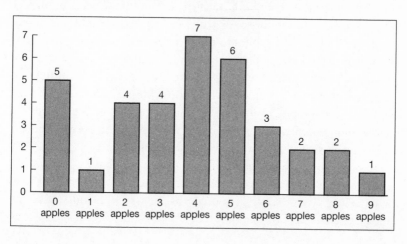

- Mean average number of apples (136 apples divided by 35 fruit bowls): 3.9
- Median average number of apples: 4.5
- Mode average number of apples: 7

FIGURES THAT SEEM TO CONTRADICT EACH OTHER

In books like *The Essential Personnel Sourcebook*, *The Essential Management and Finance Sourcebook* and *The Essential Marketing Sourcebook*, there are many figures which refer to very similar things. In some cases these figures may appear directly to contradict each other. In fact, we have taken great pains to ensure that no contradictory figures are included in any of *The Essential Business Sourcebooks*, but there are often subtle differences between statistics which are easy to overlook, and may give the impression that they cannot both be correct.

For example, suppose we are examining the composition of a particular fruit bowl which contains four satsumas and a grapefruit. We may say that:

- The contents of the fruit bowl is made up of 20% grapefruit.
- It is also made up of 50% grapefruit.

For the sake of this example, these figures are obviously deliberately unhelpful, but they may both be correct. The first, in fact, applies to the composition in numbers of fruits (four satsumas and one grapefruit), and the second applies to the composition in weight (since four satsumas weigh the same as one grapefruit). Naturally, we will explain such differences whenever there are potentially confusing figures like this in any of *The Essential Business Sourcebooks*, but if you are only looking up one piece of information, or if you are in a hurry and concentrating more on the figures than the text, then it is easy to miss such slight but crucial differences.

In order to minimise the likelihood of this happening, and make it easier to spot the reasons for such discrepancies in this book or elsewhere, I will briefly explains some of the main reasons that such apparent contradiction can occur.

Differences in the sample

Even if two surveys ask exactly the same question, it is exceptionally unlikely that they will be asking the same people. For this reason, results will always vary slightly between different surveys. Often surveys will deliberately be asking different people about the same thing – one survey may ask all workers, for instance, and another may be asking only managers. This may produce substantially different results, and these differences may even be the main point of interest in the figures.

The differences are sometimes even more subtle than this; for instance one survey may ask workplaces if they operate a certain policy, and another may workers if their workplace operates the policy. If the policy is most often operated by large workplaces with many employees, then the proportion of workers answering 'yes' is likely to be higher than the proportion of workplaces answering 'yes'.

Differences in survey characteristics

Sometimes differences may be less deliberate. One survey may have covered more large companies than another, for instance, and in many cases this will lead to different results. This does not mean that one was a survey of large companies and the other a survey of small companies, it simply means that their balance of companies of different sizes was not the same. Similarly, one survey may have been conducted by interview and another by postal questionnaire, and this will also have an effect on the results.

Another factor that may lead to differences is the time of the survey. Figures of change over time can be very useful information in its own right, but since any two surveys are likely to vary in many ways (such as what exact question was asked, who was asked and so on) it is often misleading to compare results from two totally different surveys conducted at different times.

To avoid this type of confusion, the figures in this book have been selected as the most reliable ones of all that were available. However, there may be times when two different surveys cover the same topic but ask slightly different questions, in which cases both will be included, in order to provide as much useful information as possible. In such cases, it is worth remembering that the two surveys were very probably conducted at different times and in different ways, and while both are informative and valid, they are unlikely to have produced exactly the same results.

Differences in conceptual structure

Many decisions are made when designing a survey, and this is another area where surveys can vary. If I am conducting a survey into how many people eat apples often, then I will have to define 'often'. Is it once a week, twice a week, or once a fortnight? Naturally, the choice I make in defining this term will affect what figure I arrive at at the end of the survey.

Similarly, I may be surveying how many apples people eat in a week. If I am doing this on a tick-box questionnaire, then I will have to choose what categories to provide a box for – it may be '0-3', '4-8', '8-11', '12+', or it may be '0', '1-5', '6-10', '11+'. It will be very hard to tie together the two sets of figures that I receive, and each grouping has its own strengths and weaknesses.

Similarly, I may be surveying people's favourite fruits, and listing them either by colour, or by price, or in groups such as citrus, tropical and so on. Again, I may not be able to compare the different results that I receive in any meaningful way. Each set of results will tell me something that I want to know, but will fail to tell me something else. So each set of results simply has to be taken on its own merits, and the inherent differences borne in mind when taking the results together.

NOT ADDING UP TO 100%

In this book, and elsewhere, percentage figures are often given which do not total 100%. At times this may be confusing, particularly when you want to be sure that you have complete and reliable information. Of course, there are many legitimate reasons why this can occur, and it is worth running through these quickly so that, when such a situation occurs, you will be able to see why it has happened.

More than 100%

Rounding

Some of the figures that are given as whole number percentages may originally have been calculated to one or two decimal places. This level of detail is often unnecessary, and can complicate the information that is being given, and hence the figures have been 'rounded' to the nearest whole number. This process can occasionally produce figures which total 101% or 102%, although it is rare to create any more of a disturbance than this.

For example, the composition of my fruit bowl (by weight) is:

Apples: 30.6%
Oranges: 32.7%
Bananas: 36.6%

This makes a total of 100%. However, I would like to make these statistics easier to read and take in, so I want them as whole numbers. Since the numbers after the decimal places are all greater than 5, this means that all these numbers will be rounded up, giving this composition:

Apples: 31%
Oranges: 33%
Bananas: 37%

This totals 101%. This is an unfortunate, but unavoidable, effect of rounding. Although it can be disconcerting, the only way to treat it is to simply accept that it happens, but that it causes only very minimal distortion of the statistics, since the total of the percentages very rarely comes to more than 102%.

Multiple answers

Let's consider the example given earlier in this section of the proportion of people with each given fruit in their fruit bowl:

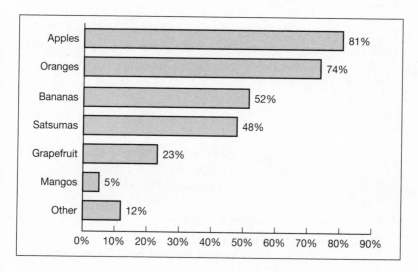

The total here is obviously much greater than 100%. The simple reason for this is that many people have more than one fruit in their bowl. Questions like this, for which each individual can give more than one answer, often end up with figures that total more than 100%. So long as we do not find that 117% of people have apples in their fruit bowl, then the data is perfectly correct.

Overlapping categories

I have found that my fruit bowl contains (by quantity), 50% tropical fruit and 70% citrus fruit. These figures seem hard to reconcile, but of course there is an explanation for this. This explanation involves grapefruit, which I class as a citrus fruit and also as a tropical fruit. My fruit bowl contains 5 satsumas, 3 bananas and 2 grapefruit. Hence there are 7 citrus fruits (satsumas and grapefruit) and 5 tropical fruits (bananas and grapefruit).

It is often useful to collect information in groupings which do not have overlaps, so as to provide a total figure of 100%. However, it may also be that two particular groups are of interest (e.g. tropical and citrus fruits), and that these groups have an overlap. If so, the figures for these groups, when added together, may total more than 100%.

Less than 100%

Rounding

The effects of rounding, as discussed previously, can produce figures which total less than 100%. On re-examining my fruit bowl, I have discovered its composition (by weight) to be:

Apples: 31.3%
Oranges: 32.4%
Bananas: 36.3%

This, again, totals 100%. After rounding, however, the figures are:

Apples: 31%
Oranges: 32%
Bananas: 36%

These figures only add up to 99%. Again, there is nothing that I can do about this rounding error, except to acknowledge that it is unavoidable, and causes only minimal distortion of the statistics.

Omitted categories

The most obvious categories which could be relevant here are 'Not Answered' and 'Don't Know'. If I ask everyone in my office whether they have apples in their fruit bowl at home, I may find that

- 72% do have apples;
- Only 25% do not have apples.

But what about the other 3%? Well, maybe they didn't know, or maybe they just didn't want to say. Maybe they all, in fact, do have apples at home, and maybe none of them do. We simply can't say, and we have to ignore them.

Sometimes figures for D/K or N/A are given, showing how many people did not respond to the question, and at other times they are not. Many survey questions, however, do not receive a full quota of answers, but the number not responding is usually fairly low and, as with rounding, does not undermine the other data to any appreciable extent.

Of course, other categories can be omitted when data is presented – any category can. If I ask my workmates what their favourite fruit is, I may find that:

- Apples are favourite for 43%.
- Bananas are the next most popular, cited by 31%.
- Oranges are prefered by only 14%.
- 4% did not know or did not answer.

This gives a total of 92%. So what about the other 8%? Well, some of them prefered mangoes, others went for satsumas or guava – there were various answers. However, the proportion who opted for each was so low that it did not seem worth including them. The information that I was trying to convey was how popular the most popular fruits are, not a full breakdown with details of fruits that were favourite with only 0.3% of people.

Although *The Essential Business Sourcebooks* try to be as comprehensive as possible, they are designed for practical use, and hence some figures may have been omitted in this way when they were not significant or relevant, and would serve only to confuse the data provided. Such detail may also have been omitted in the source literature from which the statistics were gathered. For these reasons, categories may sometimes have been omitted, giving figures that add up to less than 100%. In these cases, the data is indeed not comprehensive, but the figures that are given are no less valid for it.

APPENDIX 2

CONTACT ADDRESSES OF CONTRIBUTING ORGANISATIONS

Association of British Chambers of Commerce
9 Tufton Street, London SW1P 3QB
0171 222 1555

Association of British Factors and Discounters
1 Northumberland Avenue, Trafalgar Square, London WC2N 5BW
Tel: 0171 930 9112
Fax: 0171 839 2858

The Bank Consultancy Group
93 Wardour Street, London W1V 3TE
0171 287 0422

Barclays Bank plc
Small Business Services, PO Box 120, Longwood Close
Westwood Business Park, Coventry CV4 8JN
01203 694242

Board for Chartered Accountants in Business
ICAEW, PO Box 433, Chartered Accountants Hall, Moorgate Place
London EC2 PBJ
0171 920 8100

British Venture Capital Association
Essex House, 12–13 Essex Street, London WC2R 3AA
Tel: 0171 240 3846
Fax: 0171 240 3849
Email: bvca@bvca.co.uk

Business Strategy Review
London Business School, Sussex Place, Regent's Park, London NW1 4SA
0171 262 5050

Confederaton of British Industry (CBI)
Centre Point, 103 New Oxford Street, London WC1A 1DU
0171 379 7400

Centre For Management Buy-out Research
School of Management & Finance, Portland Building
University of Nottingham, University Park, Nottingham NG7 2RD
0115 951 5493

The Creditors Group Ltd
Bydell House, Sudbury Hill, Harrow-on-the-Hill, Middlesex HA1 3NJ
0181 422 3999

Deloitte & Touche Consulting Group
Columbia Centre, Market Street, Bracknell, Berkshire RG12 1PA
01344 54445

Dun & Bradstreet
Holmers Farm Way, High Wycombe, Bucks HP12 4UL
01494 422000

Ernst & Young Chartered Accountants
Rolls House, 7 Rolls Buildings, Fetter Lane, London EC4A 1NH
0171 928 2000
For publications, please contact Kay Sullivan, Marketing Department

The Forum of Private Business
Ruskin Chambers, Drury Lane, Knutsford, Cheshire WA16 6HA
01565 634467+

Freight Transport Association
Hermes House, St John's Road, Tunbridge Wells, Kent TN4 9UZ
01892 526171

Globus Office World plc
Caversham House, 82 Caversham Road, Reading, RG1 8AE
01734 393577

Healey and Baker
29 St. George Street, Hanover Square, London W1A 3BG
0171 629 9292

Hoffman Investigations Ltd
Van Leijenberghlaan 199a, 1082 GG Amsterdam, The Netherlands
00 31 20 642 02 37

International Centre for Banking and Financial Services
Manchester Business School, Booth Street West, Manchester M15 6PB
0161 275 6416

The Institute of Export
64 Clifton Street, London EC2A 4HB
0171 247 9812

The Institute of Logistics
Douglas House, Queen's Square, Corby, Northants NN17 1PL
01536 205500

Institute of Management Foundation
Management House, Cottingham Road, Corby, Northants NN17 1TT
Tel: 01536 204222
Fax: 01536 201651

Journal of Marketing Management
The Dryden Press, 24-28 Oval Road, London, NW1 7DX
0171 267 4466

Kidsons Impey Chartered Accountants
(Kidsons Impey is a leading UK firm of Chartered Accountants and business advisers throughout the UK)
Spectrum House, 20-26 Cursitor Street, London EC4A 1HY
Tel: 0171 405 2088
Fax: 0171 334 4734

KPMG Tax Advisers
8 Salisbury Square, London EC4Y 8BB
Tel: 0171 311 1000
Fax: 0171 311 3311

P-E International plc
Park House, Wick Road, Egham, Surrey TW20 OHW
01784 434411

Paul Chapman
144 Liverpool Rd, London, N1 1LA

Pitman Publishing
128 Long Acre, London, WC2E 9AN
Tel: 0171 447 2000
Fax: 0171 240 5771

Price Waterhouse
Southwark Terrace, 32 London Bridge Street, London SE1 9SY
0171 939 3000

PRO NED Ltd
Devonshire House, Mayfair Place, London W1X 5FH
0171 493 4567

Small Business Research Trust
School of Management, The Open University, Walton Hall,
Milton Keynes, MK7 6AA
0190 865 5831

Small Business Research Centre,
Kingston University, Kingston Hill, Surrey KT2 7LB
Tel: 0181 547 7247
Fax: 0181 547 7029

ESSENTIAL BUSINESS SOURCEBOOKS

business information for professionals

Good ideas, good strategies, good planning and good benchmarking all rely on up-to-date, accurate business facts.

How often have you wished that you had all the facts at your fingertips?

The **Essential Business Sourcebooks** have been written to provide you with these facts, giving you the power to make you and your company more successful.

The information in the books is generic, not industry specific and will apply to you, whatever business you are in.

The **Essential Business Sourcebooks** will become a vital management tool and asset to your professional life.